TIMELINE of the CIVIL WAR

THE ULTIMATE GUIDE TO THE WAR THAT DEFINED AMERICA

TIMELINE of the CIVIL WAR

THE ULTIMATE GUIDE TO THE WAR THAT DEFINED AMERICA

John D. Wright

amber
BOOKS

First published in 2007 by
Amber Books Ltd
Bradley's Close
74–77 White Lion Street
London N1 9PF
United Kingdom
www.amberbooks.co.uk

ISBN-13: 978-1-59223-722-7
ISBN-10: 1-59223-722-3

Editorial and design by
Amber Books Ltd
Bradley's Close
74–77 White Lion Street
London N1 9PF
www.amberbooks.co.uk

Project Editor: Sarah Uttridge
Picture Research: Terry Forshaw
Design: Zoë Mellors

Printed in China

PICTURE CREDITS:
Amber Books: 25, 33(both), 34(l), 48, 50, 52, 59, 62, 63, 64(r), 67, 70, 80, 81, 82(r), 84, 85, 87, 88(l), 101, 108(r), 120,
121(r), 157, 167, 172, 188, 194, 200, 218(b); Art-Tech/MARS: 38, 51, 61, 65, 71, 78, 79, 90(r), 94, 95, 99, 112(r), 113,
115, 119, 121(l), 122, 123, 124, 127, 134, 136, 141, 145, 146, 151; Corbis: 16(b), 20(b), 28, 31(l), 214(l); Defence Visual
Information Center: 7, 11(l), 15, 29, 32, 37, 41, 49, 53, 68(both), 69, 74, 75(r), 93, 105, 116, 117, 125, 126(b), 128, 137,
140, 144, 153(l), 155(both), 159, 160, 162(l), 163, 166(r), 170, 171, 177, 183, 184(l), 185, 190, 191, 193(both), 196, 199,
201, 203, 206, 207; Getty Images: 39(r), 54, 55, 60, 73(r), 77, 98, 100, 104, 107, 109, 126(t), 131, 164, 175(l), 184(r), 186,
189, 192, 198, 204; Library of Congress: 4, 5, 6, 8, 9, 10, 11(r), 12(all), 13, 14, 16(t), 17, 18, 19(both), 20(t), 21, 22,
23(both), 26, 27, 30, 31(r), 34(r), 35(r), 39(b), 43, 46, 47, 57, 58, 72, 73(l), 75(l), 82(l), 83, 89, 90(l), 91, 92(both), 96, 102,
103, 106, 111, 114(l), 118, 129, 130, 133(l), 135, 138, 143, 147, 148(l), 152(r), 154, 158, 161, 162(r), 173, 174, 175(r),
176, 178, 179, 180, 181, 197, 202, 205(both), 208, 209(l), 210(both), 211(all), 212, 213(both), 214(r), 215(both), 216, 217,
218(t), 219(all), 220, 221(all); TRH Pictures: 24, 35(l), 36, 39(l), 40, 42, 44, 45, 56, 64(l), 66, 76(both), 86, 88(r), 97, 108(l),
110, 112(l), 114(r), 132, 133(r), 139, 142, 148(r), 149, 150, 152(l), 153(r), 156, 165, 166(l), 168, 169, 182, 187, 195, 209(r).

Contents

Introduction

America's Civil War was one of the bloodiest and most talked about periods of time in American history. It was both caused by slavery and not caused by slavery. The case can be made for either argument, depending on the perspective taken.

Slavery in the South created a one-horse economy driven by cotton and ruled by an elite class whose roots usually led back to the British Isles. The North, on the other hand, had generally abolished slavery and was flourishing, its diverse economy fueled by the famous melting pot of workers from many nations. This contrast caused the two re`gions to grow apart, and disagreements over slavery and states' rights created the antagonisms that provoked the war.

Left: A cotton gin separated the seeds from raw cotton. Slaves worked hard all day 'chopping' cotton and carrying it to be weighed, ginned and baled.
Right: Lincoln became known as 'the Great Liberator'.

However, no incident related to slavery caused the outbreak of fighting. Neither did the acts of secession by Southern states. Many in the North felt that the South was not worth the trouble, and that the federal government should just let the 'wayward sisters' go. For his part, the new Confederate President, Jefferson Davis, vowed, 'We propose no invasion of the North, no attack on them, and only ask to be left alone.'

The war began because the newly independent states felt they had a right to seize US forts, naval bases and armouries within their territory. A wiser strategy would have been one of negotiation and compensation, which was, in fact, promised but never paid. The transition was fairly peaceful – the US general in charge of Texas simply handed over his military to the Texas Rangers – but a flash point was unavoidable. It happened in Charleston Harbor on 12 April 1861, when South Carolinians fired on Fort Sumter. They had seized two US forts in Charleston the previous December, but the new Republican president, Abraham Lincoln, decided to reinforce, rather than surrender, Fort Sumter.

The United States was only 84 years old when it began to break apart. Americans were intensely proud of their nation, but the Union had been uneasy because of disputes about federal versus state powers. South Carolina even argued that a state had the right to nullify any US law with which it disagreed. The matter of states' rights was deeply felt in the South and was not, as is sometimes argued, introduced merely to distract from the slavery question. States' rights continued within the Confederacy when Southerners reacted against their new nation's income tax, military conscription and other central government dictates. 'Isn't this why we left the United States?' was a frequent cry.

Slave families were often broken up at slave auctions held throughout the South.

The Institution of Slavery
The obstacle to forming a perfect Union was slavery. Unlike states' rights, this had existed in America since early colonial days. The first slaves arrived in 1619 in Virginia, but there were only about 300 by 1650. By 1715, however, the population of South Carolina had some 40 per cent more blacks than whites. It was the invention of the cotton gin – patented in 1793 by Eli Whitney of Massachusetts – that turned cotton farming into a large-scale profitable industry. The annual cotton production boomed from 178,000 bales in 1810 to more than 4 million bales just before the Civil War. This required an extensive workforce: the number of slaves increased from 1,191,354 in 1810 to 3,953,760 in 1860.

This supply of captured workers came from a 'triangular slave trade' in which British ships went first to the Atlantic coast of Africa to buy slaves and then transported them to the New World. The third voyage was back to England

1860

FEBRUARY

2 February US Senator Jefferson Davis from Mississippi presents resolutions stating that the US Government cannot prohibit slavery in the territories and must protect slave owners there.

27 February Abraham Lincoln, in a speech at the Cooper Union in New York City, declares that the Constitution provides the power to control slavery in territories.

28 February Lincoln begins a two-week speaking engagement across New England, delivering 11 speeches.

with goods from the American plantations. Joining the trade later were New England ships that operated out of Boston and other ports in the Northeast.

Eli Whitney of Massachusetts invented the cotton gin, making cotton the 'King of the South'.

The American Revolution in 1776 was of great importance to slaves. The nation's leaders now questioned the moral and economic values of the system. Thomas Jefferson denounced the slave trade in his first draft of the Declaration of Independence, but his denunciation was deleted by the Continental Congress. The document did declare that 'all men are created equal', but slaves were normally considered to be property.

About 275,000 slaves had arrived in the American colonies before 1776, and 12 of the 15 states still had them when the US Constitution was approved. At the Constitutional Convention in 1787, George Washington, Thomas Jefferson, James Madison and Alexander Hamilton wanted the document to abolish slavery, but they relented when Georgia and South Carolina threatened to stay out of the Union.

Many of America's Founding Fathers were slave-holders, including Washington, Jefferson and Patrick Henry. Indeed, eight of the first 12 US Presidents owned slaves. However, between 1787 and 1804, all the Northern states passed legislation that banned it immediately or in the years to come.

And in 1808, the nation renounced the overseas trade – though not before another 60,000 Africans had been transported. Three years later, in 1811, Britain's Parliament enacted a bill that proclaimed slave trading to be a criminal offence and instructed the Royal Navy to stop it. All this, though, did little to hinder slavery in the United States, since the country was successfully reproducing its slaves.

Nonetheless, a small but active abolitionist movement existed, ranging from the fanatic John Brown to the sophisticated William Lloyd Garrison, the editor of the *Liberator* and founder in 1832 of the New England Antislavery Society. Many Northerners applauded their work, but it took Harriet Beecher Stowe's emotional novel *Uncle Tom's Cabin*, published in 1852, to arouse passions against the evils of human bondage. 'So you're the little lady who started this big war,' Abraham Lincoln is reported to have said when she visited the White House during the conflict.

Opinion in the South was very different. The 'peculiar institution' of slavery had great support, although some 95 per cent of its

MARCH

6 March Lincoln speaks in New Haven, Connecticut, saying, 'What we want, and all we want, is to have with us the men who think slavery wrong.'

APRIL

30 April Delegates of eight slave states walk out of the Democratic National Convention in Charleston, South Carolina saying Senator Stephen Douglas of Illinois is not supportive enough of slavery.

Brutal conditions existed on slave ships with the human cargo in chains.

population were not slave-holders. Southern farmers were comparatively poor, and ample wealth was needed in 1860 to buy a slave, who could cost up to $2000. Northerners were puzzled that common white Southerners should be so determined to protect the aristocratic lifestyle of wealthy planters. Actually, a great many people in the South were indeed against secession and war; what roused them were 'arrogant Yankees' bent on revising the Southern way of life. They blamed their region's financial problems on federal tariffs imposed to protect Northern industries. They claimed that Northern industrialists kept their own workers in economic slavery. And deep in their memories were the grand landed estates of England run by the nobility, a feudal system that had produced an empire.

Attempts at Compromise

Even though slavery had been abolished in the North and abolition was becoming a popular cause, the US Government knew it must tread very softly. The South had been in the forefront of the American Revolution and had helped to structure the new nation: Virginia alone provided seven of the first 12 US Presidents.

The Missouri Compromise of 1820 allowed Missouri, which had about 2500 slaves, to enter the Union as a slave state and Maine to join as a free one. This kept Congress evenly balanced with 12 slave states and 12 free ones. The Compromise also excluded slavery from territories north of Missouri's southern boundary, keeping it far south.

The South's continuing power in Congress was reflected by the Fugitive Slave Act of 1850, in which runaway slaves could be arrested in free states and returned to their owners without a trial. And any US citizen aiding them could receive a large fine and imprisonment. This act was part of the Compromise of 1850, by which California was admitted as a free state, the trade was abolished in the District of Columbia and a decision on slavery was deferred in the territories of Utah and New Mexico.

The compromise proved fragile, because the Kansas–Nebraska Act of 1854 allowed

1860

MAY

3 May The Democratic National Convention ends without selecting a candidate, because of the slavery question.

9 May The Constitutional Union Party convention in Baltimore, Maryland nominates US Senator John Bell from Tennessee for President.

9-10 May The Illinois Republican Convention meets in Decatur and instructs its delegates to the national convention to support Abraham Lincoln, whom they nickname 'the Rail Splitter'.

Left: Harriet Beecher Stowe's novel Uncle Tom's Cabin *helped the abolitionist cause.*

those two territories and any future ones to decide for themselves if they wanted slavery. This prompted settlers from the North and South to rush into the territories to gain control, and it led to the establishment of the Republican Party to unify the anti-slavery groups.

Slave owners gained the support of the US Supreme Court in 1857 in the case of Dred Scott. A slave in Missouri, he accompanied his owner, John Emerson, to the free state of Illinois and the Wisconsin Territory, where slavery was also illegal. After four years they returned to Missouri, where Emerson died, leaving his slaves to his wife. Scott sued for his freedom in 1846, claiming he had automatically been freed while living in the free areas. A decade later, the case reached the Supreme Court, which ruled 7–2 against Scott, declaring that he was not a citizen and therefore had no right to sue in a federal court.

Right: Abolitionists grew in numbers and power in the mid-nineteenth century as the war approached.

16–18 May The Republican Convention in Chicago nominates Abraham Lincoln of Illinois as presidential candidate.

JUNE

18–23 June Democrats meet again in Baltimore, Maryland and nominate Senator Stephen Douglas of Illinois for President.

Fugitive slaves going north were helped by the 'Underground Railroad' providing safe houses.

Indeed, the court went further, arguing that Scott had not been free in the Wisconsin Territory because Congress could not prohibit slavery in any territory, and adding that the Missouri Compromise with its ban on slavery was unconstitutional. Read by Chief Justice Roger Taney, this strong support for slave-holders' rights ensured that the nation would be unable to fashion another

compromise. It also helped to unite the shocked anti-slavery voters under the Republican banner, eventually sending Abraham Lincoln to the White House.

First, however, more shocks would come. The territory of Kansas was torn apart by its own civil war between supporters of slavery and its opponents, who had rushed there after the Kansas–Nebraska Act. 'Bleeding Kansas' should have been a warning about the brewing national conflict. The territory's first legislature, which was dominated by slavery advocates, applied to become a slave state in 1855. Settlers opposed to slavery responded by setting up their own government on 15 January 1856, after which the US Congress refused to recognize either group.

The fighting also spilled over into Congress. US Senator Charles Sumner, an aggressive abolitionist from Massachusetts, spoke on 19 May 1856 against the 'rape' of Kansas by slavery supporters, insulting Senator Andrew Butler of South Carolina. Butler's nephew, US Congressman Preston Brooks, responded by viciously thrashing Sumner with a cane, right in the Senate chamber.

Dred Scott failed in his legal bid for freedom that went to the US Supreme Court.

1860

JUNE

28 June Democrats from slave states meet in Baltimore and nominate Vice President John C. Breckenridge of Kentucky for President.

NOVEMBER

6 November Lincoln is elected as US President with Hannibal Hamlin as his Vice President.

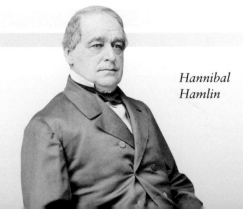

Hannibal Hamlin

John Brown Begins to March

Sumner's beating, and an attack on Lawrence, Kansas, roused the mentally disturbed abolitionist John Brown to action. He led four of his five sons and three other men to a settlement on Pottawatomie Creek, where they hacked to death five pro-slavery men. This helped unleash a wider guerrilla war across the territory. By the autumn, some 200 men had been killed, and Brown and his followers were driven from their town of Osawatomie by a force of 300 or more pro-slavery men.

Brown was not finished. He removed to Canada to hold a convention of whites and blacks in the spring of 1858, and there he announced his plans to create a free, defended area in the Appalachians of Maryland and Virginia for escaping slaves. This would later provide a base for a larger slave rebellion. The convention elected him commander-in-chief of this enterprise, and financial support rolled in from prominent abolitionists in Massachusetts and New York.

By the summer of 1859, Brown and 21 men, including five Negroes, were holed up in a rented farmhouse in Harpers Ferry, Virginia, preparing to attack the federal armoury there to secure guns and ammunition. Brown calculated that this assault would encourage slaves in the region to rise up and join the new revolution.

Their attack was launched on the night of 16 October. They seized the armoury and kidnapped 60 prominent men from the area to hold as hostages, killing the mayor in the mêlée. Instead of fleeing with the arms, Brown awaited the black insurrection that would supply reinforcements. The next day, his band was able to resist the local militia's counterattack, but the following morning saw the arrival of a small force of US Marines led by Colonel Robert E. Lee. They stormed the armoury, wounding Brown and killing ten of his followers, including two of his sons. Six more were captured and five escaped. Five of the Marines also lost their lives and nine were wounded. Among Lee's men was James Ewell Brown Stuart; known by his initials as 'Jeb', he would become a famed Confederate cavalry leader in the upcoming war.

Brown was jailed and faced trial in Charlestown, Virginia, charged with murder, insurrection and treason (to the state of Virginia). His defence cited mental illness, but

US Senator Charles Sumner was an outspoken abolitionist and radical Republican.

DECEMBER

3 December President James Buchanan tells Congress that no state has the right to secede, but that the federal government has no power to prevent this from happening.

13 November Georgia's US Senator Robert Toombs tells the Georgia legislature that secession is needed for 'the vindication of our manhood, as well as the defense of our rights'.

Brown refused to plead insanity. 'I am too young,' he stated in court, 'to understand that God is any respecter of persons.' He was convicted on 31 October 1859 and hanged on 2 December along with his six followers, who had also been captured.

Anti-slavery backers, as well as abolitionists, had few good words for Brown's bloody rebellion. The new Republican Party was quick to distance itself. 'John Brown's effort was peculiar,' noted their future presidential candidate Abraham Lincoln. 'It was not a slave insurrection. It was an attempt by white men to get up a revolt among slaves, in which the slave refused to participate. In fact, it was so absurd that the slaves, with all their ignorance, saw plainly enough it could not succeed.'

Southerners were suspicious of such disavowals and furious that Brown was now praised by such well-known New England intellects as Ralph Waldo Emerson and Henry David Thoreau. John Brown united the South against abolitionists in the same way that Harriet Beecher Stowe had united the North against slave-holders. But only in the midst of the Civil War did John Brown become a US

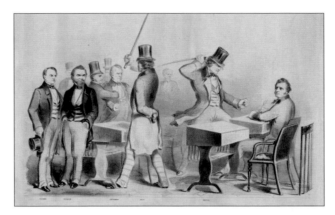

US Senator Charles Sumner was physically attacked in Congress for his abolitionist views.

hero and near saint, as Union soldiers began to sing of 'John Brown's Body' lying 'a-mouldering in the grave' while 'His soul goes marching on!' This stirring tune was made even more patriotic when it was set to the words of Julia Ward Howe's 'Battle Hymn of the Republic'.

Slavery Enters the Political Debate
The polarization of the United States was reflected in the political sphere. National parties were now disintegrating into regional ones. The Whig Party, which battled the Democratic Party

for the national vote from 1834 to 1852, gathered support from Southerners keen on states' rights. However, it also contained anti-slavery voices, which became louder after the passage of the Kansas–Nebraska Act, and the party lost its way on a national level.

Most of its members deserted to the Republican Party, which was established in 1854 to counter the political influence of Southern plantation owners. This move was less to do with the abolitionist agenda in particular than with politics in general. The Republicans gained further strength by incorporating Free Soilers and Know Nothings. The Free Soil Party had been formed to stop the spread of slavery into the territories, but it never ran a strong campaign, and drew only 5 per cent of the popular vote in the presidential election of 1852. The Know Nothing Party, also known as the American Party, took its name from the semi-secret organization of its members; when asked about its activities, a member was supposed to say, 'I know nothing'. The party was formed to restrict immigration, specifically from Catholic countries, and to restrict political office only to native-born citizens. These goals

1860

DECEMBER

11 December New restrictions at the Union's Fort Moultrie in Charleston Harbor gives access to only those known by an officer of the garrison.

17 December US Senator Benjamin Wade of Ohio tells the Senate that compromising with slave states means 'anarchy intervenes, and civil war may follow.'

had created a united party, but the surprising fervour of the slavery question during the elections of 1856 divided it fatally.

Balancing the emergence of a powerful Republican Party was the old Democratic Party, which could be traced back to Thomas Jefferson's Democratic Republican Party of 1792. Democrats had grown strong on defending states' rights, and this included opposing the federal government's involvement in the slavery question. As the nation drew back into two camps, it seemed logical to retain this political platform to gather votes from Americans who did not want the Republicans and US Government to turn the slavery debate into a crisis. In other words, the Democratic Party had obtained a Southern slant.

The 1856 election was the first presidential race to be driven by the slavery debate.

The Know Nothing Party met in Philadelph ia on 22 February to select as candidate the former Whig president, Millard Fillmore. He had signed the Fugitive Slave Act while in office, and his campaign was now swept along by the pro-slavery faction, which drove opponents into Republican hands.

The Democrats, holding their national convention in Cincinnati on 2 June, rejected their own sitting President, Franklin Pierce. Although against slavery, he courted the pro-slavery vote and had supported the Kansas–Nebraska Act that caused 'bleeding Kansas', making him a dangerous candidate. Instead, the convention chose James Buchanan, who had been serving as Minister to Great Britain, far away from the slavery argument. Morally opposed to slavery, he nevertheless agreed that the Constitution gave the states the right to choose.

The Republicans gathered for their first national convention in Philadelphia on 17 June. They selected the charismatic US Senator John C. Frémont from California. Known as 'the Pathfinder' for his explorations across the West as a US Army lieutenant, he became a popular hero and governor of California. However, he was court-martialled and found guilty of mutiny in 1848 for disobeying orders to turn over authority to a general. He regained his national popularity by more expeditions and his anti-slavery stance.

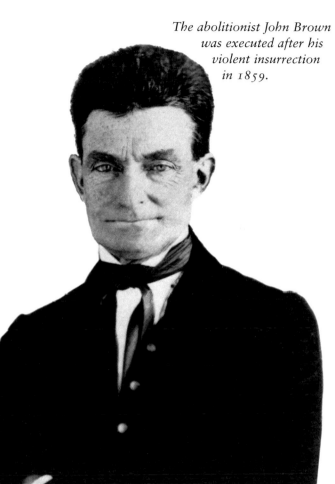

The abolitionist John Brown was executed after his violent insurrection in 1859.

18 December US Senator John Crittenden of Kentucky proposes that a constitutional amendment be passed to restore the Missouri Compromise forever.

18 December Senator John J. Crittenden of Kentucky proposes extending the Missouri Compromise line to the Pacific to divide free and slave states, but this fails.

19 December Porcher Miles of the South Carolina State Convention says Fort Sumter is an 'empty fortress' which could be seized and controlled in a single night.

US Colonel Robert E. Lee led US Marines who captured John Brown and his men at Harpers Ferry, Virginia. Lee would later command the Confederate army.

The Democrats were again returned to office, gathering the electoral votes of 14 of the 15 slave states (with Maryland's going to the Know Nothings). The Republicans swept the free states, but lost the electoral count by 174 to 114.

This sent the weak-willed James Buchanan to Washington as the slavery crisis was building. Facing the possibility of Southern secession, he gave ground to the slave-holders, upholding the Supreme Court's Dred Scott decision (made two days after his inauguration) and deciding that Kansas should have a popular vote to decide their slavery issue. (This proposal was passed by the Senate, but was then killed by the House of Representatives.) Buchanan was steering the Democrats away from the North and reducing their appeal as a national party.

Enter Abraham Lincoln

The Republicans were ready to take advantage of the country's nervousness as the congressional elections of 1858 approached. So was Abraham Lincoln.

Kentucky-born Lincoln was a lawyer who had lived in Illinois since 1830. He lost a race for the state legislature in 1832 but rebounded

1860

DECEMBER

20 December Congress convenes and each house appoints a special committee to try to work out a compromise with slave states.

Convention where ordinance of secession was passed.

20 December South Carolina secedes from the Union.

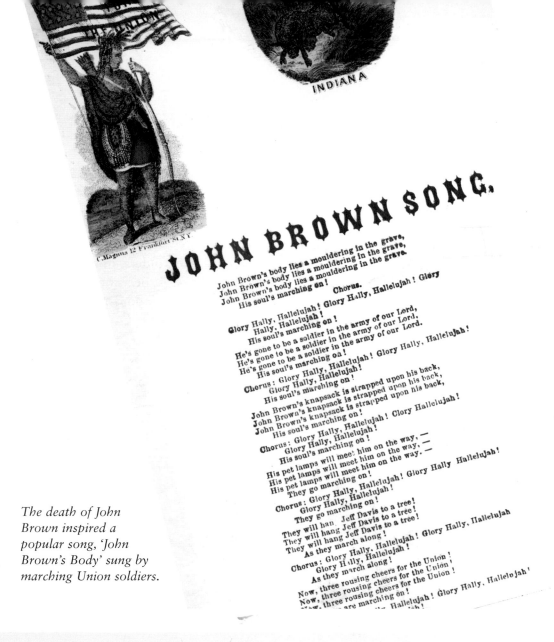

The death of John Brown inspired a popular song, 'John Brown's Body' sung by marching Union soldiers.

with a victory two years later, serving as a Whig in Illinois' lower house from 1834 to 1842. He then won a seat in the US House of Representatives (1847 to 1849), where he opposed slavery. In 1858, now a Republican, he ran for the US Senate against the Democratic incumbent, Stephen A. Douglas.

Douglas, affectionately nicknamed 'the Little Giant', had been in Congress for 15 years, serving in the House from 1843 to 1847 and in the Senate since 1847. He helped draft the Compromise of 1850 and the Kansas–Nebraska Act.

Lincoln lost to Douglas, but their seven debates around the state would make his name nationally known. Taking place between 21 August and 13 October, these focused on both candidates' opposition to slavery, with Douglas emphasizing the legalities and Lincoln addressing the immorality of owning human beings. During their second debate on 27 August in Freeport, Douglas enunciated what became known as his Freeport Doctrine. Although the Dred Scott decision meant that territories were open to slavery, Douglas stated that residents could reject it by using legislation

21 December The Charleston newspapers begin to place US news under the heading of 'foreign news'.

22 December US Congressman John Sherman (brother of William T Sherman, who would become the famous Union general) wrote Philadelphians that 'blood shed in civil war will yield its baleful fruits for generations'.

24 December Major Robert Anderson, commanding Fort Moultrie in Charleston Harbor, writes that 'if attacked by any one but a simpleton, there is scarce a possibility of our being able to hold out....'

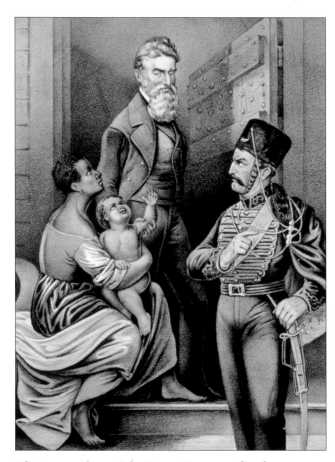

This image shows John Brown's sorrow for the victims of slavery before he was hanged.

and policing. This alienated Southerners and would later hurt his presidential bid.

It was Lincoln's eloquence and sincerity about slavery that caught the nation's attention. Indeed, his words are still remembered:

'A house divided against itself cannot stand,' he said on 16 June. 'I believe this government cannot endure permanently, half-slave and half-free. I do not expect the Union to be dissolved – I do not expect the house to fall – but I do expect it will cease to be divided. It will become *all* one thing, or *all* the other.'

During the fifth debate, on 7 October in Galesberg, Illinois, Lincoln's summary of his position contained words fearful to those Southerners considering secession: 'Now I confess myself as belonging to that class in the country who contemplate slavery as a moral, social and political evil.'

In that same debate, he rounded on Douglas' idea that states could make their own decisions about slavery:

'And I do think – I repeat, though I said it on a former occasion – that Judge Douglas, and whoever, like him, teaches that the Negro has no share, humble though it may be, in the

Declaration of Independence, is going back to the era of our liberty and independence, and so far as in him lies, muzzling the cannon that thunders its annual joyous return; that he is blowing out the moral lights around us when he contends that whoever wants slaves has a right to hold them; that he is penetrating, so far as lies in his power, the human soul, and eradicating the light of reason and the love of liberty, when he is in every possible way preparing the public mind, by his vast influence, for making the institution of slavery perpetual and national.'

Having established their anti-slavery views, both politicians assured their voters that they would not give priority to blacks. Douglas said:

'I look forward to a time when each state shall be allowed to do as it pleases. If it chooses to keep slavery for ever, it is not my business, but its own; if it chooses to abolish slavery, it is its own business, not mine. I care more for the great principle of self-government, the right of the people to rule, than I do for all the Negroes in Christendom.'

More surprising, and not so fondly remembered, was Lincoln's extended statement on

1860

DECEMBER

26 December The US garrison in Charleston Harbor is transferred from Fort Moultrie to the more secure Ft Sumter.

27 December South Carolina troops seize Charleston's Ft Moultrie on Sullivan's Island, and Castle Pinckney, another fort in Charleston's lower end.

Millard Fillmore opposed President Lincoln throughout the Civil War.

the inequality of Negroes, made during the fourth debate on 18 September in Charleston, Illinois:

'I will say then that I am not, nor ever have been, in favor of bringing about in any way the social and political equality of the white and black races, that I am not, nor ever have been in favor, of making voters or jurors of negroes, nor of qualifying them to hold office, nor to intermarry with white people; and I will say in addition to this that there is a physical difference between the white and black races which I believe will forever forbid the two races living together on terms of social and political equality. And inasmuch as they cannot so live, while they do remain together there must be the position of superior and inferior, and I as much as any other man am in favor of having the superior position assigned to the white race. ...I will add to this that I have never seen to my knowledge a man, woman or child who was in favor of producing a perfect equality, social and political, between negroes and white men.'

Two years later, Lincoln and Douglas would face each other again with a different result.

US President James Buchanan was indecisive when confronted with Southern secession.

27 December The South obtains the first vessel for its navy when US Captain N. L. Coste resigns and turns over his revenue cutter USS *William Aiken* to South Carolina.

27 December The US House of Representatives passes a resolution to appease the slave states, saying amendments to the US Constitution about slavery could only be proposed by slave states and ratified by all states.

28 December Commissioners from South Carolina arrive in Washington, DC, to demand the removal of troops from Fort Sumter.

The inauguration on 4 March 1857 of Democrat James Buchanan as US President began four years of hesitant policy in which he said secession was illegal but the federal government could not halt it.

1860

DECEMBER

28 December Charleston authorities seize the US custom house and post office.

John Buchanan Floyd

29 December US Secretary of War John Buchanan Floyd resigns after President Lincoln refuses to withdraw the US garrison from Charleston Harbor. (Floyd becomes a Confederate general.)

29 December The South Carolina commissioners write to President James Buchanan, saying US troops at Fort Sumter are 'a standing menace'. They enclose an official copy of the state's Ordinance of Secession.

A Vote for War

John Brown had been dead less than five months when the Democratic National Convention opened in Charleston, South Carolina, on 30 April. The location was chosen to demonstrate the party's strong ties with the South, but the ties proved fragile. Douglas was the front-runner, and this did not sit well with the slave states still bristling over his Freeport Doctrine. The delegates of eight Southern states walked out after Douglas refused to include a plank in the party platform saying the federal government would preserve slavery in the territories.

The wounded convention failed to name a candidate, reassembling on 18 June in Baltimore, Maryland without the firebrand Southerners to stop them from nominating Douglas. For their part, delegates from the slave states gathered in the same city ten days later to nominate Vice President John C. Breckinridge of Kentucky as their presidential candidate.

The Republicans, eager to take on the shattered Democrats, opened their convention on 16 May in Chicago, an unusual 'Far West' venue that favoured the Illinois candidate, Abraham Lincoln. First he had to survive two ballots in which he trailed Senator William H. Seward of New York, whose extreme anti-slavery views included his statement that God's law was higher than the Constitution's regarding slavery. Lincoln, considered more moderate, was chosen as the presidential candidate. (Seward later became his secretary of state.)

Lincoln clearly won the election on 6 November 1860, receiving 40 per cent of the popular vote, compared to 30 per cent for Douglas, 18 per cent for Breckenridge, and 12 per cent for Senator John Bell for the Constitutional Union Party. Lincoln's majority in the electoral college was 180 votes over the other three's combined 123.

Since Lincoln ran on a platform that promised to restrict slavery, the stunned South made preparations to leave the Union. *The Richmond Whig* called his victory 'the greatest evil that has ever befallen this country'. Not all agreed, including the future vice president of the

COL. JOHN C. FREMONT.
Hoisting the American Flag on the highest Peak of the Rocky Mountains.

John Frémont was the Republican anti-slavery candidate in 1856, losing to James Buchanan.

30 December President Buchanan replies to the commissioners' letter, positively refusing to withdraw troops from Fort Sumter.

30 December Charleston authorities seized the US arsenal and send troops to occupy Fort Moultrie and Castle Pinckney.

Confederacy, Alexander Stephens of Georgia. On 14 November, he told that state's legislature:

'In my judgment, the election of no man, constitutionally chosen to that high office, is sufficient cause for any state to separate from the Union. It ought to stand by and aid still in maintaining the Constitution of the country. To make a point of resistance to the government, to withdraw from it because a man has been constitutionally elected puts us in the wrong.'

Others could see the coming storm, and chief among them was the lame-duck president, James Buchanan, who was still seeking compromises to avoid secession and war. In his last message to Congress on 3 December, he noted:

'The fact is that our Union rests upon public opinion and can never be cemented by the blood of its citizens shed in civil war. If it cannot live in the affections of the people, it must one day perish. Congress possesses many means of preserving it by conciliation, but the sword was not placed in their hand to preserve it by force.'

But nothing could stop the impetuous South Carolinians, who had no intention of waiting for Lincoln's inaugural speech or his early actions as President. The state, led by its fiery

governor, W.H. Gist, held a convention in Columbia on 20 December and unanimously passed an ordinance of secession. Six days later, under cover of night, the federal government moved its small garrison in Charleston Harbor from the vulnerable Fort Moultrie to the more secure Fort Sumter. The following day, South Carolina troops in Charleston occupied Moultrie and another fort, Castle Pinckney.

Two days after the secession, Abraham Lincoln sat down and penned a letter to Alexander Stephens of Georgia, who was still trying to keep his state in the Union. He wrote:

'Do the people of the South really entertain fears that a Republican administration would, *directly* or *indirectly*, interfere with their slaves, or with them, about their slaves? If they do, I wish to assure you, as once a friend, and still, I hope, not an enemy, that there is no cause for such fears.'

On the last day of this fateful year, President Buchanan vowed to

....

Stephen Douglas was defeated by Abraham Lincoln for the presidency in 1860.

1860

DECEMBER

31 December US Senator Judah Benjamin from Louisiana makes a speech to Senate members saying he believes there would not be a peaceable secession but 'you can never subjugate us'.

defend Fort Sumter against any attack. A letter soon arrived from South Carolina commissioners who warned, 'By your course, you have probably rendered civil war inevitable. So be it.' They and the President knew that any federal attack on South Carolina would cause other Southern states to break away and join her. This would lead to the disruption of trade, transportation and the other essentials of American life. In commercial dealings, the South owed the North some $300 million, which Southerners believed would be forfeited, causing ruin and bankruptcy in the North.

Northerners, as well, misread the coming troubles. 'Whenever any considerable section of our Union shall deliberately resolve to go out,' wrote the *New York Times* on 9 November 1860, 'we shall resist all coercive measures designed to keep it in.'

Military action to keep it in would begin in five months and cost more American lives than any other war in the nation's history.

The victorious ticket of Abraham Lincoln and Hannibal Hamlin led to Southern secession.

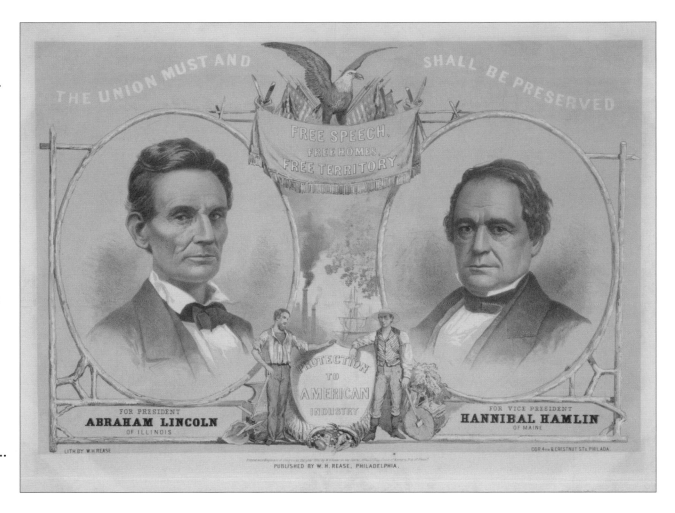

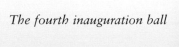

The fourth inauguration ball

31 December US President James Buchanan announces that Ft Sumter will be defended against any attack.

Chapter One
1861

South Carolina proved to be the loose thread that unravelled the United States. January of 1861 saw five more states secede: Mississippi on the 9th, Florida the 10th, Alabama the 11th, Georgia the 19th, and Louisiana the 26th.

Texas followed on the first of February, despite a fervent plea by Governor Sam Houston, who said, 'I am for the Union without any "if". He added:

'I tell you that, while I believe with you in the doctrine of States Rights, the North is determined to preserve this Union. They are not a fiery, impulsive people as you are, for they live in colder climates. But when they begin to move in a given direction ... they move with the steady momentum and perseverance of a mighty avalanche.'

He also accurately warned that Southern independence would cost 'the sacrifice of countless millions of treasure and hundreds of thousands of lives'.

When Texas seceded, Houston made the official announcement but urged his state to stay independent of the Confederacy. When he refused to take the required loyalty oath to the Confederacy, he was removed from office.

It is worth remembering that Southerners were not as joyous at leaving the Union as is often depicted. 'Secession is nothing but revolution,' wrote US Lieutenant Colonel Robert E. Lee to his son in 1860. And writing to his first cousin, Martha Custis Williams,

Left: Engineers of the 8th New York State Militia were among thousands of men suddenly at war. Right: Governor Sam Houston failed to keep Texas in the Union.

This idealized, allegorical painting depicts President Abraham Lincoln as the saviour of the troubled nation that was splitting apart in 1861.

on 22 January 1861, he declared:

'I am unable to realize that our people will destroy a government inaugurated by the blood and wisdom of our patriot fathers, that has given us peace and prosperity at home, power and security abroad, and under which we have acquired a colossal strength unequalled in the history of mankind. I wish to live under no other government, and there is no sacrifice I am not ready to make for the preservation of the Union save that of honour.'

Virginia Clay, wife of US Senator Clement Clay of Alabama, said the saddest day in her life was when her husband renounced his allegiance to the United States. And in Jackson, Mississippi, both men and women wept when a state ceremony lowered the US flag, the only banner they had ever known. As previously noted, the South had played a major part in winning the Revolution, its army being led by General George Washington of Virginia, and in creating a type of republic admired throughout the world. Although a schism had developed with the North, it would not prove easy to denigrate the United States of America and shoot at the Stars and Stripes.

1861

JANUARY

1 January The Union Army's new Department of the Pacific is created with headquarters in San Francisco.

1 January The US Navy lists only one steamer available for the defence of its entire Atlantic coast.

2 January North Carolina seizes Ft Macon at Beaufort, forts at Wilmington, and the US arsenal at Fayetteville.

3 January Georgia takes over Ft Pulaski, which guards Savannah.

3 January Delaware, a slave state, votes to stay in the Union.

4 January A Day of Special Humiliation, Fasting, and Prayer is observed – the response of President James Buchanan to the approaching civil war.

5 January US Senator Jefferson Davis and other Southern senators urge states in the South to secede and begin organizing a Southern Confederacy.

6 January New York Mayor Fernando Wood recommends that the city secede and remain neutral during the war.

Deep pockets of loyalty existed throughout the region. Western Virginia later broke away to form a new US state loyal to the Union. Only 30 per cent of eastern Tennessee's population favoured secession, and many young men travelled to Kentucky to enlist in the US Army. North Alabama was a hotbed for Unionists, with Winston County trying to secede from Alabama as the Free State of Winston.

In fact, none of the seceding states had called for a popular vote, leaving the decision in the hands of delegates to special state conventions. Together, they numbered 854 men, of whom 697 voted to leave the Union and 157 voted to stay. (Texas did hold a state-wide referendum three weeks after seceding, which approved the convention's decision by three to one.)

Strangely, the concept of secession had followers in the North. Delaware, which permitted slavery, took a vote to secede that failed. In New York City, which had important commercial dealings with Southern planters, Mayor Fernando Wood sent a message to his council on 7 January calling for the city to secede from the Union when the nation broke up.

The North Unites

Events, however, were unfolding that would unite the North. January saw additional seizures of forts in North Carolina, Georgia and Florida. More critical was the decision by President Buchanan to finally act. On 9 January, two days after Mayor Wood's proposal and five days after Buchanan had led 'A Day of Special Humiliation, Fasting, and Prayer', he ordered the US steamer *Star of the West* to carry provisions and reinforcements for Fort Sumter. He was careful to select an unarmed merchant ship to avoid provoking South Carolina, but the state's guns fired 17 shots at the helpless ship before it could enter Charleston Harbor, splintering planks and denting its hull with two cannon shots.

On 12 January, the steamer returned to New York – and a shocked North. Indeed, this could have gone down in history as the beginning of the Civil War had not President Buchanan downplayed the event, believing federal coercion was as unconstitutional as secession. (Confederates would later capture the *Star of the West* and sink it in the Yazoo River in Mississippi to block Union access to Fort Pemberton.)

Stephen Mallory, a former US senator, became the Confederacy's secretary of the navy.

8 January US garrison in Ft Barrancas in Pensacola, Florida repels men attempting to capture the fort.

9 January South Carolinians fire on the US steamer *Star of the West* which President Buchanon had ordered to take reinforcements and supplies to Ft Sumter.

9 January Mississippi secedes from the Union.

10 January Florida secedes from the Union.

10 January US Senator Stephen Mallory of Florida resigns from Congress to join the Confederacy.

11 January Alabama secedes from the Union.

12 January US Navy Yard at Pensacola Bay, Florida surrenders to Florida forces.

12 January US steamer *Star of the West* returns to New York from Charleston, bearing marks on her hull from two Confederate cannon shots.

19 January Georgia secedes from the Union.

Not all members of the government were as meek as Buchanan. General John A. Dix, US Secretary of Treasury, won Northern hearts with his 'American flag' dispatch of 20 January. This was his response to a New Orleans captain who refused an order from Dix's agent to turn over his cutter for its transfer to New York. Dix telegraphed an order for his arrest as a mutineer and added, 'If anyone attempts to haul down the American flag, shoot him on the spot'. (The message was intercepted by Confederates in Mobile and New Orleans and never reached the agent, but its eventual publication would lift Northern spirits.)

On 4 February, 21 states sent delegates to a Washington Peace Conference in the nation's capital and spent the entire month trying to find a compromise on slavery that would satisfy the South. What made this conference so important was that it was initiated by the Virginia legislature; even so, the seven seceded states failed to attend. The compromise, which did include an amendment that Congress could never ban slavery in any state, was sent to Congress on 27 February and approved, but the Southern states were in no mood to wait for

Political cartoons of the era were rough and right to the point. This one shows the seceding Southern states riding off towards certain disaster.

1861

JANUARY

21 January Jefferson Davis resigns from the US Senate.

26 January Louisiana secedes from the Union.

29 January Kansas admitted to the Union as a non-slave state.

29 January US Secretary of the Treasury John Dix sends orders to the government in New Orleans to shoot anyone attempting to haul down the American flag.

FEBRUARY

1 February Texas secedes from the Union.

4 February Provisional government convenes in Montgomery, Alabama.

4 February US Senator Judah Benjamin from Louisiana resigns from the Senate. (He becomes the first Confederate Attorney General and, later, Secretary of War.)

4–27 February Washington Peace Conference is held in the nation's capital by 21 states to resolve the slavery dispute. Recommendations, presented to Congress, are unacceptable to both sides.

possible ratification by all the states.

A more monumental event also occurred on 4 February, when representatives of the seceding states convened in Montgomery, Alabama, to form a provisional government. Delegates from Texas, which had seceded only three days before, arrived after the other six states had organized the new government. On 8 February, the official name of the Confederate States of America was chosen (after the suggestion of one Georgia delegate was rejected – the Republic of Washington). That same day, a Constitution was announced, based on the US Constitution, but preserving slavery and giving more rights to the states. The slave trade itself was banned and no mention was made of states being able to secede from the Confederacy. This Constitution would be formally adopted on 11 March by the Confederate Congress.

The Confederacy Chooses a President

On 10 February, the new government selected former senator and Secretary of War Jefferson Davis of Mississippi as President and former Congressman Alexander H. Stephens of Georgia as Vice President. The two men would prove to have a mutual dislike for each other, with Stephens calling Davis 'weak and vacillating, timid, petulant, peevish, obstinate', and spending little time in Richmond for official duties.

Jefferson Davis, previously US Secretary of War, was chosen as the Confederate President.

Jefferson Davis was a second-generation Southerner whose grandfather had moved to Georgia from Pennsylvania. Jefferson, like Abraham Lincoln, was born in Kentucky and moved as a child with his family to Mississippi. He studied at Transylvania College in Kentucky, leaving to take up an appointment to West Point, then spent seven years as a lieutenant on the Northwest frontier, fighting in the Black Hawk War. In 1835, he married the daughter of Colonel Zachary Taylor (who was later to become President) and resigned to settle in Mississippi on a 404ha (1000 acre) cotton plantation, Brierfield.

His wife died of malaria three months after their marriage, and in 1845 he married Varina Howell and was elected to Congress. However, he resigned to fight in the Mexican War under Taylor and was wounded at Buena Vista. Offered an appointment as brigadier general, he declined in order to become a senator. He again resigned to run, unsuccessfully, for governor of Mississippi. From 1853 to 1857 he served as secretary of war under President Franklin Pierce, and then returned to the Senate to champion states' rights and the extension of slavery. At

8 February Confederate government chooses the name Confederate States of America and announces its new constitution – based on the US Constitution but preserving slavery and states' rights.

8 February The US arsenal at Little Rock, Arkansas surrenders to state troops.

9 February The Confederate government elects Jefferson Davis as provisional President and Alexander H. Stephens as provisional Vice President.

11 February President-elect Lincoln leaves his hometown of Springfield, Illinois, telling a gathering of local people that he does not know if he will ever return.

18 February The Confederacy's provisional officers are inaugurated in Montgomery, and 'Dixie', the new unofficial anthem, is played.

21 February The Confederate government appoints Leroy Walker as Secretary of War and Stephen Mallory as Secretary of the Navy.

21 February President-elect Lincoln stops in Philadelphia and is warned of a plot against him.

22 February Lincoln arrives in Washington, DC by secret train, having skipped a stop in Baltimore, Maryland in response to the warning.

A large crowd turned out on the cold, windy day of 4 March to view President Lincoln's inauguration on the steps of the Capitol building whose dome was unfinished.

this time, he was not an avid supporter of secession, but after Lincoln's election he urged his state to secede. Indeed, he resigned his Senate seat on 21 January 1861.

The day after Mississippi left the Union, Davis told his Senate colleagues that 'Mississippi's gallant sons will stand like a wall of fire around their state'. He added that he was leaving the Senate 'not in hostility to you, but in love and allegiance to her, to take my place among her sons'. In his resignation speech, he explained, 'Secession is to be justified upon the basis that the states are sovereign', and warned: 'There will be peace if you so will it, and you may bring disaster on every part of the country if you thus will have it.'

On 10 February, Davis was cutting roses with his wife in their garden when a slave handed him a telegram notifying him of his selection as Confederate President. His expression was such that his wife 'feared some evil had befallen our family', and he told her of its contents 'as a man might speak of a sentence of death'. Davis had already been appointed major general in command of his state's militia and he wished to receive a top military

1861

FEBRUARY

23 February Three weeks after Texas secedes, its citizens vote three to one in favour of secession.

23 February President-elect Lincoln visits Mathew Brady's studio for his inaugural photograph.

25 February Judah Benjamin becomes Attorney General of the Confederate government.

MARCH

2 March Tennessee Senator Andrew Johnson (later US President) declares that if he were President he would hang anyone who fought the Union.

4 March Lincoln is inaugurated as President of the United States. In his address, he states, 'I have no purpose … to interfere with the institution of slavery.'

4 March The Confederate Congress approves the First National Confederate flag, nicknamed the Stars and Bars.

4 March Gideon Welles, US Secretary of the Navy, reports that the US Navy has 90 vessels but that only 42 are in commission, carrying 555 guns.

5 March Three Confederate commissioners arrive in Washington, DC. Their request to present their credentials are rejected by US Secretary of State William Seward.

command in the Confederacy. He was sincerely dismayed to be given the almost insurmountable challenge of leading the new government.

He had been chosen because of his extensive experience, but Davis was also known to be in frail health and was virtually blind in one eye, and this cold and aloof man had an abrasive and cantankerous nature. After assuming the presidency, he was obsessed with details and with keeping control of military decisions.

Two Presidents Inaugurated

A day after Davis' telegram arrived, President-elect Abraham Lincoln was leaving his hometown of Springfield, Illinois. He was a popular figure and the town gathered at his doorstep to see him off. He told them:

'I now leave, not knowing when, or whether ever, I may return with a task before me greater than that which rested upon Washington. Without the assistance of that Divine Being who ever attended him, I cannot succeed. With that assistance, I cannot fail.'

Privately, he told his law partner, William Herndon, 'If I live, I am coming back some time and then we'll go right on practising law as if

Confederate President Jefferson Davis was inaugurated on 18 February in Montgomery, Alabama.

nothing had happened.' And he left Herndon with one of his famous homespun sayings, this time concerning the seceding states: 'I only wish I could have got there to lock the door before the horse was stolen. But when I get to the spot, I can find the tracks.'

On 18 February, Jefferson Davis, Alexander Stephens, and other provisional Confederate officials were inaugurated in Montgomery on the steps of the Capitol. Davis had arrived two days before to cheering throngs and, at his inauguration, he was introduced by former US Congresssman William Yancey of Alabama, who enthused, 'The man and the hour have met!' The new Constitution meant that Davis, selected but not elected by popular vote, would serve a six-year term without possibility of re-election.

In his inaugural speech, Davis said that the Confederacy 'illustrates the American idea that governments rest on the consent of the governed, and that it is the right of the governed, and that it is the right of the people to alter or abolish them at will whenever they become destructive of the ends for which they were established'. Stephens, the new Vice President, was more straightforward: 'Our new

6 March The Confederate government establishes the Provisional Army of the Confederate States.

11 March The Confederate Congress formally adopts the Constitution of the Confederate States of America.

16 March The Confederate Congress creates the Confederate States Marine Corps, led mostly by former US Marines.

21 March Confederate Vice President Stephens speaks in Savannah, Georgia, insisting that 'the Negro is not equal to the white man', and that slavery is 'his natural and normal condition'.

27 March The State Rangers are organized as a Virginia militia to operate in the western part of the state behind Union lines.

Gideon Welles, Secretary of the Navy

government is founded on the opposite idea of the equality of the races' and 'rests upon the great truth that the Negro is not equal to the white man'.

The festivities were accompanied by thundering cannon, fancy drill demonstrations and a presidential carriage pulled by six grey horses. Music at the inaugural ceremony included the South's new unofficial anthem, 'Dixie', which had been composed in New York as a minstrel song by Dan Emmett of Ohio. Crowds also sang 'Farewell to the Star-Spangled Banner'.

Three days later, Abraham Lincoln was in Harrisburg, Pennsylvania, on the way to his own inauguration. During this stop, however, he was warned of a plot to assassinate him by Allan Pinkerton, a Scottish-born private detective. During the war, Pinkerton would create the organization that became the Secret Service, and later he would establish his famous detective agency.

Lincoln's advisers convinced him to skip a scheduled stop in Baltimore, Maryland, which had great Southern sympathies, and to go directly by a secret overnight train to

Washington. He arrived wearing a felt hat as disguise, and in the coming days he would have to suffer jokes and political cartoons about his undignified arrival.

His inauguration as the 16th President came on a cold and windy day, 4 March. Spirits were raised because the slave

state Missouri had just rejected secession by an overwhelming vote of 89 to 1. In his speech under the portico of the unfinished Capitol, Lincoln promised not to interfere with slavery where it existed, quoting from a previous

The Confederate 'Stars and Bars' flew over battered Fort Sumter, South Carolina, after its evacuation on 14 April.

1861

APRIL

6 April President Lincoln informs South Carolina that he will send provisions to Ft Sumter in Charleston Harbor, but that he will reinforce or rearm it only if attacked.

11 April Confederate Gen P.G.T. Beauregard demands the surrender of Ft Sumter. Maj Robert Anderson, commander of the fort, refuses.

12 April Confederate troops bombard Ft Sumter.

13 April Maj Anderson surrenders Ft Sumter.

13 April Pensacola, Florida, becomes the first Southern port to be blockaded as the USS *Sabine* arrives offshore.

14 April Maj Anderson evacuates his troops from Ft Sumter.

15 April President Lincoln calls for 75,000 troops for three months' service to suppress 'insurrection', and summons a special session of Congress.

Despite the fierce shelling of Fort Sumter, the garrison was defended without loss of life.

speech: 'I have no purpose, directly or indirectly, to interfere with the institution of slavery in the states where it exists. I believe I have no lawful right to do so, and I have no inclination to do so.' He added, 'Those who nominated and elected me did so with the full knowledge that I had made this and many similar declarations, and had never recanted them.'

He also denied the right of a state to secede: 'Physically speaking, we cannot separate. We cannot remove our respective sections from each other, nor build an impassable wall between them. A husband and wife may be divorced, and go out of the presence and beyond the reach of each other, but the different parts of our country cannot do this.'

He promised not to initiate a war, addressing Southerners:

'In *your* hands, my dissatisfied fellow countrymen, and not in *mine* is the momentous issue of civil war. The government will not assail *you*. You can have no conflict without being yourselves the aggressors. *You* have no oath registered in Heaven to destroy the government, while *I* shall have the most solemn one to "preserve, protect, and defend" it.'

Lincoln's Early Unpopularity

For some time, the 'sophisticates' of Washington, New York and other Eastern cities looked down their noses at their new leader. Though impressed by his speeches, they disparaged his common ways, his embarrassingly candid remarks, and his unrefined jokes and stories. And there was the matter of his tall, gangling figure and a face

General P.G.T. Beauregard commanded the Confederate attack on Fort Sumter.

16 April President Lincoln signs an act that abolishes slavery in the District of Columbia.

16 April President Lincoln forbids any trading with states that secede.

16 April Union troops abandon Harpers Ferry Arsenal and Armory in Virginia after setting a fire that destroys its 17,000 muskets.

17 April Virginia secedes from the Union.

17 April Confederate President Davis issues a proclamation inviting private armed vessels to attack US ships of commerce on the high seas.

18 April Lt Col Robert E. Lee, a Virginian, declines Lincoln's offer to command the US Army.

18 April Virginia seizes the arsenal at Harpers Ferry.

18 April The Sixth Massachusetts Regiment (the first mustered to defend Washington, DC) reaches New York City.

19 April President Lincoln announces blockade of Confederate ports from South Carolina to Texas.

19 April A Baltimore mob stones the soldiers of the Sixth Massachusetts regiment passing through the city to Washington, DC; four soldiers and 12 civilians die.

19 April The New York Seventh Regiment 'National Guard' sets out to defend Washington, DC.

described by many as the ugliest they had ever encountered – hardly a look that could be called presidential.

But Lincoln had overcome more than this in his 52 years. His father was an illiterate Kentucky farmer and Abe, born in 1809, grew up in humble conditions. The family moved to Indiana and then Illinois, where he became a rail-splitter while fencing his father's farm. In the coming years, he would work variously as a flatboatman, storekeeper, postmaster and surveyor. He enlisted for the Black Hawk War of 1832, but later said he fought more mosquitoes than Indians. He then taught himself law, passed the law exam and in 1837, settled in Springfield, the new state capital where he made a name for himself as a shrewd and honest lawyer.

Lincoln was elected to the Illinois state legislature four times from 1834 to 1840. He was opposed to slavery but not with the fervour of an abolitionist. When he later served in Congress (1847–9), he proposed an unpopular bill to free slaves in the District of Columbia but only with the approval of 'free white citizens'. He also opposed the Mexican War before his term ended. He left Congress at the age of 40 to resume his legal career. He stayed out of politics for the next five years until the Kansas–Nebraska Act revived his enmity against slavery and led him to win a seat in the state legislature, where he opposed the spread of slavery to territories. He then resigned to oppose Stephen A. Douglas in the 1858 Senate race. He was unsuccessful, but this was his first big step towards the presidency.

US General Benjamin Butler (seated middle, facing right) and his staff. He led his troops into Maryland to occupy Annapolis on 21 April and suppress support for the Confederacy.

1861

APRIL

20 April Baltimore's mayor sends three citizens to President Lincoln, requesting that no other troops pass through their city, to avoid further street battles.

20 April Col Lee resigns his commission in the US Army, saying, 'I cannot raise my hand against my birthplace, my home, my children.'

20 April Union forces abandon Norfolk Navy Yard in Virginia and partially destroy it before Virginia's troops move in.

20 April A Union Meeting, held in New York's Union Square, passes a resolution that urges citizens to help save the nation from 'universal anarchy and confusion'.

20 April The US Government seizes copies of telegraphs kept on file for the past year throughout the nation, to locate message-senders hostile to the government.

20 April Citizens are arrested under the US Secretary of State's warrant, without process of law, and imprisoned in Baltimore, New York and Boston.

Norfolk Navy Yard

Married since 1842, Lincoln had four sons. His wife, Mary Todd, was quick-witted but temperamental, and in the coming national tragedy, she would prove to be both a great comfort and source of distress.

The Federal Government Talks Tough

The day after his inauguration, three Confederate commissioners arrived in Washington to present their credentials – as befits a foreign country. US Secretary of State William Seward refused their request,

US Major Robert Anderson surrendered Fort Sumter.

The USS Sabine *under Captain Henry Adams was the first Union ship to blockade a Confederate port on 13 April off Pensacola, Florida, where it reinforced Fort Pickens.*

saying that the move represented 'an unjustifiable and unconstitutional aggression' and adding that they were still citizens of the United States.

The Union would not fire the first shot of the war, but Lincoln added that he intended to hold the federal forts ringing the South, a declaration that virtually dared the Confederacy to take them by force. The first test would

21 April Thomas Jackson takes Virginia Military Institute (VMI) cadets to Richmond, Virginia, to train mobilized troops. (Jackson later earns the nickname 'Stonewall'.)

21 April Union Gen Benjamin Butler leads his force to Annapolis, Maryland. Governor Thomas Hicks protests the presence of 'Northern troops' on his soil.

22 April Robert E. Lee leaves his home, Arlington House, on the Potomac River. The US Government seizes the estate, which later becomes Arlington National Cemetery.

22 April US Lt Joseph Wheeler resigns his commission to join the Confederate Army as a lieutenant.

23 April Virginia commissions Robert E. Lee as a major general, in command of the state's forces.

24 April Virginia begins a military alliance with the Confederate states.

24 April The USS *Niagara* reaches Boston from Japan and is sent to Charleston Harbor.

26 April Confederate troops seize Ft Smith, Arkansas.

27 April President Lincoln extends the port blockade to North Carolina and Virginia.

27 April Virginia Col Thomas Jackson takes command of Harper's Ferry and organizes troops from the Shenandoah Valley. They later become the 'Stonewall Brigade'.

This illustration shows the Sixth Massachusetts Regiment having to defend itself from stoning by a pro-Confederate mob as it marched through Baltimore, Maryland.

be Fort Sumter, whose small force of 100 had held out for three months and now needed more supplies. Lincoln worried about taking action that would upset the eight slave states remaining in the Union, while the Confederates of South Carolina were waiting for the defenders to succumb to hunger. Lincoln did consider surrendering the fort to the Confederacy in return from a promise by Virginia, on the very doorsteps of Washington, not to secede. But weakness was not part of Lincoln's nature, and he quickly dismissed the idea.

Therefore, on 6 April, the US President informed South Carolina that he was sending provisions to the fort but not troops or arms, unless it were attacked. Both the state and the Confederacy were suspicious of Lincoln's intentions. An attack by US warships had already been anticipated, and the new Confederate Army's Brigadier General Pierre Gustave Toutant Beauregard had been sent to Charleston. After receiving Lincoln's announcement, the Confederate government sent a telegram on 10 April, ordering Beauregard to take the fort. An official demand for surrender was made the next day.

1861

APRIL

29 April Confederate President Davis addresses a special session of the Provisional Confederate Congress, praising South Carolinians for capturing Ft Sumter and 'securing their own tranquillity'.

29 April Maryland's government votes not to secede from the Union.

29 April The Confederate Provisional Congress meets in Montgomery (until May 21).

MAY

3 May President Lincoln calls for 42,000 volunteers for three years, ordering the regular army to increase by 22,700 men and the navy to add 18,000 seamen.

6 May Arkansas secedes from the Union.

7 May Tennessee enters a military alliance with the Confederate states.

9 May US Gen David Twiggs surrenders Texas with its forces and supplies to the Texas Rangers. He later becomes a Confederate general.

Some leading Confederates did realize the danger of using force. The Confederate Secretary of State Robert A. Toombs warned President Davis that an attack on the fort was 'suicide, murder, and you will lose us every friend at the North. You will wantonly strike a hornet's nest which extends from mountains to ocean; legions, not quiet, will swarm out and sting us to death. It is unnecessary; it puts us in the wrong; it is fatal.'

Commanding the fort was US Major Robert Anderson, a Kentuckian who had owned slaves and supported slavery but was against secession. At West Point, he had taught artillery to Cadet Beauregard, who was about to use it against him. Anderson was ill-equipped to withstand the force assembled against him, and Fort Sumter's heavy guns had been positioned toward the sea rather than the city.

Anderson refused to surrender, but added that he would vacate the fort on 15 April if the Confederates did not attack and no orders were received from Washington. General Beauregard

As war broke out, Union troops moved in to fortify Washington from an expected attack.

10 May The Maryland legislature passes a resolution protesting the war against the Confederacy and resolving to take no part in it.

10–11 May Union forces seize Missouri militia in Camp Jackson near St Louis, causing riots in the city.

11 May The US Army's Department of the Ohio (Ohio, Indiana, western Pennsylvania, and western Virginia) is organized, with Gen George McClellan in command.

13 May US Gen Benjamin Butler's troops seize Baltimore, Maryland.

13 May Queen Victoria proclaims Britain's neutrality in the war but withholds official recognition of the Confederacy, granting them the status of 'belligerents'.

14 May William Tecumseh Sherman accepts an appointment as colonel in the 13th Infantry of the US Army.

14 May Union troops of Gen Butler occupy Baltimore and Ft McHenry.

16 May The Confederate Congress authorizes a $10 military enlistment bounty.

Union barricades go up in occupied Alexandria, Virginia in 1861 to protect the railroad from Confederate cavalry.

1861

MAY

20 May North Carolina secedes from the Union.

21 May Richmond, Virginia, is chosen as the permanent capital for Confederacy.

21 May Robert E Lee's nephew, Lt Fitzhugh Lee, resigns as instructor at the US Military Academy to join the Confederate army.

22 May Gen Butler's Union force occupies Ft Monroe in Virginia, establishing a new command on the Atlantic coast.

23 May Three slaves find refuge in Ft Monroe, and Gen Butler refuses to return them, saying the Confederate state has no right to US laws.

24 May Union troops enter Virginia, and Alexandria is occupied by an amphibious expedition from the Washington Navy Yard.

24 May US Col Elmer Ellsworth removes the Confederate flag from a hotel in Alexandria, Virginia and is murdered by the innkeeper, who is later killed by Union troops.

The campfire was better than the battlefield for Americans who were 'seeing the elephant' (the war).

replied that the bombardment would commence the next morning, 12 April – which it did, at 4.30 a.m. The first shot, a 25cm (10in) mortar, was fired by Captain George S. James. The fort took a battering, but Anderson's men held out for 34 hours, returning shots until their ammunition ran low. He surrendered at 7 p.m. on 13 April, having done as much as he could.

No one had died, but when the US troops began a 100-gun salute to their flag after the surrender, a gun burst, killing one private and wounding five. Anderson then marched his men out to the tune of 'Yankee Doodle'.

In a dispatch to the US Secretary of War Simon Cameron, Anderson noted that he had defended the fort 'until the quarters were entirely burned, the main gates destroyed by fire, the gorge walls serious injured, the magazine surrounded by flames, and its door closed from the effect of heat, four barrels and three cartridges of powder only being available, and no provisions remaining but pork'.

The North Responds

The Union defeat galvanized the North. As Oliver Wendell Holmes would write two years later, 'The first gun that spat its iron insult at Fort Sumter smote every loyal American full in the face'. It also made an instant hero of Major Anderson, whom Lincoln would promote to brigadier general on 15 May.

Lincoln responded instantly to the surrender. On the same day, 13 April, he instructed the USS *Sabine* to move into position off Pensacola,

A Southerner killed Union Colonel Elmer Ellsworth but was then shot dead by a US soldier.

Fort Monroe

26 May The Confederacy creates the Department of the Peninsula and the Army of the Peninsula, commanded by Gen J.B. Magruder.

26 May US Supreme Court Chief Justice Roger Taney rules that President Lincoln cannot suspend the writ of habeas corpus. The President, however, ignores this ruling.

26 May Union Gen George McClellan informs West Virginians that US troops will not interfere with their slaves and will crush any attempts by slaves to rebel.

27 May The *New York Tribune* urges 'On to Richmond' – a phrase the newspaper will often repeat.

27 May Union Gen Irvin McDowell is appointed to command a new military department comprising Virginia east of the Alleghany Mountains.

29 May The Confederate capital is transferred from Montgomery to Richmond, Virginia.

The skirmish at Fairfax Court House, Virginia, on 1 June saw US General Charles Tompkins kill Captain John Q. Marr, the first Confederate to die in battle.

Florida, to begin the first blockade of a Confederate port – part of the 'Anaconda Plan' of General Winfield Scott to strangle Southern trade. The next day, as Anderson evacuated his troops from Sumter, the President called for 75,000 troops to serve for three months to put down the 'insurrection' and also summoned a special session of Congress. Then, on 16 April, the President signed a bill that abolished slavery in the District of Columbia (although runaway slaves from Union states continued to be imprisoned there). On 19 April, he announced the blockade of all Confederate ports from South Carolina to Texas, and the following day authorized the government to seize copies of telegrams to identify possible enemies.

On 20 April, New York's Union Square saw throngs gather for a Union Meeting that passed a resolution urging citizens to help rescue the nation from 'universal anarchy and confusion'. Former US Senator Robert J. Walker of Mississippi, warned: 'We have no country, no flag, no Union; but each state at its pleasure, upon its own mere whim or caprice, with or without cause, may secede and dissolve the Union.'

1861

JUNE

1 June The first Confederate war death is Capt John Q. Marr, killed at Fairfax Court House, Virginia during a skirmish.

1 June Confederate Gen Beauregard warns that Union armies have abandoned civilized warfare and now seek 'your honor and that of your wives and daughters'.

2 June Confederate Gen Beauregard takes command of the Potomac Department, and the name changes to the Army of the Potomac.

2 June The Confederate gunboat CSS *Savannah* escapes through the Union blockade of Charleston Harbor.

3 June The CSS *Savannah* captures the US brig *Joseph* carrying a cargo of sugar from Cuba.

3 June The US man-of-war USS *Perry* captures the CSS *Savannah*. The ship and crew are sent to the port of New York.

3 June Union forces defeat Confederate outposts at Philippi, West Virginia in the war's first skirmish between opposing armies.

4 June The Confederates retreat quickly from Philippi, West Virginia, an action that becomes known as 'the Philippi Races'.

Around this time, Lincoln also gave the word to arrest citizens around the country without process of law, thus suspending the writ of habeas corpus that protected citizens from being arrested without lawful grounds or a trial. In this, the President was ignoring a ruling by the US Supreme Court Justice Roger B. Taney of Maryland, who ruled on 26 May that the President had no right to suspend the writ.

The North's strongest fear at that moment was an attack on its capital, which virtually bordered the Confederacy. Troops from several states rushed to its defence, the first being the Sixth Massachusetts Regiment. As it marched through Baltimore on 19 April, Southern sympathizers known as 'plug uglies' attacked the troops, killing four and wounding 36. Twelve civilians also died in the mêlée. Two days later, the US Army moved in retribution: General Benjamin Butler marched forces into Annapolis, Maryland, even as Governor Thomas Hicks officially protested the 'Northern troops' occupying his state. On 29 April, Maryland nevertheless voted to remain in the Union. General Butler helped guarantee its loyalty on 14 May by occupying Baltimore,

known for its concentration of rebels, and Fort McHenry in the harbour.

It has been argued that hot-headed South Carolinians dragged the Confederacy into a war that could have been avoided. It is doubtful that President Lincoln would have mobilized an army to invade the South if US forts, arsenals, and other facilities had been allowed to coexist with Confederate ones.

The first roar of cannon also activated the South. Virginia seceded on 17 April, Arkansas on 6 May, North Carolina on 20 May and Tennessee on 8 June. The Confederacy had now reached its maximum of 11 states, although 13 stars appeared on the battle flag designed by General Beauregard, in anticipation that Kentucky and Missouri would join.

The Resignation of Robert E. Lee
Especially devastating to the Union cause was the loss of Robert E Lee. Four days after Sumter fell, President Lincoln offered him the command of the entire US Army. Lee

US General George McClellan, shown with his wife, Ellen, led the Army of the Potomac in a hesitant manner.

5 June Confederate Gen Beauregard proclaims to the people of Virginia that 'A reckless and unprincipled tyrant has invaded your soil'.

8 June Tennessee secedes from the Union.

8 June Kentucky declares its state military forces are neutral.

9 June Mary Ann 'Mother' Bickerdyke begins working as a nurse in Union hospitals.

10 June Confederate forces repulse a Union incursion at Big Bethel, Virginia in the first full land battle of the war.

10 June Union Capt Judson Kilpatrick becomes the first regular army officer wounded in the war, at Big Bethel, Virginia.

13 June The United States Sanitary Commission is established to help improve medical treatment and sanitary conditions in military hospitals.

waited to see if his native Virginia would secede. It did, and on 22 April he left his beautiful home, Arlington House, on the Potomac River across from Washington, never to return. Its grounds would later be used for the US military's Arlington National Cemetery.

Earlier that year, he had written to his cousin to say that if Virginia left the Union, 'I shall go back in sorrow to my people and share the misery of my native state.' When secession came, he resigned to take command of all of Virginia's military forces. 'Save in defense of my native state, I never desire again to draw my sword,' he said in his resignation letter of 20 April to General Winfield Scott. As for the delay of his resignation, 'It would have been presented at once but for the struggle it has cost me to separate myself from a service to which I have devoted the best years of my life, and all the ability I possessed.'

Lee was among 197 US officers who now resigned to lead Confederate troops, and another 99 came out of retirement to fight with the South. In all, a total of 270 officers resigned to fight the United States, the nation that allowed them to go into the

Aquia Creek, a tributary of the Potomac River, saw an inconclusive battle when three Union ships bombarded Confederate batteries from 29 May until 1 June.

1861

JUNE

14 June Virginia's Governor John Letcher proclaims that the majority of the state should rule the state, and that Western Virginians should join the Confederate army.

15 June Union troops under Capt Nathaniel Lyon occupy the state capital of Jefferson City, Missouri.

11–19 June Loyal Unionists in western Virginia form their own state government.

17 June Confederates defeat Union soldiers on a reconnaissance mission at Vienna, Virginia.

17 June Capt Lyon's Union troops rout secessionist militia at Boonville, Missouri.

17 June Confederate Col Thomas Jackson is promoted to a brigadier general.

17 June Ulysses S. Grant is appointed colonel of the 21st Illinois Volunteer Infantry Regiment.

27 June Some 38,600 Union troops are gathered in and around in Washington, DC.

A railroad bridge lies in ruins after the Battle of Blackburn's Ford, Virginia, on 18 July.

Confederate military instead of incarcerating them in US prisons.

Robert E. Lee belonged to an aristocratic Virginia family that had supplied a governor of the colony and soldiers and statesmen for the American Revolution, including his own father, Lieutenant Colonel Henry 'Light-Horse Harry' Lee. In 1831, Robert married Mary Custis, the daughter of George Washington's adopted son. Inheriting slaves from his wife's family, he freed them. He graduated from West Point first in artillery and tactics and second in his class overall, having received no demerits. Lee then joined the US Corps of Engineers for more than 15 years. He was a captain when the Mexican War began, and was assigned to General Winfield Scott's personal staff. Lightly wounded, he gained a reputation for brilliant strategy and tactics. After the war, Lee served from 1852 to 1855 as superintendent of West Point before becoming a lieutenant colonel of a cavalry regiment in Texas, fighting both Indians and Mexicans. It was he who led the Marine forces that captured John Brown at Harper's Ferry.

At the beginning of the Civil War, Lee was 54, a large, handsome man with a serious countenance that sometimes relaxed into a winning smile. He was known as a gentleman, having an easy dignity, humility, selflessness and a high personal character. His idealism inspired idealism. He never referred to the Union forces as the enemy but rather as 'those people'. He stands out as one of the two great noble and benevolent figures of the war; the second is Abraham Lincoln.

A seasoned military man, Lee knew that the South stood no chance against the army he was leaving. The 11 Confederate states faced 23 states that had a white population four times as large (22 million versus 5.5 million) and which produced about 90 per cent of the nation's industrial products. Factory employment stood at 1.3 million in the North and only 110,000 in the South. The Confederacy had agricultural land, a great regional spirit – and too much confidence. The North had a navy, marines, and an old, well-organized army with a military academy; the South had none of these. Northern arsenals were filled with 530,000 small arms; contrasted, Southern arsenals held just 135,000 – 125,000 of which were old muskets requiring alterations.

JULY

1 July Since March 4, 1861, a total of 259 US Navy officers have resigned their commissions or been dismissed.

1 July The US Navy has 82 ships of war in commission, carrying 1100 guns and 13,000 men, as well as officers and Marines.

2 July President Lincoln suspends the writ of habeas corpus for special cases.

4 July President Lincoln addresses a special session of Congress, which authorizes a call for 500,000 men.

4 July US Secretary of War Simon Cameron announces that 260,000 men are in active service, including 165,000 volunteers signed up for three years.

11 July Union troops drive Confederate forces from Rich Mountain, West Virginia.

13 July Confederate Gen Robert Garnett becomes the first general of either side to be killed, at a skirmish near Carrick's Ford, West Virginia.

16 July Union forces under Gen Irvin McDowell move from camps near Washington, DC towards Manassas, Virginia.

The First Battle of Bull Run (or Manassas), the war's first major battle, included cavalry charges, a tactic that later gave way to trench and fortification warfare.

The Confederates Miscalculate

There were only two ways the Confederacy could have won its cause: for the US government to conclude that its citizens did not believe that secession and slavery were worth their own blood and money; or for the Confederacy to draw Great Britain, France and other countries to its cause.

The latter point was badly misjudged by President Davis and his cabinet. They believed that Europeans were so dependent on Southern cotton they would have to intervene, at the least demanding the end of the blockade. In fact, a surplus of cotton existed in Britain in 1861 and supplies were being developed in Egypt and other countries.

It was more realistic to believe that the North would tire of the conflict, particularly if there were an extended war. Southerners felt they could fight defensive battles indefinitely in the steamy expanses of their region, which were unknown to the invaders. This plan nearly worked during the first half of the conflict, as public opinion in the North turned progressively against the war in response to a series of setbacks suffered by Union troops.

1861

JULY

18 July Engagement at Blackburn's Ford, Virginia (Confederate name: the Battle of First Bull Run).

19 July Union Gen George McClellan tells his soldiers that Union men 'are more than a match for our misguided and erring brothers'.

19 July Confederate Secretary of State Robert Toombs resigns, to become a brigadier general in command of a Georgia brigade. He is replaced by Robert Hunter.

20 July The Confederate Provisional Congress meets in Richmond (until 31 August).

21 July The war's first major battle won by Confederates at the First Battle of Bull Run, Virginia (Confederate: First Manassas). Casualties: Union about 3000; Confederate, 1982.

21 July Mathew Brady takes the war's first photographs at Bull Run.

22 July President Lincoln appoints Gen George McClellan to command the Division of the Potomac that operates around Washington, DC.

22 July The US Congress passes a resolution stating that the war is 'to preserve the Union' not to abolish slavery.

26 July The CSS *Sumter* reaches Venezuela, having captured the USS *Abby Bradford* and sent it to New Orleans.

President Davis addressed a special session of the Provisional Confederate Congress on 29 April, giving special praise to the 'noble state' of South Carolina for capturing Fort Sumter:

'We feel that our cause is just and holy. We protest solemnly, in the face of mankind, that we desire peace at any sacrifice save that of honor. In independence, we seek no conquest, no aggrandizement, no cession of any kind from the states with which we have lately confederated. All we ask is to be let alone – that those who never held power over us shall not now attempt our subjugation by arms. This we will, we must resist, to the direst extremity.'

Tennessee would be the last state to leave the Union. The four border states, which had slaves, were caught in the middle and wisely chose the strong side. Delaware had voted unanimously on 3 January to stay. Maryland, as mentioned, voted not to secede on 29 April but then passed a resolution on 10 May to take no part in the war, which it protested. This neutrality was soon ended by the imprisonment of many of its state officials. On 8 June, Kentucky also proclaimed its military forces to be neutral, though these were incorporated in the Union

The Confederate rout of Union forces at the First Battle of Bull Run (or Manassas) created panic among the Washington elite who had turned out expecting a Union victory.

27 July Gen McClellan assumes command of Union troops in the vicinity of Washington, DC, and organizes the new Army of the Potomac, the largest US army.

27 July Texas troops of Col John Baylor capture Ft Fillmore at San Augustine Springs, New Mexico.

30 July Union Gen Benjamin Butler writes to US Secretary of War Simon Cameron, justifying his refusal to return fleeing slaves on the grounds that they are 'contraband of war'.

AUGUST

2 August Union Gen George McClellan offers war correspondents suitable information and telegraph services in return for an agreement to publish nothing to aid the enemy.

3 August The first ascent from a balloon made from USS *Fanny* at Hampton Roads, to observe Confederate batteries on Sewell's Point, Virginia.

3 August Union ships shell Galveston, Texas.

3 August Union Col William T. Sherman is promoted to brigadier general of volunteers.

army after a few months. Missouri was mostly pro-Union, but it was home to many Confederate supporters and saw numerous home-grown battles within its borders during the war.

The Confederacy moved its capital from Montgomery to Richmond, Virginia, on 21 May, a decision made to honour Virginia's importance but which also turned the state into the war's major battleground. Its location only 160km (100 miles) from Washington prompted

both sides to mass their forces in the area to protect their capitals. The move also assured Richmond's destruction at war's end, while Montgomery remained virtually unscathed.

The First Casualties of War

In May, responding to the crisis, Lincoln scheduled a special session of Congress for two months later, a move that allowed him to prepare for war without having to confer with Congress over the details. By May 24, Union troops had crossed the Ohio

into Virginia to encourage Unionists in the western part of the state. They also crossed the Potomac to occupy Robert E. Lee's home and moved into Alexandria, Virginia, where US Colonel Elmer Ellsworth was killed by an innkeeper named Jackson for removing a Confederate flag placed on the inn's roof. Jackson was then shot dead by a US soldier. Both Ellsworth and Jackson became martyrs to their separate sides. In New York, a new volunteer unit was formed as 'Ellsworth's Avengers'.

The South was shaken by such an audacious and quick invasion. Confederate General Beauregard, who had captured Fort Sumter, rushed a force of 35,000 troops into Virginia to meet the threat. On 1 June, he issued a proclamation to shock and inspire Virginians:

'A reckless and unprincipled tyrant has invaded your soil. Abraham Lincoln, regardless of all moral, legal and constitutional restraints, has thrown his Abolitionist host among you, who are murdering and imprisoning your citizens, confiscating and destroying your

Memorials were erected on the Bull Run battlefield before the Civil War had ended.

1861

AUGUST

5 August US Congress passes the nation's first income tax, to finance the war.

6 August US Congress passes the Second Confiscation Act – anyone who uses their slaves in military service against the Union will forfeit the slaves.

6 August The special session of the US Congress ends after 33 days.

7 August President Lincoln appoints Col Ulysses Grant as a brigadier general of volunteers at Cairo, Illinois.

7 August Confederates led by Gen Magruder burn the village of Hampton, Virginia, to keep it from being used to house Union troops.

10 August Confederates win the Battle of Wilson's Creek, Missouri. Union Gen Nathaniel Lyon is killed, becoming the first Union hero of the war.

12 August The Confederate government negotiates a treaty with Indians in its territory, creating an Indian alliance.

21 August Some 4000 Cherokees hold a mass meeting at Tahlegue in the Indian Territory to pledge their support of the Confederate cause.

William T. Sherman progressed from US colonel to general, earning a fierce reputation.

property, and committing other acts of violence and outrage, too shocking and revolting to humanity to be enumerated. All rules of civilized warfare are abandoned, and they proclaim by their acts, if not on their banners, that their war-cry is "Beauty and Booty." All that is dear to man – your honor and that of your wives and daughters – your fortunes and your lives, are involved in this momentous contest.'

His message, however, failed to convince Unionists in western Virginia who were elated at the federal force. This poorer section of the state had long been jealous of the rich eastern planters – and the tax exemptions they enjoyed. Too late, on 14 June, Virginia's Governor John Letcher promised to drop the exemption. He urged those in the west to join the Confederate army, saying the eastern part of the state 'is ready to share with you all the burdens of government'.

By then, however, West Virginians were meeting at Wheeling to form their own state government. By 19 June, they had established their own government and elected a governor of what would become, on 20 June 1863, the 35th state, West Virginia.

The advance over the Ohio led to the war's first battle death. Confederate Captain John Q. Marr was killed on 1 June during a skirmish at the village of Fairfax Court House, Virginia. On 3 June, at Philippi, some 290km (180 miles) northwest of Richmond, the Union army, led by Major General George B. McClellan, collided with a small Confederate force under Brigadier General Robert S. Garnett. The Confederates retreated so quickly that their flight was known locally as the 'Philippi Races'. The two armies

---

23 August Mrs Rose O'Neal Greenhow, a Confederate spy, is sentenced to house arrest in Washington, DC.

29 August Union forces capture Ft Hatteras and Ft Clark, North Carolina, as well as Hatteras Inlet, after two-day naval bombardment.

30 August US Gen John C. Frémont establishes martial law in Missouri and frees the slaves of owners against the Union.

31 August Col George Washington Custis Lee, Gen Lee's oldest son, is appointed aide-de-camp to Confederate President Jefferson Davis.

SEPTEMBER

2 September President Lincoln revokes Gen Frémont's emancipation of Missouri slaves and transfers him.

3 September Confederate troops invade Kentucky and seize Columbus.

Union General Irvin McDowell led his troops to defeat at the first Bull Run.

clashed again on 13 July at Garrick's Ford, where Garnett was killed, becoming the first general officer on either side to die in battle.

McClellan's small victory was hailed by Northerners, who were convinced that the Southern rebellion would be short-lived. The *New York Tribune* and other Northern newspapers took up the cry of 'On to Richmond'. It is worth bearing in mind that one purpose of the invasion was to stop the Confederate Congress from gathering for its first session in Richmond, due to begin on 20 July.

The Confederates Fight Back
On 16 July, Union Major General Irvin McDowell received further instructions. He was to move his troops from their camps around fortified Washington to engage General Beauregard's Confederates near the town of Manassas, Virginia (close to the small stream of Bull Run). This was only 40km (25 miles) west of Washington, and there were now 38,600 soldiers concentrated in the area. However, Lincoln's three-month recruits were nearing the end of their enlistment and McDowell protested that his volunteer men were not sufficiently

trained to take the offensive. Lincoln assured him, 'You are green, it is true, but they are green also. You are all green alike.'

McDowell was supported by the army of General Robert Patterson, who had orders to stop Beauregard's troops being reinforced by General Joseph Johnston. Based some 89km (50 miles) northwest of Manassas, Johnston was also to take overall command of the Confederate troops, some 32,000 men strong. They faced a Union force numbering about 37,000.

Sections of the two armies met initially on 18 July at Blackburn's Ford. The Union's reconnaissance force was repulsed, suffering 83 casualties to the Confederates' 68. The US Army reports described the engagement as an 'affair'; for the Confederates, this victory was the 'First Battle of Bull Run'.

Union General Patterson failed to halt Johnston's army from joining Beauregard's. Patterson withdrew to Harper's Ferry, claiming he had no orders to attack, and Johnston's men arrived at Manassas on 20 July by rail, the war's first movement of troops by rail to immediately influence the outcome of a battle. On the train was General Thomas Jackson, who

1861

SEPTEMBER

4 September Union forces under Gen Ulysses S.Grant occupy Paducah, Kentucky.

5 September The Western Sanitary Commission is established in St Louis, Missouri to help medical care and sanitary conditions for hospitalized soldiers in the West.

7 September Union troops capture Ship Island off Biloxi, Mississippi.

10 September Confederates withdraw after an engagement at Carnifex Ferry, West Virginia. Union Gen William Rosecrans is slightly wounded.

11 September Kentucky's legislature unsuccessfully demands the unconditional withdrawal of Confederate troops.

11–13 September In Gen Robert E. Lee's first campaign of the war, his troops attack but fail to capture Cheat Mountain, West Virginia.

would earn a famous nickname during the upcoming battle, which is known to the North as the First Battle of Bull Run and to the South as the First Battle of Manassas.

On 21 July, before the troops engaged, Washington senators and congressmen, other officials, and sightseers were arriving in buggies and carriages, eager to watch the 'show'. Settled on a grassy slope a few miles away with their binoculars, they were ready to cheer on the expected rout of the Southerners; some even brought along picnic baskets and champagne. At least 50 correspondents arrived from Northern newspapers and 26 from Southern ones.

McDowell's larger army took the initial advantage, pushing back Beauregard's troops until they met resistance from the Virginia division. This was commanded by General Jackson, who stood resolutely at the back of a plateau called Henry House Hill at the edge of woods. Noticing him, Confederate General Barnard Bee inspired his retreating troops by exclaiming: 'There is Jackson standing like a stone wall. Rally behind the Virginians.' Within an hour, Bee was mortally wounded, but he had

created the war's most renowned nickname, for 'Stonewall' Jackson.

For the troops, the battle was descending into confusion. The two armies were not decked out in the distinctive blue and grey uniforms that would later be worn, and the soldiers were often sporting similar colours, which were becoming dusty from the fight. When Confederates advanced on Union batteries on the plateau through the smoke, the Northerners thought they were their own troops and withheld fire, allowing the 33rd Virginia to shoot down every gunner at the 12 cannon.

The battle moved back and forth on Henry House Hill. Still McDowell's large force looked ready to overwhelm the Confederates until Johnston's army came up. McDowell mismanaged his attack, failing to bring up his many reinforcements from the other side of the Bull Run. Four of his eight brigades did virtually nothing during the battle. Johnston's vigorous attack scattered the green Union soldiers, and by the late afternoon they were crossing the Bull Run in a panic, intermingling with civilians.

Their desperate flight was recorded by William Howard Russell, war correspondent for

Confederate General Thomas Jackson earned his nickname by standing like a 'Stonewall' at Bull Run.

12–20 September Missouri state troops, supporting the Confederacy, besiege and capture Lexington, Missouri.

13 September Chicago churchmen visit President Lincoln asking for an emancipation proclamation. He tells them that this would drive border states to the Confederacy.

13 September US Lt J.H. Russel from the *Colorado* raids Pensacola Navy Yard, burning a ship.

17 September The US Navy captures Ship Island, Mississippi.

17 September Judah Benjamin appointed Secretary of War for the Confederacy, replacing Leroy Walker.

OCTOBER

1 October Confederate naval force captures USS *Fanny*. It later becomes CSS *Fanny*.

1 October Confederate President Davis confers with his generals, turning down their request for 20,000 additional troops to invade Maryland.

the *Times* of London:

'Soon I met soldiers who were coming through the corn, mostly without arms; and presently I saw firelocks, cooking tins, knapsacks, and greatcoats on the ground, and observed that the confusion and speed of the baggage-carts became greater, and that many of them were crowded with men, or were followed by others, who clung to them. … Men literally screamed with rage and fright when their way was blocked up. On I rode asking all, "What is all this about?" And now and then, but rarely, receiving the answer, "We're whipped;" or, "We're repulsed." Faces black and dusty, tongues out in the heat, eyes staring – it was a most wonderful sight.'

Russell's 'wonderful' in this case meant 'full of wonder or amazement', but Lincoln disliked his reporting and the North gave him the abusive nickname of 'Dr Bull Run Russell.' Secretary of War Stanton refused to allow Russell to accompany the US Army, and he returned to England after penning his last US dispatch on 3 April 1862.

Bull Run gave Americans the first photographs of war, taken by Mathew Brady.

These were the first of the 3500 shots he would take throughout the war, and he would eventually hire 20 teams of photographers. The battle also introduced the use of flags to signal, a system that became known as 'wigwag'. Confederates used it to send information back and forth about the enemy's movements, which was used by Johnston to rush troops to threatened areas.

As the battlefield cleared, Confederate President Davis arrived from Richmond to congratulate his army. For his part, General Jackson asked him for 10,000 more men to pursue the retreating enemy all the way to Washington to end the war, but Davis lacked both men and supplies, a weakness that would hobble the Confederacy throughout the war.

The North Responds

Bull Run made the South overconfident and stunned the North. It was, as noted in *Harper's* 1866 history of the war, 'a victory as decisive and complete as is recorded in the annals of war'. Union casualties numbered 3051 (including 481 killed) to the Confederates' 1982 (378 killed). The war would now not be over in

Union General John Frémont lost his command for delving into politics.

1861

OCTOBER

2 October US Senator John C. Breckinridge of Kentucky flees that state before being expelled from Congress and arrested as a traitor. He joins the Confederate army.

4 October US Navy authorizes construction of its first ironclad warship, which will later be named the *Monitor*.

7 October Confederate Brig Gen 'Stonewall' Jackson is promoted to major general.

8 October A Confederate force attacks the Sixth New York Regiment camped on Santa Rosa Island in Pensacola Harbor, burning the camp and taking supplies.

9 October Union troops repel Confederate attack on Santa Rosa Island in Pensacola Harbor, Florida.

13 October Confederate troops under Gen Turner Ashby make a daring raid on Harper's Ferry, Virginia. Shells fired on the village burn mills and storehouses.

three months, as predicted, and new emergency measures were needed. On 22 July, the day after the battle, the US Congress authorized the enlistment of 500,000 volunteers. At the same time, it tried to appease the slave-holding border states by passing a resolution declaring that the war was being fought not to abolish slavery but to preserve the Union. Congress also levied the nation's first income tax to finance the war – 3 per cent of income over $800.

Lincoln's response was to shuffle his generals. McDowell was removed from command and Patterson, who had failed to keep Johnston out of the battle, was mustered out. McClellan was put in command of all troops protecting Washington, and in early August two new brigadier generals were appointed: Ulysses S. Grant and William T. Sherman, who was promoted from colonel.

The following months brought more bad news to the White House. On 10 August, an outnumbered force of Confederates nonetheless won the Battle of Wilson's Creek in Missouri,

The Battle of Wilson's Creek saw the first Union general killed, Nathaniel Lyon.

17 October Confederate Secretary of the Treasury Christopher Memminger reports that treasury notes totalling $100 million have been issued to carry on the war.

21 October Confederates ambush Union troops moving to engage them, at Ball's Bluff, Virginia, near Leesburg.

21 October Union troops of Col Joseph Plummer rout Confederates at Frederickstown, Missouri. The next day, Plummer is promoted to brigadier general.

22 October The Confederacy creates the Department of Northern Virginia, commanded by Gen Joseph Johnston.

24 October William Brownlow, a Tennessee Unionist, publishes the final edition of his *Knoxville Whig*. He is later arrested, and in March 1862 he is expelled to the North.

31 October Missouri's 'Rebel Legislature' meets at Neosho and votes to secede from the Union.

during which the first Union general was killed – Nathaniel Lyon. He had till then been campaigning successfully to rid southern Missouri of Confederate forces. This defeat prompted General John Frémont to establish martial law in Missouri, threaten death to Confederate guerrillas and proclaim freedom for all slaves owned by Missouri secessionists. The latter proclamation moved into political territory, angering President Lincoln, who revoked it and removed Frémont from his command. (The general, aware of the likely response, posted guards to stop the order from arriving, but it was delivered by an army captain disguised as a farmer.)

On 3 September, Confederates under General Leonidas Lafayette Polk, an Episcopalian bishop, invaded Kentucky and seized Columbia. The victory would subsequently prove to be a costly tactical mistake, upsetting Kentucky's supposed neutrality and causing a movement of Union troops into the state. The next day, General Grant, without orders, moved 96km (60 miles) from his base in Cairo, Illinois, to Paducah, Kentucky an important town where the Tennessee River meets the Ohio. Then, on

North Carolina's Confederate General Leonidas Polk invaded Kentucky on 3 September.

7 September, the hero of Fort Sumter, Robert Anderson, now a general, moved his troops from Cincinnati, Ohio to Louisville, Kentucky.

As winter loomed in Virginia, Union troops were making little progress and sometimes stumbling into defeats. On 13 October, General Turner Ashby's Confederate troops raided Harper's Ferry, held by the Union, and attacked the village with shells that burned mills and storehouses. Worse came on the 21st at Balls Bluff, where the Union Colonel Edward Baker, Lincoln's friend and a former congressman, led his troops into an ambush by a Confederate force under Colonel Nathan Evans, who had fought at Bull Run. The Union losses were 921 to the Confederates' 149.

President Lincoln responded by accepting the standing offer of General Winfield Scott to retire as general-in-chief of all US armies, and replacing him with General George B. McClellan. The relief was felt throughout the military. McClellan was 35 years old and a rising star from the Mexican War, inspiring fierce devotion among his troops. Scott, on the other hand, was 75, weighed more than 136kg (300lb), suffered from gout, and could no longer

1861

NOVEMBER

1 November Lincoln appoints Gen McClellan as General-in-Chief of all US forces after the resignation of 75-year-old Gen Winfield Scott.

7 November Confederate troops led by Gen Leonidas Poke and Gen Gideon Pillow repulse the Union troops of Gen Grant at Belmont, Missouri.

7 November The US Navy and Army capture Port Royal Harbor, South Carolina and establish a base on Hilton Head Island.

8 November The US Navy seizes two Confederate commissioners heading to England on the British ship *Trent,* initiating the diplomatic 'Trent Affair' with Britain.

11 November Observation of Confederate forces is made by the Union Balloon-Boat G. W. *Parke Curtis* in the Potomac River.

ride. Known as 'Old Fuss and Feathers', because he loved military pomp, he had been a hero of the War of 1812. His best days were obviously past, although it was his idea to blockade Southern ports.

The War Turns International

The drama of the war now switched to the sea. The US Navy was doing a thorough job of sealing the enemy ports and recapturing forts that could be used as blockade bases off North Carolina, South Carolina and Mississippi. More help was coming, as the US Congress on 4 October approved construction of the nation's first ironclad warship, the *Monitor*.

The tightening blockade sealed off the cotton

The US government set up schools for contrabands (freed slaves), like this one in Arlington, Virginia.

12 November The ship *Fingal* (later CSS *Atlanta*), purchased in England, runs the Union blockade to enter Savannah with military supplies.

18 November An unofficial convention in Russellville, Kentucky declares the state independent and elects George Johnson governor.

18 November The Confederate Provisional Congress meets in Richmond (until 17 February 1862).

19 November Confederate President Davis asks his Congress for a railway linking the east and west through the interior of the Confederacy. This is soon built.

19 November Julia Ward Howe writes the poem 'The Battle Hymn of the Republic' after seeing a review of Union troops outside Washington, DC the previous day.

22 November The Confederate government establishes authority over its Indian territory.

23 November A Union garrison repulses a Confederate attack on Ft Pickens on Santa Rosa Island, Pensacola, Florida.

President Lincoln's friend, US Colonel Edward Baker, was ambushed and killed during his 'slight demonstration' against Confederate troops at Balls Bluff, Virginia.

trade, and the help that the Confederacy had expected from Europe was not forthcoming. President Davis decided it was time to establish strong diplomatic ties, appointing James M. Mason of Virginia as his envoy to England and John Slidell of Louisiana to France. Some blockade runners were breaking through the Union fleet, and the two envoys made it out of Charleston Harbor during a storm. Landing in Havana, Cuba, they transferred to a British mail steamer, *Trent,* heading for England. Just out of Cuban waters, however, the US Navy sloop *San Jacinto* fired at the *Trent* and boarded it, arresting Mason and Slidell.

The envoys were taken to prison in Fort Warren in Boston Harbor, and the city welcomed the captain of the Trent, Charles Wilkes, as the war's latest hero. Congress also thanked him for his 'brave, adroit, and patriotic conduct in the arrest of the traitors'.

Not so the British. Indeed, it was a similar act on the high seas that had started the War of 1812, when the culprits were the British. Now they wanted an apology and the release of the envoys, and they backed up these demands by putting their navy on a war

1861

NOVEMBER

25 November Confederate Secretary of War Judah Benjamin orders 'traitors of East Tennessee' to be tried and, if found guilty, 'executed on the spot by hanging'.

26 November Cavalries have a skirmish at Dranesville, Virginia.

DECEMBER

1 December The Union army in Kentucky numbers about 70,000, including some 20,000 Kentuckians.

2 December US Congress convenes for its regular session, with President Lincoln asking for a military railroad to be constructed.

2 December US Secretary of War Simon Cameron reports that 660,971 men are in active service in the US Army, including 640,637 volunteers signed up for three years.

10 December Gen Felix Zollicoffer's Confederates force Union troops under Gen Albin Schoepf out of Somerset, Kentucky.

alert and sending 11,000 troops to Canada.

The Confederacy was, of course, delighted. President Davis said that the US sailors had acted worse than barbarians. The *Times* of London wrote that Captain Wilkes epitomized the characteristics of Americans: 'Swagger and ferocity, built on a foundation of vulgarity and cowardice…' Queen Victoria's husband, Prince Albert, joined in mediations between the two governments, softening his country's harsh language. Some US officials, aware that their nation was undefeated in the two previous wars with Great Britain, wanted to take the fight to them again. Lincoln's cabinet was opposed to releasing the envoys, and Secretary of State William Seward even suggested to the President that a war with Britain might drive the South back into the Union.

'One war at a time,' replied Lincoln, who called the Confederate prisoners 'white elephants'.

Meeting on Christmas Day, Lincoln and his cabinet devised a face-saving compromise, which the British accepted: the two envoys would be released, but the United States would maintain its right to have made the arrest.

The Union Naval vessel 'San Jacinto' captures two Confederate commissioners travelling on the British mail steamer 'Trent' from Havana to Europe during the American Civil War.

16 December Confederate Gen Zollicoffer urges Kentuckians to help him drive Union forces out of the state.

18 December Union troops surround and capture more than 1500 enemy soldiers near Milford, Missouri, along with arms and ammunition.

20 December Troops of Union Gen Edward Ord defeat those of Gen 'Jeb' Stuart near Dranesville, providing the Army of the Potomac with its first important victory.

20 December Radical Republicans in the US Congress establish Joint Committee on the Conduct of the War to oversee Lincoln, whom they consider too conciliatory.

21 December President Lincoln signs legislation providing for a Navy Medal of Honor.

26 December Confederate commissioners seized on 8 November from the British ship *Trent* are released after Britain threatens war. 'One war at a time,' says Lincoln.

Chapter Two
1862

The year began with the Trent affair being brought to an end. By letting the Confederate commissioners sail for Europe on 1 January, Lincoln avoided confrontation with Great Britain. And by holding the prisoners for nearly two months, he had cooled Union opposition to their release.

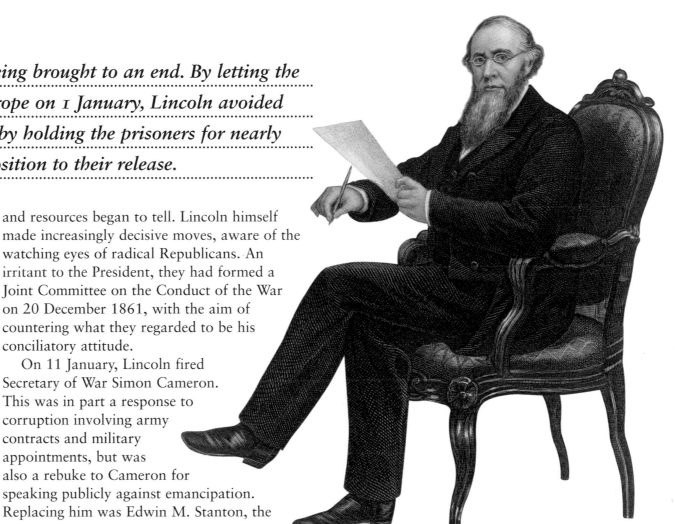

The Confederates hailed the move as a significant victory, but the envoys had virtually no influence on the governments of the respective countries – Mason in Britain and Slidell in France – and neither received official diplomatic recognition despite their presence throughout the war.

During 1862, the South would continue to win battles and to protect Richmond, but the Union's overwhelming strength in manpower

Left: Confusion reigned at the Battle of Seven Pines or Fair Oaks, Virginia.
Right: Edwin Stanton succeeded Simon Cameron in 1862 as US Secretary of War.

and resources began to tell. Lincoln himself made increasingly decisive moves, aware of the watching eyes of radical Republicans. An irritant to the President, they had formed a Joint Committee on the Conduct of the War on 20 December 1861, with the aim of countering what they regarded to be his conciliatory attitude.

On 11 January, Lincoln fired Secretary of War Simon Cameron. This was in part a response to corruption involving army contracts and military appointments, but was also a rebuke to Cameron for speaking publicly against emancipation. Replacing him was Edwin M. Stanton, the

*The Battle of Logan Cross Roads, Kentucky, on 19 January 1862 was
a Union victory by Ohio troops led by General G.H. Thomas.*

McClellan had built up and trained the formidable 110,000-man Army of the Potomac, the Union's main force on the Eastern front. But he was vain and arrogant, and he worried about his place in history, fearful of losing to the inferior Confederate troops. His hesitation to attack, which he justified by overestimating the enemy's numbers, became legendary. The Joint Committee on the Conduct of the War wanted him replaced, but Lincoln resisted the pressure despite the difficulty it caused him. 'If General McClellan does not want to use the army,' he once complained, 'I would like to borrow it for a time, provided I could see how it could be made to do something.'

McClellan ignored the President's order to advance, causing Lincoln to write him that 'it is indispensable to you that you strike a blow'. For his part, McClellan assured his soldiers that the long delay was needed. On 14 March, he told them:

'Soldiers of the Army of the Potomac! For a long time I have kept you inactive, but not without a purpose; you were to be disciplined, armed, and instructed; the formidable artillery you now have, had to be created; other armies were to move and accomplish certain results. I have held you back that you might give the death-blow to the rebellion that has distracted our once happy country.'

Two Union Generals

George Brinton McClellan, one of the war Democrats selected by Lincoln, was considered to be a brilliant soldier and moulder of men. He entered West Point at the age of 16, graduating second in his class and voted 'most likely to succeed'. He served in the engineering corps during the Mexican War, taught engineering at West Point, was assigned to report on the

bustling 'war Democrat' who had been the US Attorney General under President Buchanan.

On 22 February, Lincoln ordered all US troops to advance. His purpose was to spur General George McClellan into action.

1862

JANUARY

1 January The two Confederate commissioners seized from the *Trent* sail for Europe – James Mason to Great Britain and John Slidell to France.

1 January Confederate troops bombard Ft McRea in Pensacola Harbor but inflict little damage.

1 January Union Gen John Schofield issues an order to suppress his soldiers 'plundering and robbing peaceable citizens and [...] wantonly destroying private property' in Missouri.

4 January Confederate forces capture Bath, Virginia.

8 January Cavalries skirmish at Charleston, Missouri.

9 January Flag Officer David G. Farragut is appointed to command the Western Gulf Blockading Squadron, beginning the New Orleans campaign.

11 January President Lincoln appoints Edwin M. Stanton as Secretary of War, replacing Simon Cameron.

Crimean War, then resigned his commission to become a railroad civil engineer. When the war began, he was commissioned as a major general of volunteers, commanding the Department of the Ohio. He led his troops to victories over Confederates in western Virginia and was made a major general in the regular army.

Nicknamed 'Young Napoleon', McClellan thought well of himself. After his appointment, he wrote to his wife, 'Who should have thought, when we were married, that I should so soon be called on to save my country?' His optimism, his certainty of ultimate victory, pleased his men but annoyed other officers and Secretary of War Stanton.

In stark contrast to McClellan was the quiet, anonymous General Ulysses S. Grant, who commanded a district in the 'West', with headquarters in Cairo, Illinois. True, his first action had been unimpressive: on 7 November 1861, he led his troops down the Mississippi on transports to launch a confused attack on Belmont, Missouri, and was driven back by Confederate reinforcements. But Grant was slowly gaining a reputation among his men for his directness, tenacity, and battlefield tactics.

Most of all, and unlike McClellan, he craved action: ordered to make only a show of force towards Belmont, he turned it into a full attack.

Born Hiram Ulysses Grant, he was raised in Georgetown, Ohio. A lazy boy, he was teased by schoolmates, who made a pun of his middle name – 'Useless'. He attended West Point under the name Ulysses Simpson Grant because his local congressman made the error on his recommendation. He graduated 21st of 29 in his class. In 1848, Grant married Julia Dent, the sister of a West Point classmate and the daughter of a Missouri slave owner. The couple had three sons and a daughter.

He fought in the Mexican War, and was promoted to captain, but he later called it 'one of the most unjust ever waged by a stronger against a weaker nation'. He served in that conflict alongside Captain Robert E. Lee.

After serving at Sackets Harbor, New York, and Detroit, Michigan, Grant was assigned to Fort Vancouver and the West Coast. Missing his wife and children, he began to drink. In 1854, after arguing with his commander, he was forced to resign his commission to avoid a court-martial. He tried farming in Missouri on 24ha

Union General John Schofield commanded the Military District of Missouri in 1862.

12 January Confederate ships, including fire ships, attack the Union fleet blockading New Orleans, but cause little damage.

14 January The poem 'Battle Hymn of the Republic' by Julia Ward Howe is first published, in the *New York Herald Tribune*.

16 January The Union commissions seven armoured river gunboats for western operations.

19 January Union troops win a victory over Confederates at Logan Cross Roads (also called Mill Springs), Kentucky.

20 January John Ericsson, designer of the Union's first ironclad warship, chooses the name *Monitor* because it will be a 'severe monitor' to southern leaders.

22 January The Confederate Congress increases the military enlistment bounty from $10 to $50.

(60 acres) given to him by his father-in-law, working three slaves and calling his log farmhouse 'Hardscrabble' because both the land and life were difficult. He next turned his hand to bill-collecting and real estate. Failing here too, he moved to Galena, Illinois, to work in his father's leather shop.

When war broke out in 1861, Grant helped to organize Galena's first volunteer company. He wanted a regular command, but General McClellan had no time to interview him. It was the governor of Illinois who appointed him colonel of the 21st Illinois Infantry and, on 7 August, he became a brigadier general of volunteers and was assigned to Paducah, Kentucky.

Grant was not a complainer by nature, and during the war he accepted things as they were and tried to improve them in a businesslike way. He seldom if ever made the same mistake twice. He was stubborn but relied heavily on his subordinates. Grant did not believe in fuss and bother, showing up at Lee's surrender in a simple, rumpled uniform – a contrast to Lee, who turned up in full dress with shining sword.

Union gunboats under Commodore Andrew Foote shelled Fort Henry in Tennessee on 2 February 1862, giving General Ulysses S. Grant his first major victory.

Grant's Victory

For some time, Grant had been urging attacks on two Tennessee forts near the Kentucky line: Fort Henry on the Tennessee River and Fort Donelson on the Cumberland. Now, in the new year, he received approval from his commanding officer, General Henry Halleck.

Fort Henry was not a difficult target. On 2 February, Grant shipped 17,000 troops up the Tennessee River on transports protected by seven gunboats. He then sat back as Commodore Andrew Foote's fleet shelled the fort. Some of the Confederate defenders retreated to Fort Donelson 18km (11 miles)

1862

JANUARY

27 January President Lincoln orders all US forces to advance by 22 February. This is a prompt to the hesitant Gen McClellan, who ignores the order.

30 January USS *Monitor*, the Union's first ironclad warship, is launched.

30 January Confederate Gen 'Stonewall' Jackson threatens to resign in a letter to Secretary of War Judah Benjamin, who had overruled one of his orders. (Benjamin backs down.)

31 January US Congress creates the United States Military Railroads system.

General Grant first became a Union hero when he took Fort Donelson in Tennessee and captured 14,000 prisoners after demanding 'unconditional and immediate surrender.'

away, but others stayed – and surrendered on 6 February.

Grant pursued the enemy to Fort Donelson – which would prove a tougher nut to crack. It rested on high ground and had been reinforced, its defenders now numbering some 15,000. This time, the same Union gunboats were pounded to pieces by the Confederates – two were sunk and the rest badly damaged – while Commodore Foote was wounded. But Grant, in command of 25,000 men, had no thoughts of giving up the fight, especially since the fort's commander was General John Buchanan Floyd. A former US Secretary of War under President Buchanan, he had been accused of building up arms in federal arsenals so that Confederates could capture them when war came.

On 15 February, the Confederates emerged from the fort to engage in a pitched battle on grounds layered in snow and ice. After they withdrew inside, Grant concluded that a long winter siege would be required to take the fort, but that night General Floyd and his second-in-command, General Gideon Pillow, fled in a steamer, accompanied by a small force. They left the command to General Simon Bolivar Buckner,

FEBRUARY

4 February The CSS *Sumter* escapes from Southampton, England after being blockaded by the USS *Tuscarora*.

4 February Confederate Secretary of War Judah Benjamin orders all military commanders to impress saltpetre at 40 cents a pound. It is needed to manufacture gunpowder.

6 February Union troops led by Gen Grant, and backed by gunboats, capture Ft Henry on the Tennessee River, Tennessee.

7–8 February The US Navy and Army capture the Confederate garrison on Roanoke Island, North Carolina.

10 February A US fleet destroys the Confederate 'Mosquito Fleet' off Elizabeth City, North Carolina.

13 February The West Virginia Constitutional Convention votes that 'no slave or free person of color' can enter the state to become a permanent resident.

who had brought in the relief forces. He and Grant had been at West Point together and served together in the army, and Buckner now decided to surrender. He was opposed by Lieutenant Colonel Nathan Bedford Forrest, who would become one of the South's renowned cavalry leaders. Buckner therefore allowed Forrest to escape with his own command and several hundred more before asking Grant for the surrender terms.

'No terms except an unconditional and immediate surrender can be accepted,' Grant replied. 'I propose to move immediately upon your works.' (It was this stance that won Grant the affectionate nickname of 'Old Unconditional', and the famous play on his initials of 'Unconditional Surrender'.) The Confederate commander, complaining about the 'ungenerous and unchivalrous terms', surrendered on that day, 16 February.

Grant captured more than 14,000 prisoners from Fort Donalson, the largest amount so far in the war. It had taken him less than two weeks to take both forts, and he went on to take the state capital of Nashville on 23 February. Washington's rising star was now promoted from brigadier to major general.

The Confederates Respond

On 22 February, even as Grant was making inroads in Tennessee, the Confederate government was inaugurating its permanent government in Richmond, between flurries of snow and pouring rain. Nor were Grant's victories the only gloomy news the new government had to face. Confederate forces evacuated Kentucky and Missouri; Roanoke Island in North Carolina was captured by General Ambrose Burnside; and it seemed that the great Army of the Potomac was about to be unleashed on Richmond.

So the faces under umbrellas on that inauguration day – the 130th anniversary of George Washington's birth – were not the joyous ones that had watched with excitement when Davis took his first oath in Montgomery a year before. Now the crowd was sombre as he kissed the Bible and admitted, 'Events have demonstrated that the government had attempted more than it had the power successfully to achieve. Hence, in the effort to protect by our arms the whole territory of the Confederate States, seaboard, and inland, we have been so exposed as recently to suffer great

disasters.' He intimated that troops had to be enlisted for longer terms, and, as always, called on a higher power: 'My hope is reverently fixed on Him Whose favor is ever vouchsafed to the cause which is just.'

....

Andrew Johnson was US military governor of Tennessee before he became vice president.

1862

FEBRUARY

13–16 February Gen Grant's troops capture Ft Donelson on the Tennessee River in Tennessee. Grant earns the nickname 'Unconditional Surrender' – a response to his demand, and one that which fit his own initials ('U.S.').

14 February Union troops of Gen Henry Halleck occupy Springfield, Missouri.

17 February Brig Gen Grant is promoted to major general of volunteers.

17 February The US Senate passes a resolution to create a Medal of Honor.

18 February The Confederate (Regular) Congress meets in Richmond (until 21 April).

18 February Union Gen Ambrose Burnside and Flag Officer L.M. Goldsborough proclaim to North Carolinians that 'comparatively few bad men' are to be blamed for causing 'the desolating war'.

Not all the news was bad, but the military success occurred far away in New Mexico, where Texas troops won the Battle of Valverde on 21 February. The 3700-strong Confederate Army of New Mexico was organized by General Henry Sibley, the inventor of the popular tent and stove used by the US Army. His victory allowed him to proclaim New Mexico and Arizona as Confederate property. In January, he took 2600 soldiers up the Rio Grande and at Valverde, near Fort Craig, he engaged a Union force of 3810, including Colonel Christopher 'Kit' Carson. The Texans made a charge with lances, which was unsuccessful, but then launched a frontal attack that won the day. The Union dead numbered 68, while Sibley lost just 36.

Along its coasts, the Confederacy was beginning to build an offensive navy, and on 5 March it launched its own ironclad ship, the CSS *Virginia*, at the Norfolk Shipyard. This was a reconstruction and rechristening of the USS *Merrimack* (often later spelled *Merrimac*), a wooden steamer scuttled by Union forces when they had withdrawn from the yard. The Confederate navy raised it from the bottom of the harbour and made a rough job of refitting it with 10cm (4in) iron plates, 10 guns, and an iron ram beneath the waterline. The iron came from the Tredegar Iron Works in Richmond, and some of the money was raised by Virginia women of the Ladies Defense Association selling personal items such as jewellery and silver plate.

A Severe Monitor

Word quickly reached the North about this winter project, and the US Navy speeded up the building of its own ironclad, the USS *Monitor*, completing it in 101 days. It was the brainchild of John Ericsson, a Swedish engineer who had lived in the USA for 23 years. Many believed an iron-plated ship would sink, so the *Monitor* attracted many nicknames, including 'Ericsson's folly', 'Ericsson's iron pot', 'cheesebox on a raft', 'wash-tub on a raft' and, in reference to its round turret over a flat deck, 'hat on a shingle'. But Ericsson had already chosen its name on 20 January, some 10 days before its launch, reflecting his belief that the ironclad would serve as a 'severe monitor' to Southern leaders.

On 5 March, the same day that the *Virginia* left its port, the *Monitor* sailed from New York to confront her. Three days later, before the

US General Henry Halleck went to Washington, DC, in 1862 as general-in-chief.

20 February Confederate troops evacuate their fortifications at Columbus, Kentucky, held since 3 September 1861.

20 February President Lincoln's 11-year-old son, Willie, dies from fever.

20 February Union Navy Flag Officer David Farragut arrives on Ship Island, 105km (65 miles) from New Orleans, to await Gen Benjamin Butler and prepare to take the city.

20 February US Capt David Farragut arrives at Ship Island off Biloxi, Mississippi to take command of the West Gulf squadron.

24 February Confederates are victorious at the Battle of Valverde, New Mexico, thanks to Texas troops of the Army of New Mexico, led by Gen Henry H. Sibley.

22 February Permanent government officials of the Confederate States of America are inaugurated in Richmond.

22 February The first Confederate prisoners arrive at Camp Morton in Indianapolis. This former fairground will house 3700 prisoners within days.

22 February President Lincoln appoints Andrew Johnson as military governor of those parts of Tennessee under US control.

23 February Union forces occupy Nashville, Tennessee and hold it throughout war.

Union General Ambrose Burnside popularized the hair style that was soon called 'sideburns'.

Union Admiral David Farragut captured New Orleans and opened up the Mississippi.

Union ironclad arrived, the *Virginia* came out at its top speed of 8km/h (5mph) to take on three Union ships that were part of the blockade. It headed straight for the USS *Cumberland*, the US Navy's most powerful frigate, whose flurry of broadsides bounced off the iron 'like India rubber balls', as a Union officer recalled. The *Virginia* rammed the enemy vessel, which sank fast, and then turned on the fleeing USS *Congress*, raking her with shells that killed the commander and set her on fire. Also wounded was the *Virginia's* commander, Admiral Franklin Buchanan (who was later defeated at the Battle of Mobile Bay by Admiral David Farragut). Finally, the Confederate ship ran the USS *Minnesota* aground. The Union had lost 250 sailors.

Navy men on both sides now realized that the era of

wooden warships was dead. They also wondered if victory was even possible in a battle between ironclad ships. The first one in history would happen the next day in Hampton Roads, often referred to as the battle between the *Monitor* and the *Merrimack* (note the use of the latter's original Union name).

The *Monitor* arrived on the scene at 1 a.m. on 9 March. And at 8 a.m., the two ships engaged, the two vessels lumbering around each other like clumsy whales. Spectators watched from the shores, each ship easily identifiable, thanks to the *Monitor's* round turret and the *Virginia's* slanted upper housing. The ships collided five times, hammering the protective metal with all kinds of shot: shell, cannister,

---

1862

FEBRUARY

24 February As President Lincoln's cabinet meeting ends, Gen Benjamin Butler says, 'Goodbye, Mr President. We shall take New Orleans, or you will never see me again.'

MARCH

3 March A Union fleet captures Fernandina, Florida.

3 March US Asst Adj Gen N.H. McLean issues a warning in St Louis, Missouri, that members of Confederate guerrilla bands 'will be hung as robbers and murderers'.

5 March Gen Beauregard takes command of the Confederacy's Department of the Mississippi. He tells his soldiers to return home if they are not up to the task.

5 March The Confederate ironclad CSS *Virginia* is launched at Norfolk Shipyard. It is the old wooden USS *Merrimack*, a steamer scuttled by Union forces.

5 March The USS *Monitor* leaves New York to seek the enemy.

6 March President Lincoln sends Congress a message advocating 'compensated emancipation' to free slaves and reimburse their owners. This is aimed at slave-holding Union border states.

grape, musket and rifle balls. One shot that hit the *Monitor's* pilothouse temporarily blinded its commander, John L Worden, and his ship began to drift. Assuming that it was withdrawing, the *Virginia* now headed home to repair leaks.

If the battle itself ended in a draw, the Union had nonetheless checked the power of the Confederate ironclad and saved its blockade. And although the *Virginia* would approach the Union fleet three times more to renew the battle, the *Monitor* sailed away each time, aware that she offered the only protection for the Union's wooden warships. In fact, the two ships would never meet again: the *Virginia* was run aground and burned by her own crew on 11 May to prevent her capture by Union forces occupying Norfolk; and the *Monitor* would founder and sink during a gale off Cape Hatteras on the last day of the year, for the loss of 16 lives.

The Union was quick to initiate a building programme, and produced many more improved *Monitor*-type vessels. As for the Confederacy, it had to rely on its wooden navy.

The union victory at Pea Ridge, Arkansas saw Indians fighting with Confederates.

7–8 March Battle of Pea Ridge (Confederate name: Elkhorn Tavern), Arkansas is a Union victory. Union scout 'Wild Bill' Hickok is present, as is a Confederate Cherokee cavalry.

8 March The Confederate ironclad *Virginia* sinks the Union Navy's *Cumberland* and *Congress* wooden warships at Hampton Roads, Virginia.

8 March Confederate Col John H. Morgan leads a cavalry raid around Nashville, Tennessee.

9 March The world's first battle between ironclad warships, the Union's *Monitor* and Confederate's *Virginia* (former USS *Merrimack*), ends in draw at Hampton Roads, Virginia.

10 March Worried about Union Gen George McClellan's army, Gen Joseph Johnston evacuates his Confederate troops from Manassas, Virginia, burning materials that cannot be carried away.

11 March President Lincoln removes Gen McClellan's title of General-in-Chief, but keeps McClellan in command of the Army of the Potomac.

11 March The US military Department of the Mississippi is created, to be supervised by Gen Henry Halleck.

The Presidents Act

During March, both Presidents were busy fulfilling their roles as Commanders-in-Chief. Lincoln's message to Congress on 6 March included the sad thought that in a continuing war 'it is impossible to foresee all the incidents which may attend and all the ruin which may follow it'. He also advocated a 'compensated emancipation', which would reimburse states who freed their slaves. This was aimed at the border states, and both houses passed the resolution by large majorities:

'*Resolved*, That the United States ought to co-operate with any State which may adopt a gradual abolishment of slavery, giving to such State pecuniary aid, to be used by such State in its discretion to compensate for the inconveniences, public and private, produced by such change of system.'

Lincoln's patience with the hesitant General McClellan was nearly exhausted, and on 11 March he removed McClellan's title of General-in-Chief, while allowing

Union gunboats for the Mississippi fleet were built at Carondelet, Missouri, near St Louis.

1862

MARCH

13 March Gen Robert E. Lee begins serving as military adviser to Confederate President Davis (holding the role until 1 June).

13–14 March New Madrid, Missouri, is captured by Union force.

14 March Union troops led by Gen Ambrose Burnside, with naval support, capture New Bern, North Carolina. They occupy it until war's end.

15 March The Union creates the Department of the South for South Carolina, Georgia and Florida.

17 March The Confederate ship *Nashville* runs the blockade out of Beaufort, North Carolina.

17 March Union Gen McClellan begins to move his army towards Richmond.

23 March Confederate troops led by Gen Thomas 'Stonewall' Jackson attack a larger Union force at Kernstown, Virginia, but are forced to retreat.

23 March Santa Fe, New Mexico is captured by Confederates led by Gen Sibley.

him to remain commander of the Army of the Potomac. Six days later McClellan began to move toward Richmond. To avoid a frontal attack against entrenched Confederate defenses, McClellan conducted an amphibious turning movement. Lincoln was happy McClellan was finally moving, but the President had lingering fears for the safety of Washington.

For his part, President Davis appointed General Lee as his military adviser on 13 March. In truth, Davis had too much confidence in his own ability to make military decisions, after his experience in the Mexican War and having served as US Secretary of War (at which time he spurred the Army to adopt the rifled infantry musket). Indeed, he had just sent Lee, an engineer, on a thankless four-month job of supervising the fortification of the many islands and inlets along the Confederacy's Atlantic shore. The role earned him the nickname of 'Ace of Spaces'. This new assignment in Richmond 'under the direction of the President' put Lee in charge of 'the conduct of the military operations in the armies of the Confederacy', but it gave him no real authority over any of them.

Confederate General Henry Sibley had invented a tent and stove used by the US Army.

Confederate Losses

On the western fringe of the Confederacy, General Sibley was meeting trouble. Advancing into New Mexico, he intended to take California, and on 23 March his troops captured Santa Fe. However, the Union forces were growing, and when faced by an army twice his size, Sibley retreated – all the way to San Antonio, Texas, where he arrived after losing 1700 men.

More worrying for the Confederacy were events in Tennessee. On 7 April, General John Pope's Union army captured the enemy's Island Number 10 in the Mississippi River on the Tennessee–Kentucky border, taking about 5000 prisoners.

Nashville had been taken and General Grant now had in his sights General Albert Sidney Johnston's Confederates, who were retreating toward Corinth, Mississippi. Grant decided to wait for the additional troops of General Don Carlos Buell before attacking Corinth, and made camp at Pittsburg Landing on the west side of the Tennessee River, near the Mississippi line. Few defences were put into place, since an attack was not expected from the retreating

23 March Union Gen Benjamin Butler arrives on Ship Island to join US Navy forces planning to attack New Orleans.

26–28 March Indecisive skirmishes in Apache Canyon, New Mexico near Santa Fe, lead to a retreat of Gen Sibley's Confederates.

31 March Union Gen David Hunter takes command of the Department of the South.

APRIL

1 April The Confederacy has all recruits serving in the field and revokes all leaves of absence.

4 April Canal construction off Mississippi River completed by Union troops under Gen John Pope to bypass Confederate guns on Island No. 10, south of New Madrid, Missouri.

4 April Gen McClellan's Army of the Potomac begins the Peninsular Campaign against Richmond, Virginia.

Above: The first battle of ironclad ships saw the USS Monitor *and CSS* Virginia *(formerly USS* Merrimack*) fight to a draw at Hampton Roads, Virginia.*

....

Left: The USS Monitor *was affectionately nicknamed 'hat on a shingle', 'wash-tub on a raft', 'cheesebox on a raft' and 'Ericsson's iron pot'.*

Rebels. Johnston knew this and, wanting to catch the enemy before Buell arrived, he began moving his 40,000 men through woods towards the 33,000 Union troops.

On 6 April at 8 a.m., the Confederates surprised the soldiers of General William T. Sherman, who were whiling away this Sunday near Shiloh Church. Earlier, a confident Sherman had informed Grant, 'I do not apprehend anything like an attack upon our positions.'

Thus began the Battle of Shiloh, which means 'place of peace'; it is also sometimes known as

1862

APRIL

5 April Union forces of Gen McClellan begin a siege of Yorktown, Virginia. Within a month, it will be successful.

6–7 April The Battle of Shiloh, Virginia is won by Gen Grant's army. The Confederates are led by Gen Beauregard, replacing the killed Gen Albert Johnston. Casualties: Union 13,047; Confederate 10,690.

7 April Gen Pope's Union troops cross the Mississippi River to block the retreat of Confederates, who surrender 3500 men at Tiptonville, Missouri.

7 April Confederates surrender the garrison on Island No. 10 in the Mississippi River, south of New Madrid, Missouri.

9 April President Lincoln, frustrated by the inaction of Gen McClellan in Virginia, telegraphs him that the failure to move 'is but the story of Manassas repeated'.

10 April Slavery is abolished in Washington, DC.

the Battle of Pittsburg Landing. The half-starving Confederate troops, who had eaten nothing for a day, stopped to pick up food from the Union camp even as the fierce three-hour battle continued, breaking up into smaller confusing skirmishes. The Confederate forces still had not adopted a grey uniform, and Beauregard's troops even wore blue, drawing fire from their own side.

Only by mid-morning did General Grant arrive, having placed his own headquarters 16km (10 miles) away. He ordered his troops to take cover at a sunken road in a dense thicket and to hold it at all costs. The Confederates launched dozens of attacks on this position, which became known as 'the hornet's nest' because of the bullets and shells buzzing in all directions. The Union ranks finally gave under the fire from 62 cannon, and they surrendered.

Johnston, one of the best Confederate commanders, was shot in the leg and bled to death. General Beauregard replaced him, and suspended action as the day ended. During the night, however, Buell finally arrived with his reinforcements, bringing fresh troops to the Union army, so that it was now overall twice

The USS Cumberland *was sunk by the Confederate's ironclad* Virginia *on 8 March at Hampton Roads, Virginia, beginning the end of dominance by wooden warships.*

10–11 April Ft Pulaski, Georgia, guarding Savannah at the mouth of the Savannah River, falls to Union forces after constant bombardment.

12 April Union raiders steal train engine 'General' between Atlanta and Chattanooga. It is recaptured at the Georgia–Tennessee state line by Confederates pursuing in engine 'Texas' running backwards.

14 April A joint attack by the Union army and navy captures Newbern, North Carolina. It remains under Union control for the rest of the war.

16 April The Confederate Congress passes the Conscription Act, the first in American history, requiring three years' service for white males aged 18–35.

16 April Congress passes an act providing compensated emancipation in the District of Columbia.

19 April Camden, North Carolina falls after it is attacked by the Union army and navy.

the size of the Confederates. As dawn broke, Grant's men pushed forward and retook nearly all the ground they had lost. By late afternoon, the Confederates were withdrawing back to Corinth, while the cavalry of Lieutenant Colonel Nathan Bedford Forrest conducted a vigorous rearguard action to keep the enemy at bay, despite

President Lincoln selected General John Pope to head the new Army of Virginia.

Forrest being seriously wounded. The Union troops would soon follow, laying lay siege to Corinth for a month before General Beauregard evacuated it at the end of May.

This second large battle of the war saw more than double the number of soldiers fall than in all the previous engagements combined. Union casualties totalled 13,047, while the Confederates lost 10,694. Some of the wounded were trapped in tracts of woodland that caught on fire, and they burned to death. On both sides, the number of deaths was virtually the same: 1754 for the North and 1723 for the South. 'Death was in the air,' wrote the *New York Tribune's* correspondent, 'and bloomed like a poison-plant on every foot of soil.' The *Cincinnati Times* reported: 'On either side the battle was fought with a desperation which I could not have believed to exist in the minds of men.'

Grant himself wrote in his memoirs that: 'Shiloh was the severest battle fought at the West during the war, and but few in the East equalled it for hard, determined fighting. I saw an open field in our possession on the second day over which the Confederates had made repeated charges the day before, so covered with dead that

it would have been possible to walk across the clearing, in any direction, stepping on dead bodies, without a foot touching the ground.'

Shiloh was judged to be a draw in fighting terms, but a Union victory inasmuch as it forced the Confederates to withdraw. Still, much of the Northern press and public criticized Grant for being caught unaware and for losing so many men, and a false rumour circulated that he had been drunk. Looking back after the war, he called the battle 'perhaps less understood, or, to state the case more accurately, more persistently misunderstood, than any other engagement between National and Confederate troops during the entire rebellion'.

President Lincoln had to brush off an effort to replace Grant with General Halleck. 'I can't spare this man,' he retorted. 'He fights!'

War on the Railroads

Down in Georgia during this time, one of the war's most adventurous, and perhaps comical, raids was getting underway. Captain James Andrews, a Union spy, led 21 Union soldiers dressed in civilian clothes on a mission to steal a Confederate train locomotive on the railroad

1862

APRIL

21 April The Confederate Congress hastily adjourns as its members become anxious about Union movements towards Richmond.

24 April The Union fleet, commanded by Flag Officer Farragut, destroys the Confederate flotilla below New Orleans.

25 April New Orleans, the Confederacy's largest and richest city, surrenders to Union forces.

25 April Union army–navy forces capture Ft Macon at the entrance to Beaufort Harbor, North Carolina, giving the Union control of the entire North Carolina coast.

26 April Ft Macon, North Carolina, protecting Beaufort, surrenders after Union siege of over a month.

27 April Union troops raise the American flag over the New Orleans Mint, but a local cuts it down. Flag Officer Farragut threatens to shell the city.

line between Atlanta and Chattanooga. This was accomplished on 12 April when they captured the 'General' and its cars as its crew and passengers were having breakfast in Big Shanty (now Kennesaw).

They were pursued by a conductor for the Western & Atlantic Railroad and a roundhouse foreman, both men running on foot before encountering a handcar with its crew and jumping aboard. Continuing the chase, the Southerners switched to two different locomotives, but were forced on foot again after the raiders destroyed some track. Luckily, they then met a train pulled by the 'Texas'. Loading it with volunteers, they accelerated backwards to chase the General, avoiding obstacles that Andrews left on the track, including crossties and a burning boxcar. Eventually, the 'Texas' overhauled the other locomotive at the Tennessee line, where Andrews and his men abandoned their mission and dashed into a forest. They were captured, and Andrews and seven others hanged. The survivors were among the first to be awarded the Medal of Honor, which was also given posthumously to those executed.

The fierce Battle of Shiloh on 6 and 7 April in Virginia resulted in a total of nearly 24,000 casualties, including the death of Confederate General Albert Johnston.

28 April The month-long siege of Corinth, Mississippi begins.

28 April Two Confederate forts protecting New Orleans – Ft St Philip and Ft Jackson – surrender.

29 April Union troops capture Bridgeport, Alabama.

MAY

1 May Brig Gen Sherman is promoted to Major General of volunteers.

3 May Gen McClellan's troops near Yorktown, Virginia, send up an observation balloon. It draws Confederate fire, which misses.

4 May Yorktown, Virginia falls and is occupied by Union troops under Gen McClellan. They encounter a new weapon laid by Confederates – land mines.

4 May Confederate Gen 'Stonewall' Jackson begins the Shenandoah Valley Campaign in Virginia. Within a month, it will succeed.

Fort Pulaski, guarding Savannah, Georgia, fell on 11 April after a two-day Union bombardment.

Both Sides Legislate

Four days after the 'General' was seized, the US Congress passed the act that provided compensated emancipation in the District of Columbia, whose slaves had been freed on 10 April.

Meanwhile, in Richmond, the Confederate government was turning a soldier's voluntary service into an obligation. On 16 April, its Congress passed the Conscription Act, the first ever in America, predating by a full year similar legislation enacted by the Union. White males between the ages of 18 and 35 were now required to serve for three years, and the existing one-year enlistments were extended to three years. Conscription provoked disgust throughout the South, since it was at odds with states' rights. Vice President Stephens opposed it, and Governor Joseph Brown of Georgia was one of several governors who believed his troops should fight only in Georgia and that the act was unconstitutional. He wrote to President Davis: 'No acts of the Government of the United States prior to the secession of Georgia struck a blow at constitutional liberty so fell as has been stricken by the conscript acts.'

Exemptions existed for teachers, civil officials, railroad workers, and others needed on the home front. For those who failed to qualify, the conflict became 'A rich man's war, a poor man's fight'. The soldiers, of course, hated conscription. Private Sam Watkins of the First Tennessee Regiment would later recall: 'A soldier had no right to volunteer and to choose the branch of service he preferred. He was conscripted. From this time till the end of the war, a soldier was simply a machine, a conscript. It was mighty rough on rebels. We cursed the war, we cursed [General Braxton] Bragg, we cursed the Southern Confederacy. All our pride and valor had gone, and we were sick of war and the Southern Confederacy.'

Such dissent, fuelled by the way the war was going, was not lost on their commanders. On 25 July, Bragg himself wrote to General Samuel Cooper, the Confederate Army adjutant and inspector general, with a stark warning: 'Conscripts cannot be got from the region held by the Yankees, and soldiers will desert back to

1862

MAY

4–5 May The Battle of Williamsburg, Virginia ends with a Confederate retreat and Union occupation. Casualties: Union, 2239; Confederate, 1603.

8 May Confederate troops under Gen 'Stonewall' Jackson repulse the enemy at McDowell, Virginia.

9 May Norfolk, Virginia is abandoned by Confederate troops, who join in the defence of Richmond.

10 May Union force occupies Norfolk, while Confederates destroy Norfolk Navy Yard.

10 May Pensacola, Florida is occupied by Union troops after Confederates destroy Pensacola Navy Yard and withdraw.

10 May The Confederate fleet at Memphis, Tennessee sails up the river to engage a Union squadron, but retreats after an hour-long battle.

11 May CSS *Virginia* runs aground and is burned by her crew off Craney Island, Virginia to prevent her capture.

12 May Union fleet, under Flag Officer Farragut, occupies Baton Rouge, the capital of Louisiana.

12 May Natchez, Mississippi surrenders to Flag Officer Farragut's force.

Union troops gathered to view a captured Confederate cannon during the Peninsular Campaign in which US General George McClellan failed to take Richmond, Virginia.

their homes in possession of the enemy. Some do so from disaffection, some from weariness with the war, and some to protect their families against a brutal foe.'

The Surrender of New Orleans

The 'brutal foe' was now ready to capture New Orleans, the South's largest, richest city and its busiest port. Grant had concluded that it must be taken in order to control the Mississippi and to cut the Confederacy in two. Since 20 February, Flag Officer David Farragut had been waiting on Ship Island 105km (65 miles) from the city, delaying the attack until General Benjamin Butler's arrival, on 25 March.

To sail from the Gulf of Mexico up the Mississippi to New Orleans, Farragut's fleet of 24 ships had to battle past two forts, Jackson and St Philip, which had a line of ship hulks blocking the river between them. A week of shelling gained nothing, so Farragut decided to run the gauntlet in the darkness, moving at 2 a.m. on 24 April. The enemy guns thundered into action, setting his flagship, *Hartford*, on fire. The crew extinguished it, and all but four of the Union ships eventually passed the forts.

13 May Robert Smalls and seven other slaves seize the steamship *Planter* in Charleston Harbor and turn it over to the Union blockade squadron.

14 May Gen McClellan halts his advance 32km (20 miles) from Richmond to await reinforcements, despite having overwhelming troop numbers.

15 May The Union's James River Flotilla, including the *Monitor*, sails to within 12.8km (8 miles) of Richmond but is repulsed by batteries at Drewry's Bluff.

15 May Union Gen Benjamin Butler, commanding troops occupying New Orleans, issues orders to treat as prostitutes any woman who insults Union soldiers.

15 May The Virginia State Line, a Virginia militia, is established.

20 May President Lincoln signs the Homestead Act, providing western land to settlers who have never borne arms against the Union or aided its enemies.

The Battle of Baton Rouge

The city's last defence was a squadron of eight ships, but Farragut's men sank four of them. The next day, New Orleans surrendered, Mayor John Monroe sending a simple message: 'Come and take the city; we are powerless.'

The occupation proved tense. When Union troops raised the US flag over the New Orleans Mint and a civilian cut it down, Farragut threatened to shell the city. The attitudes and behaviour of both sides tended to be aggressive. Writing in her journal on 9 May about the occupying troops, Julia LeGrand noted: 'These people are treated with the greatest haughtiness by the upper classes and rudeness by the lower.' And a Confederate journalist in a federal prison in New Orleans wrote to President Davis on 13 September to complain: 'The wives and families of our citizens are frequently ejected from their houses to make way for coarse Federal officers and the Negro women, whom they appropriate as their wives and concubines.'

Unfortunately for the city's citizens, the Union military governor was General Butler.

Union troops manned mortars during their successful month-long siege of Yorktown, Virginia.

1862

MAY

24–30 May In four engagements, Gen Jackson's forces drive Gen Banks' troops from the Shenandoah Valley.

23 May Confederate Gen 'Stonewall' Jackson's troops defeat those of Gen Nathaniel Banks at Front Royal, Virginia, assisted by information from the Confederate spy Belle Boyd.

24 May The Union army's portable telegraph system is first employed in the Peninsular Campaign.

25 May President Lincoln telegraphs Gen McClellan that 'you must either attack Richmond or give up the job, and come back to the defense of Washington'.

27 May The Battle of Hanover Court House, Virginia, drives Confederates from that area.

29–30 May Gen Beauregard evacuates Corinth, Mississippi, ending a month-long Union siege.

Soldiers had some calm days at US General George McClellan's headquarters at Yorktown, Virginia.

The same man who had once advocated US Senator Jefferson Davis as the Democrats' strongest candidate for the White House now proved to be an extremely harsh dictator. He hanged the local man who had cut down the US flag; he took property from anyone refusing to swear allegiance to the Union; he even acquired the nickname of 'Spoons' for supposedly stealing some silverware from local homes.

On 15 May, upset by female insults towards Union troops – one woman in the French Quarter emptied her chamber pot over Admiral Farragut below – Butler issued his infamous General Order Number 28:

'As the Officers and Soldiers of the United States have been subject to repeated insults from the women calling themselves ladies of New Orleans, in return for the most scrupulous non-interference and courtesy on our part, it is ordered that hereafter when any Female shall by word, gesture, or movement, insult or show contempt for any officer of the United States, she shall be regarded and held liable to be treated as a woman of the town plying her avocation.'

A Union observation balloon is inflated with hydrogen at the battle of Seven Pines or Fair Oaks, Virginia.

This, of course, confirmed Southerners' prejudices about uncivilized Yankees. General Beauregard fired back his own General Order Number 44 expressing his outrage:

'Men of the South! Shall our mothers, our wives, our daughters, and our sisters, be thus

JUNE

30 May Union troops return to Front Royal, Virginia to rescue prisoners held from the 23 May engagement and to arrest Confederate spy Belle Boyd.

31 May– 1 June Battle of Seven Pines and Fair Oaks, Virginia is inconclusive, but Confederate Gen Joseph Johnston is severely wounded. Casualties: Union 5031; Confederate 6134.

1 June Gen Lee is given command of wounded Gen Johnston's Army of the Potomac and renames it the Army of Northern Virginia.

2 June Mrs Rose O'Neal Greenhow, who has continued to spy for the Confederate cause while under house arrest in Washington, DC, is banished to the South.

4 June Confederates evacuate Ft Pillow, Tennessee, on the Mississippi River.

outraged by the ruffianly soldiers of the North, to whom is given the right to treat, at their pleasure, the ladies of the South as common harlots? Arouse friends, and drive back from our soil, those infamous invaders of our homes and disturbers of our family ties.'

The Army of the Potomac Moves

Back in Virginia, McClellan's massive army was finally moving, and everyone wondered if it could be stopped. Some 400 ships carried more than 100,000 men of the Army of the Potomac to Fort Monroe at the end of the Virginia peninsula. The land advance of the 'Peninsular Campaign' began on 4 April, and the next day encountered a 13km (8 mile) Confederate defensive line at the Warwick River.

McClellan could have easily overrun these 17,000 troops, but his nature was again to delay

The Confederate Fort St Philip below New Orleans defended itself with 40 guns, forcing the Union fleet to pass by without capturing it.

The Union fleet fired 2,997 mortar shells at Fort Jackson below New Orleans on 18 April. A week's bombardment did little damage.

1862

JUNE

6 June A naval battle on Mississippi River results in the surrender of Memphis, Tennessee.

7–8 June Union artillery attack on Chattanooga accomplishes nothing.

9 June Confederates repulse the enemy at Port Republic, Virginia.

12–15 June Confederate Gen. 'Jeb' Stuart's cavalry undertakes raids around Gen McClellan's position in Virginia, destroying property and capturing prisoners.

16 June Confederates repulse Union advance on Charleston at Secessionville, South Carolina. Because his advance violated orders, Union Gen Henry Benham is relieved of command and arrested.

and set up a formal siege. His fears about the strength of the opposition were intensified when Confederate General John Magruder marched his men in a circle through a clearing, to give the impression that they were a larger army. McClellan immediately telegraphed Washington for more troops. This delay allowed the Rebels to bring up reinforcements for a total of 60,000. On 9 April, Lincoln reminded his general: 'The country will not fail to note – is noting now – that the present hesitation to move upon an entrenched enemy is but the story of Manassas repeated.'

Finally, on 4 May, McClellan was ready to attack – only to find that the enemy had withdrawn the previous night to better defences near Richmond. The Union army followed and occupied Yorktown, where they encountered a weapon used for the first time in warfare – land mines. These were shells buried by the Confederates a few inches below ground with a friction primer so that they exploded when stepped upon.

The next day, a fierce battle developed at Williamsburg, in which the Union lost 2200 men to the Confederates 1700. Yet the strong

New Orleans surrendered to Admiral David Farragut's fleet of 24 ships on 25 April, beginning a bitter occupation of the South's largest and richest city and busiest port.

19 June US Congress passes an act banning slavery in federal territories but not in the states.

24 June Union Gen Thomas Williams begins to construct a canal on a bend of the Mississippi so that ships can pass 9.6km (6 miles) away from Vicksburg's guns.

25 June First of the Seven Days Battles around Richmond, Virginia occurs at Oak Grove, with inconclusive results.

26 June Mechanicsville, second of the Seven Days Battles, sees Confederate attacks, but neither side makes important gains.

18 June Confederates evacuate Cumberland Gap, Tennessee, which is then occupied by Union forces.

26 June President Lincoln appoints Gen John Pope to command the Army of Virginia, the new name for the Army of the Potomac.

Army of the Potomac prevailed, pushing the Southerners out of Norfolk. The armies faced each other near Richmond until 31 May, when the Chickahominy River flooded, isolating part of McClellan's troops.

This confusion prompted Confederate General Joseph Johnston to launch a strong attack, which developed into the Battle of Seven Pines or Fair Oaks. It was a blundering affair, in which the Confederates suffered 6134 casualties for the Union's 5031. Johnston was severely wounded, but this would prove a considerable disadvantage to the Union: President Davis quickly replaced him with General Lee, who arrived at 2 p.m. on 1 June to order a return to the original Confederate positions.

The overcautious General McClellan continued his slow advance, but he had been shaken by the battle, writing to his wife that he was 'tired of the sickening sight of the battlefield with its mangled corpses and poor wounded'. Ultimately, his campaign would fail: Lee replaced Johnston's defensive tactics with an offensive strategy that pushed McClellan's superior army back to the Potomac.

It was also Lee's idea that General

Military camps were a common sight throughout the war in Virginia's fertile Shenandoah Valley, where Confederate General 'Stonewall' Jackson conducted brilliant operations in May and June.

'Stonewall' Jackson should conduct an offensive campaign through the Shenandoah Valley, tying up nearly 60,000 Union troops that McClellan desperately wanted for his advance on Richmond. Beginning on 5 May, Jackson used brilliant tactics and manoeuvres to confuse and defeat the enemy. Using his wartime philosophy to 'always mystify, mislead, and surprise the enemy', the general also kept his own men in the dark about the next day's orders: he would

1862

JUNE

27 June At Gaines' Mill, third of the Seven Days Battles, Gen Lee's troops drive Union forces back.

27 June Gen William Rosecrans assumes command of the Union's Army of the Cumberland.

27 June Confederate Gen Braxton Bragg replaces the ill Gen P.G. Beauregard as commander of the Army of Tennessee.

27–28 June Minor action at Garnett's and Golding's Farms, fourth of the Seven Days Battles, results in a slight withdrawal of Union positions.

28 June Union fleet, under Flag Officer Farragut, passes heavy batteries at Vicksburg, Mississippi to join the Union fleet in the upper river.

29 June At Savage's Station, fifth of the Seven Days Battles, Confederate attacks force Union forces to withdraw during the night.

30 June Gen McClellan's troops retreat after major action with Gen Lee's forces at White Oak Swamp or Glendale, the sixth of the Seven Days Battles. Casualties: Union, 2853; Confederate, 3615.

march them east towards Richmond, then order them onto trains going west. One moment, he seemed to be advancing on Maryland; the next, he looked certain to attack Washington. On 25 May, a nervous Lincoln telegraphed McClellan: 'I think that the time is near at hand when you must either attack Richmond or give up the job and come back to the defense of Washington'.

In the month-long Shenandoah Valley Campaign, Jackson's 'Stonewall Brigade' won five consecutive battles, outmanoeuvring three Union armies led by generals – John Frémont, Irvin McDowell and Nathaniel Banks. As Banks said, 'It is impossible to know what work lies before us. I feel the imperative necessity of making preparations for the worst'. And his fears were confirmed just two weeks later, on 23 May, when Jackson routed his forces at Front Royal. The war correspondent for the *New York Times* nicknamed the Confederate general 'the mountain fox' and others called him 'the wizard of the valley'.

'Stonewall' Jackson

Jackson, a devout Christian and devoted husband, wrote regularly to his wife, Mary Anna, during the dangerous campaign. 'You must not expect long letters from me in such busy times as these,' he apologized on 2 June, 'but always believe your husband never forgets his little darling.'

Jackson himself became the darling of the Confederacy. Beloved by his men, he was known for his eccentricities, wearing his Mexican War cap into battle, sucking lemons, laughing soundlessly with his mouth open, and always maintaining a bolt-upright position – to keep his internal organs in proper alignment, he insisted.

Although Union troops had more casualties at the Battle of Williamsburg, Virginia, on 4 and 5 May, they forced the Confederates to withdraw during the North's Peninsular Campaign.

JULY

1 July Although Union guns devastate the enemy at Malvern Hill, last of the Seven Days Battles, Gen McClellan withdraws and leaves Richmond safe. Casualties: Union, 3214; Confederate, 5355.

1 July Almost 5000 Confederate cavalry attack at Booneville, Mississippi, but Col Philip Sheridan counterattacks with just 827 Union troops and routs the enemy.

1 July The Union's freshwater and saltwater fleets meet for the first time on the Mississippi River near Vicksburg.

2 July US Congress passes legislation requiring each military officer and government official to swear allegiance to the Constitution.

4–28 July Confederate Col John Morgan conducts his first cavalry raid into Kentucky. His two regiments capture and parole 1200 prisoners.

7 July Gen McClellan writes a letter to President Lincoln, telling him how to run the war.

7 July Union Gen Benjamin Butler, occupying New Orleans, hangs William Mumford, in punishment for cutting down the American flag on 27 April.

Union General Nathaniel Banks was a former US Congressman and governor of Massachusetts.

He had strong religious convictions, never smoke or drank, and refused to eat peppers because they made his left leg ache.

Born Thomas Jonathan Jackson in rural Virginia, he was orphaned while young and raised by an uncle. Graduating from West Point in 1846 in the top third of his class, he served heroically in the Mexican War. After being promoted to major and assigned to duty in New York and Florida, he resigned in 1851 to become a professor of artillery and natural philosophy at the Virginia Military Academy. He and his cadets (who called him 'Tom Fool') were present at the hanging of John Brown. When the Civil War began, Jackson brought a battalion of cadets to Richmond to be drillmasters for new recruits. He then became a Confederate colonel in charge of Harper's Ferry, where he organized and trained his brigade, composed of five Virginia regiments from the Shenandoah Valley. On 17 June 1861, he was promoted to brigadier general and at Bull Run earned his famous nickname. Another promotion followed on 7 October, to major-general, and he was sent to the Shenandoah Valley, where he proved his brilliance.

McClellan Hesitates Again

In the last week of June, Lee began to punch back at McClellan, in what became known as the Seven Days Campaign near Richmond. The first engagement happened when the armies clashed on 25 June at Oak Grove, a day-long battle without a decisive result. The next day, McClellan was setting up his cannon for a barrage on Richmond when Lee's troops, under General Ambrose Hill, attacked the Union troops of General Fitz-John Porter, losing nearly 1500 Confederates to the enemy's 360. It was Porter, however, who withdrew 8km (5 miles) east, to secure a good position at Gaines' Mill. The following day, Lee's army attacked again, finally chasing Porter's force over the Chickahominy River but suffering too many casualties – 8750 to the Union's 4000.

After three further engagements, McClellan retreated to Malvern Hill, setting up 250 cannon in this strong position. Lee ordered his men to charge up the hill, and the Union artillery cut them down. The action was later summarized by Confederate General Daniel Hill: 'It was not war, it was murder.' Lee had lost 5300 men to McClellan's 3200.

1862

JULY

9 July President Lincoln visits Gen McClellan at Harrison's Landing, Virginia.

11 July President Lincoln appoints Gen Henry W. Halleck as General-in-Chief in Washington, DC – a post held by Lincoln for the four previous months.

11 July Col John Morgan's Confederate cavalry captures Lebanon, Kentuckyand destroys Union provisions, including sugar and coffee.

13 July Gen Nathan Bedford Forrest's Confederate cavalry takes Murfreesboro, Tennessee and its Union garrison, and breaks up the railroad track needed for a Union advance on Chattanooga.

14 July President Lincoln approves the Senate's resolution for a Medal of Honor for military bravery, to be awarded to noncommisioned officers and enlisted men.

14 July Union Gen Pope takes command of the Army of Virginia, but alienates his troops in his address by accusing them of talking constantly of 'lines of retreat'.

Mapping out a campaign strategy could be both tedious and argumentative. These Union generals hard at work are (left to right) Philip Sheridan, James Forsyth, Wesley Merritt, Thomas Devin and George Armstrong Custer.

15 July The CSS *Arkansas* attacks and passes the Union fleet above Vicksburg, partially disabling USS *Carondelet* and USS *Tyler*.

16 July Union's David Farragut is promoted to Rear Admiral, the first person to hold that rank in the US Navy.

17 July US Congress passes its Second Confiscation Act, declaring that all slaves of owners supporting 'the rebellion' will be for ever free.

18 July Confederate Gen Adam Johnson tricks a Union garrison intosurrendering at Newburgh, Indiana, by attacking with 12 men and false 'artillery' made of stove pipe.

21 July Union Gen Sherman takes command of the District of Memphis.

22 July President Lincoln submits first draft of the Emancipation Proclamation to his cabinet, but is persuaded to postpone it until the Union's military fortunes improve.

22 July The two governments agree a prisoner exchange.

In spite of this and his officers urging him to counterattack, McClellan continued to retreat until he was encamped on Harrison's Landing on the James River. He had technically not lost most of his battles, but Lee's enthusiastic charges and ample deceptions had baffled and frightened the indecisive Union general.

Nonetheless, his arrogance was still intact. His army, he declared, had 'fought an overwhelming enemy by day, and retreated from successive victories by night' before winning 'the ever-memorable victory at Malvern, where they drove back, beaten and shattered, the entire Eastern Army of the Confederacy.'

On 7 July, he wrote Lincoln a letter instructing him on how the war should be run. This was a blatant, and unwise, attempt to usurp the President's powers. 'A declaration of radical views, especially upon slavery, will rapidly disintegrate our present armies,' he advised, before defining what the very purpose of the war should be: 'It should not be a war looking to the subjugation of the people of any state, in any event. It should not be at all a war upon population but against armed forces and political organizations. Neither confiscation of property, political

US General William Rosecrans of Ohio commanded the Army of Occupation in West Virginia in 1862.

executions of persons, territorial organization of states, or forcible abolition of slavery should be contemplated for a moment.

During Lincoln's 8-9 July visit to McClellan's encampment, McClellan handed Lincoln the letter. Lincoln considered such a policy of conciliation to have already been proven a failure. Though having the option of removing McClellan, he chose instead to hand over his own title of general-in-chief to General Henry Halleck. This put future military decisions in the hands of the general who had taken charge of the disorganized military Department of the Missouri and turned out successful armies, including the one led by General Grant. Known as 'Old Brains', Halleck proved to be an

Waiting for battle could be gruelling, as in this Union camp during the Peninsula Campaign.

1862

JULY

31 July Confederate guns at Coggin's Point on Virginia's James River fire on the Union Fleet near Harrison's Landing, but little damage is done.

AUGUST

5 August President Lincoln's brother-in-law, Confederate Capt Alexander Todd, is mistakenly shot dead by his own side near Baton Rouge.

5 August Union forces repulse Confederate attempt to recapture Baton Rouge, Louisiana.

5 August The CSS *Arkansas* develops engine trouble on the Mississippi while attempting to join Confederates attacking Baton Rouge, Louisiana. It is blown up to avoid capture.

9 August Confederate troops of Gen Jackson defeat the enemy at Cedar Mountain, Virginia.

13 August Union nurse Clara Barton attends to both the Union and Confederate wounded on the field.

13 August London, Kentucky is captured by a Confederate cavalry brigade.

A field hospital at Savage's Station, Virginia, on 29 June shows the misery of the battlefield victims who were being treated near the graves of those killed.

impressive administrator, but one so out of touch with field affairs that his officers often ignored his orders. He also had an irascible nature that offended many and, like McClellan, he hesitated about sending armies into battle.

All Change!

The summer of 1862 saw many other changes of command, to give promising generals an opportunity. On 26 June, General John Pope was assigned to head the Union's new Army of Virginia. The next day, General William Rosecrans assumed command of the Union's Army of the Cumberland. And on 21 July, General Sherman took command of the District of Memphis. Meanwhile, on the Confederate side, General Braxton Bragg replaced the ill Beauregard at the head of the Army of Tennessee.

These strategic shifts all went smoothly except for Pope's introduction to his men. Addressing them on 14 July, he accused them and their beloved General McClellan of lacking the will to fight. 'I hear constantly of taking "strong positions and holding them" or "lines of retreat" and of "bases of supplies". Let us discard such ideas. The strongest position a

14 August President Lincoln proposes to a committee of northern black leaders that the government will pay freed slaves to emigrate.

15 August The Confederate Congress convenes in Richmond (until 13 October). President Davis tells them that the Union army threatening Richmond was defeated thanks to Confederate conscription.

20 August Horace Greeley's editorial in *New York Tribune*, titled 'A Prayer of Twenty Millions', urges Lincoln to enact emancipation.

20 August Northern black leaders reject President Lincoln's proposal to pay them to settle in other countries, saying that this 'served the cause of our enemies'.

22 August Lincoln responds to Greeley's editorial by stating, 'My paramount object … is to save the Union, and it is not either to save or to destroy slavery.'

22–23 August Confederate Gen Stuart's cavalry raids Gen Pope's camp near Catlett's Station, Virginia, capturing more than 300 prisoners, including staff officers, as well as money and information about his army.

soldier should desire to occupy is one from which he can most easily advance against the enemy.' And, in case his message needed clarification, he concluded, 'Success and glory are in the advance, disaster and same lurk in the rear.'

Nine days later, Pope became one of the first generals to imply his approval of plundering by his soldiers, authorizing a general order that 'it is not expected that their force and energy shall be wasted in protecting private property of those most hostile to the Government'.

Despite their troubles, the Confederates took courage from Lee's offensive strategy and the battlefield successes of their two

....

Confederate General Nathan Bedford Forrest conducted famous raids.

flamboyant cavalry leaders, General Nathan Bedford Forrest and Colonel John Morgan. Both men were acting separately to confound General Buell's advance towards Chattanooga, Tennessee. Forrest led 1000 men from that city on 6 July, and a week later captured an entire Union brigade of 1040 troops at Murfreesboro, as well as its stores, valued at nearly $1 million. He then destroyed railroad bridges to Chatanooga, an action that also blocked the force sent to capture him.

Morgan spent most of July taking his two regiments on raids around Kentucky, across more than 1600km (1000 miles) of territory. He captured and paroled 1200 prisoners while losing only 100 of his own men.

Particularly encouraging to Southern hearts was the strange success of General Adam Johnson, who crossed the Ohio River with a guerrilla band of 12 men to capture Newburgh, Indiana and its Union garrison. They accomplished the first capture of a town over the Mason–Dixon Line by threatening to shell the town with 'artillery' composed of stove pipe and charred logs placed on wagon wheels.

Lincoln Faces the Issue of Slavery

This was also the summer when President Lincoln again had to grapple with the slavery question, as battlefield successes slowed and abolitionist pressures grew. 'Things had gone from bad to worse,' he later recalled, so that 'we had about played our last card, and must change our tactics, or lose the game. I now determined upon the adoption of the emancipation policy.' This, he believed, would bring the abolitionists behind him, wreck the Southern economy, and help win Britain's support. He prepared the draft without his cabinet's knowledge and submitted it on 22 July, but was persuaded to postpone until the army had gained a solid victory.

1862

AUGUST

24 August The Confederate cruiser *Alabama*, built in Liverpool, England, is commissioned at sea near the Azores.

26 August Franklin Buchanan is promoted to Admiral, the top-ranking officer in the Confederate navy.

26 August Confederate Gen 'Stonewall' Jackson leads his troops between the Union army of Gen John Pope and Washington, DC.

29–30 August The Second Battle of Bull Run (Confederate: Second Manassas), Virginia is won by Confederates led by Gens Lee, Jackson and James Longstreet over the Union force of Gen Pope.

30 August At Richmond, Kentucky, Confederates under Gen Edmund Kerby Smith defeat the Union army of Gen M.D. Manson. Casualties: Union, 5353; Confederate, 451.

SEPTEMBER

1 September Confederates win the Battle of Chantilly (or Ox Hill), Virginia under Gens Lee and Jackson. Two Union generals are killed: Isaac Stevens and Philip Kearny.

Another solution presented itself: to eliminate the black problem by settling freed slaves in other countries. On 12 July he told representatives from the border states, 'Room in South America for colonization can be obtained cheaply.' He added that when large numbers of freed slaves agreed to this, the others 'will not be so reluctant to go'. Indeed, on 14 August, he called in free Negro leaders to consider his proposal, offering that the government would pay for this emigration. Six days later, they turned it down, saying that the move 'served the cause of our enemies'.

During this, the President was confronted by his persistent gadfly Horace Greeley, the powerful owner and editor of the *New York Tribune*. Before the war, Greeley had written that the South should be allowed to secede. Early in the war, he had called for a quick peace. Now, on 19 August, Greeley wrote a provocative editorial titled 'A Prayer of Twenty Millions'. In effect an open letter to Lincoln, it urged him to enact emancipation, and pointed out that the public was 'sorely disappointed and deeply pained by the policy you seem to be pursuing with regard to the slaves of rebels'.

The editorial further accused Lincoln of being 'strangely and disastrously remiss in the discharge of your official and imperative duty' and of being 'unduly influenced by the councils, the representations, the menaces, of certain fossil politicians hailing from the Border Slave States'. As for slavery itself, Greeley was damning, writing that the President seemed 'never to interfere with these atrocities'.

Worried about the influence of the powerful publisher, Lincoln fired back a letter three days later, saying he agreed neither with those people who declared that they would not save the Union unless they could also save slavery, nor with those who would not save the Union unless they could also destroy slavery. 'If I could save the Union without freeing any slave, I would do it,' he vowed. 'If I could save it by freeing all the slaves, I would do it – and if I could do it by freeing some and leaving others alone, I would also do that.' In a summary statement, Lincoln shocked abolitionists: 'My paramount object is to save the Union and not either to save or destroy slavery.'

Exactly one month later, however, the pragmatic President would issue his Emancipation Proclamation.

John H. Morgan, then a Confederate colonel, led a cavalry raid into Kentucky on 4 July.

---

2 September Gen Pope orders his Union army to retreat to the edge of Washington, DC.

2 September President Lincoln relieves Gen Pope of the command of the Army of Virginia, replacing him with Gen McClellan, and reverts to calling it the Army of the Potomac.

2 September Gen Lee's army is joined at Chantilly, Virginia by the troops of Gen D.H. Hill. This gives him a total of 70,000 men, compensating for the loss of 30,000 men to battle, disease and straggling.

5 September Gen Lee's army crosses the Potomac River into Maryland, his first invasion of a Union state.

5 September Gen Braxton Bragg's Confederate troops enter Kentucky.

5 September The CSS *Alabama* captures its first US commercial ship, the whaler *Ocmulgee*, in the Azores. Her crew is taken as prisoners and the ship burned.

6 September An engagement occurs at Washington, North Carolina.

13 September Union Gen McClellan is given a copy of battle plans lost by Confederate Gen Lee, but McClellan hesitates, fearing a trap.

The Union Takes a Beating

Before that happened, Union troops would come to grief on the battlefield – ironically at the place that was a symbol of Union's failures, Bull Run.

Lincoln's new military adviser, General Halleck, devised a fresh plan to combine McClellan's army with the new one led by Pope: the two would meet in Washington and march together on Richmond. This information, however, fell into Confederate hands on 22 August, when General Jeb Stuart made a daring cavalry raid on Pope's own camp near Catlett's Station, Virginia.

Lee now acted boldly, dividing his army and sending Stonewall Jackson's troops on 26 August to move around Pope's force to stand between them and Washington. The purpose was to force Pope to retreat, but he had no intention of being made to look weak like McClellan. He sent his army directly after Jackson, who had by then captured the Union supply depot at Manassas Junction. The Confederate general was again too clever, evading and confusing the enemy until 29 August, when Pope finally sent his men on a direct attack. The Second Battle of Bull Run had begun, and raged fiercely for two days. The Rebels beat back wave after wave of the enemy before Jackson withdrew some of his tired troops.

Pope assumed this was the beginning of a retreat and informed General Halleck in Washington that he would pursue. It was a bad mistake, but worse still, he had forgotten about Lee. The purpose of Jackson's manoeuvres had been to delay long enough for Lee's army to arrive on Pope's other side. And on 30 August, Lee sent General Longstreet's army to attack. Pope, fighting in both directions with his vastly larger army, had no choice but to admit defeat, retreating on 2 September to the outskirts of Washington.

The Confederate ironclad CSS Arkansas *became disabled on 5 August sailing to help retake Baton Rouge, Louisiana. It was blown up to avoid capture by the enemy.*

1862

SEPTEMBER

14 September The Battle of South Mountain, Maryland is won by Union troops led by Gen Jesse Lee Reno, who is killed. Casualties: Union, 1813; Confederate, 2685.

15 September Harper's Ferry, Virginia captured by Gen Jackson's Confederate troops.

16 September Confederates led by Gen Braxton Bragg capture Munfordville, Kentucky and its garrison.

17 September The Battle of Antietam (Sharpsburg), Maryland, the war's bloodiest day, is a draw, but Lee halts invasion of Maryland. Casualties: Union, 12,410; Confederate, 13,724.

17 September Union forces at Cumberland Gap, Tennessee are cut off and forced to abandon the garrison.

19 September Union success at the Battle of Iuka, Mississippi forces Confederate troops to retreat.

19 September Gen Lee crosses back into Virginia.

Union General William T. Sherman (centre) and his excellent staff played an important role in the Battle of Shiloh on 6 and 7 April and later in December supported General Ulysses Grant's first moves in his Vicksburg campaign.

20 September Union troops cross the Potomac River to attack Gen Lee's forces at Blackford's Ford, Virginia, but are driven back with losses.

22 September President Lincoln issues his Emancipation Proclamation to take effect 1 January 1863, liberating slaves in the Confederacy but not in border states loyal to the Union.

23 September Northern newspapers publish the Emancipation Proclamation.

25 September Confederates withdraw from Sabine City, Texas after a bombardment by Union ships.

26 September Confederate Gen Braxton Bragg in Bardstown, Kentucky issues a proclamation to those fighting for the Union, insisting that 'The Union is a thing of the past'.

26 September The Confederate Congress' Committee on Foreign Affairs recommends that President Davis open the Mississippi River and Southern markets to Northwestern states. (This never takes effect.)

Confederate General James 'Pete' Longstreet was called 'my old war horse' by General Robert E Lee.

The Second Battle of Bull Run was a repeat Confederate victory fought over the same Virginia territory. The Southerners were greatly outnumbered but won by superior leadership.

This crushing blow was worse than the first Battle of Bull Run, the Union casualties numbering 16,054 to the Confederates' 9197. It again demonstrated the superiority of Southern generals. Pope was removed from his command, but McClellan, who had hesitated and arrived with his army a day after the battle, was once more surprisingly given overall command. 'Again I have been called upon to save the country,' he wrote to his wife, Ellen.

Far away in England at this time, a further problem was brewing for the Union. Under a secret contract, a private shipyard had built *Enrica* at Birkenhead, on the River Mersey. It

1862

SEPTEMBER

27 September The first Union regiment of free blacks is formed: the First Regiment Louisiana Native Guards.

27 September The Confederate government extends its conscription law to call into service all men between the ages of 35 and 45.

29 September Union Gen William Nelson is shot dead by Union Gen Jefferson C. Davis at Louisville, Kentucky during an argument. A court-martial later acquits Davis.

30 September Confederates lose an engagement at Newtonia and are forced out of Missouri.

OCTOBER

1 October The Union's Western Gunboat Fleet is transferred from the War Department to the Navy.

1 October Confederate Gen 'Jeb' Stuart's first cavalry raid into Pennsylvania.

had been launched on 15 May, unarmed, for a 'trial voyage'. This fooled no one, and the US minister to Great Britain protested. However, the ship eventually sailed to the Azores in the North Atlantic and on 24 August was commissioned at sea as the Confederate cruiser *Alabama*. Its captain was Commander Raphael Semmes, who would sail it around the world for two years, virtually destroying US commerce on the high seas.

Britain was also moving close to recognizing the Confederacy. Expecting another Union defeat, its government offered to mediate in the war.

A Second Waterloo

On 5 September, encouraged by his success at Bull Run, General Lee moved his army across the Potomac to Maryland, for his first invasion of a Union state. He headed for a position that would threaten both Washington and Baltimore. By 7 September, he had advanced 64km (40 miles) northwest of Washington and was at the town of Frederick. The next day he issued a proclamation to the citizens of Maryland: 'The people of the Confederate States have long watched with the deepest sympathy the wrongs and outrages that have been inflicted upon the citizens of a Commonwealth allied to the states of the South by the strongest social, political, and commercial ties.' He added that the South had long wished to help Maryland throw off 'this foreign yoke' and for that reason 'our army has come among you and is prepared to assist you with the power of its arms in regaining the rights of which you have been despoiled'.

Eager to take more territory, including Harper's Ferry in Virginia, Lee took another bold step. Dividing his army into four sections,

Tired soldiers view the railway wreckage after the Second Battle of Bull Run.

3 October In one of the few bayonet charges of the war, Union troops rout Confederates at Corinth, Mississippi.

4 October Richard Hawes is inaugurated in Frankfort, Kentucky as the unofficial Confederate governor of Kentucky.

5 October Galveston, Texas captured by US Navy force.

8 October The Battle of Perryville, Kentucky is a tactical Confederate victory, but troops under Gen Braxton Bragg withdraw from the state. Casualties: Union, 4211; Confederate, 3396.

10 October Confederate Major Gen 'Stonewall' Jackson is promoted to Lieutenant General and given the command of the new 2nd Corps of the Army of Northern Virginia.

he gave each written instructions on how all his armies would move. One officer used his to wrap a cigar – and then forgot it as the army left Frederick. It was found by a Union soldier, who conveyed it immediately to a delighted McClellan. Now aware that Lee's smaller army was divided into even smaller fragments, he said enthusiastically, 'Here is a paper with which, if I cannot whip Bobby Lee, I will be willing to go home.'

Yet, instead of attacking, McClellan considered his options for 16 hours, even wondering if the orders were an elaborate bluff left behind on purpose. In that time, Lee had been informed of the 'Lost Order', and was pulling his troops back together as the Union general approached with an army that outnumbered Lee's by 70,000 to 39,000. The two forces came together at 6 a.m. on 17 September at Antietam Creek, 29km (18 miles) west of Frederick. The ensuing battle proved to be the war's bloodiest day, known to the North as the Battle of Antietam, and to the South as the Battle of Sharpsburg (the town where Confederate troops had gathered).

Artillery thundered

The Battle of Antietam was called 'the bloodiest single day of the war' with 4,808 men killed.

The dead rest in peace after the Battle of Antietam in Maryland which forced General Robert E. Lee to withdraw his troops to Virginia.

on both sides as charges and counter-charges took their toll. Confederate Colonel John B. Gordon recalled about one part of the battlefield, 'the green corn that grew upon it looked as if it had been struck by a storm of bloody hail'. Another Confederate, Major Henry Kyd Douglas, called it 'a dreadful scene. The dead and dying lay there on the field like harvest sheaths. ... Prayers were mingled with oaths, and midnight hid all distinction between blue and gray'.

1862

OCTOBER

11 October The Confederate government amends the Conscription Act to exempt people in charge of 20 or more slaves.

13 October Gen John Pemberton is given command of the Confederacy's Department of Mississippi, Tennessee, and East Louisiana.

22 October Confederates reoccupy the garrison at Cumberland Gap, Tennessee, which was abandoned by Union forces on 17 September.

22 October Confederates repulse Union attack on Yemassee, South Carolina.

26 October Gen McClellan's army crosses the Potomac River into Virginia.

28 October The first black regiment to see combat, the 79th US Colored Infantry from Kansas, is involved in action at Island Mounds, Missouri.

Another horrific scene occurred at a sunken road, where for three hours General Edwin Sumner's Union troops stormed the line held by the troops of General Daniel Hill. Bodies piled up two and three deep, while men grabbed rifles from the hands of the dead to continue an uninterrupted hail of bullets. Union staff officer, standing with McClellan to watch the Union attacks on the road, recalls the general's comment: 'By George, this is a magnificent field, and if we win this fight it will cover all our errors and misfortunes for ever.'

George Smalley, correspondent to the *New York Tribune,* wrote of Antietam: 'It is the greatest fight since Waterloo.'

McClellan again mismanaged the situation, not committing his full force at any one time, but allowing Lee to position and reposition to match each assault until the fight came to a standstill. But the fighting was costly for the Confederates, who lost 13,724 casualties (a third of their total that day) to the Union's 12,410 (a sixth). Lee considered a counterattack but was talked out of it by Generals Jackson and Longstreet. Still, he waited a day to withdraw the night of the 18th. McClellan,

for his part, did not pursue, deciding his men were too injured and exhausted, despite the arrival of 12,000 fresh troops.

The battle was so close that Lee could tell his troops it was a success: 'History records few examples of greater fortitude and endurance than this army has exhibited, and I am commissioned by the President to thank you in the name of the Confederate States for the undying fame you have won for their arms.' In fact, Antietam was a blow that forced Lee back into Virginia on the 19th. Indeed, it has sometimes been described as the real turning point of the war.

....

*Confederates captured
Harpers Ferry on
15 September.*

Healthy horses were vital not only to the cavalry but to all divisions of the army. Here a blacksmith shoes a horse at the headquarters of the Union's Army of the Potomac.

The Emancipation Proclamation

Although he was again upset by McClellan's lack of leadership and pursuit, President Lincoln was quick to call the battle a Union triumph, and he used it to announce his Emancipation Proclamation five days later, on 22 September. In practice, it freed no slaves, since the proclamation applied only to areas under the control of the Confederacy and not to the Union border states or to Southern regions under Union occupation. However, it had an important psychological impact. Set to take effect on 1 January 1863, it held out the promise that a Union victory would lead to freedom for all slaves. It was certainly viewed this way in Great Britain, which backed away from any overt support for the South, though many in its government remained hopeful that the South could retain its freedom.

The Times of London, in fact, continued its anti-Union stance, saying Lincoln's proclamation 'has the fatal demerit of being insufficient to please the ultra-abolitionists, and of being more than enough to offend the Southern slave-owner, the Northern Pro-slavery party, and the advocates of State rights, and all that large class

1862

NOVEMBER

17 November Britain's minister in Washington, DC informs his government that the Democrats want to end the war even at the risk of losing the Southern states.

21 November Union Gen Edwin Sumner demands the surrender of Fredericksburg, Virginia, threatening a bombardment. Almost the whole population evacuates.

23 November A grand military display is held in New Orleans and 28,000 troops are reviewed, including a regiment composed of 1400 'free colored men'.

24 November Confederate President Davis appoints Gen Joseph E. Johnston to command the Army in the West.

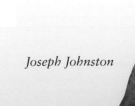

Joseph Johnston

of persons, American as well as Irish, who have a social, a political and an economic objection to the Negro, and who, though refusing to enslave him, would absolutely expel and banish him from their territories, as in Illinois and Wisconsin, and who would deny him all social status, as in New York and Pennsylvania.'

An important event came on 28 October at Island Mounds, Missouri, where the 79th US Colored Infantry from Kansas became the first black regiment to see combat. The very first regiment of Negroes had, in fact, been formed only in the previous month, on 27 September, by General Butler in New Orleans, the First Regiment Louisiana Native Guards consisting of 1,500 freed slaves from that city. The Confederate government would eventually respond, on 23 December, with an order that slaves found to be serving with Union forces, as well as with their officers, should be dealt with under state laws, a situation that implied execution.

Victory and Despair

As winter arrived, more commands were shifted. The Confederacy promoted Stonewall Jackson to lieutenant general on 10 October and placed him

President Lincoln visited General George McClellan at Antietam, Maryland, on 4 October. It was to be their last ever meeting, with Lincoln soon relieving him of his command.

28 November Confederate Gen Wade Hampton leads a cavalry raid, capturing 92 enemy soldiers, at Hartwood Church, Virginia.

28 November Union troops come off best during a skirmish with the enemy at Cane Hill, Arkansas.

29 November The Kearny Medal for Officers is created for all those who 'honorably served in battle' under Union Gen Philip Kearny, killed 1 September 1862.

DECEMBER

1 December Official US reports show that Union states have furnished 1,355,087 troops to the war by this date.

1 December President Lincoln's message to the US Congress says he favours sending freed slaves to other nations if they wish to go.

7 December The Battle of Prairie Grove, Arkansas, won by Union forces.

7 December Confederate Col John Morgan's cavalry captures Hartsville, Tennessee and its garrison.

7 December The CSS *Alabama* captures a US steamer carrying 140 US Marinesand 500 other passengers, but releases it, unable to take so many prisoners.

Union soldiers begin crossing a bridge over the Rappahannock to burning Fredericksburg, Virginia.

in charge of the new 2nd Corps of the Army of Northern Virginia. On 30 October, the Union replaced General Buell with General Rosecrans as commander of the Army of the Cumberland.

Of more impact, President Lincoln again relieved McClellan as commander of the Army of the Potomac of 5 November, angered that it took six weeks after Antietam for McClellan to bring his Army over the Potomac to Virginia. His replacement was General Ambrose Burnside, who had previously turned the command down.

Anxious to make a good impression, Burnside got his army of 120,000 men moving on 15 November. Two days later, he had reached the Rappahannock River, across from Fredericksburg, Virginia, which was halfway between Washington and Richmond. Since the river was high, he waited for pontoons, which took six days to arrive. He then waited for another three weeks, giving Lee time to position 75,000 troops on Marye's Heights, which overlooked the town from the south.

1862

DECEMBER

10–13 December Gen Hampton's cavalry raids Dumbries, Virginia capturing a wagon train with its 50 guards.

11 December Gen Burside's Union troops bombard Fredericksburg, Virginia, and cross the Rappahannock River to capture the town.

12 December The ironclad USS *Cairo* becomes the first ship sunk by a Confederate mine ('torpedo'), electrically detonated on the Yazoo River near Haines Bluff, Mississippi.

13 December Gen Lee's Confederate troops rout Gen Burnside's overwhelmingly larger army at Fredericksburg, Virginia. Casualties: Union, 12,700; Confederate, 5300.

Union forces ford the Rappahannock River on 11 December to occupy deserted Fredericksburg, Virginia after they had shelled it. The rise and fall of the river played a key role in several of the war's campaigns. The Union had formed the Department of the Rappahannock on 4 April.

In no mood for a siege, Burnside shelled Fredericksbug on 11 December, then crossed the river under sniper fire to captured the now deserted town. Two days later, he made a suicidal mistake, trying to surprise Lee by rushing his troops up the sloping open field toward the most formidable position of the high Confederate guns – which picked the soldiers off with lethal precision. The Southerners were impregnable behind a 1.2m (4ft) wall that ran over 800m (875yd) long. Even so, Burnside continued into the night, sending assault after assault. 'A chicken could not live in that field when we open on it,' said a Confederate artillery commander, Lieutenant Colonel Edward Alexander.

Lee, watching the carnage, thought in more general terms: 'It is well that war is so terrible. We should become too fond of it.'

14 December Union Gen Nathaniel Banks arrives in New Orleans to command the Department of the Gulf, relieving Gen Benjamin Butler.

16 December–1 January Gen Nathan Bedford Forrest's Confederate cavalry raids western Tennessee, including Lexington, Jackson and Trenton.

17 December Gen Grant expels all (merchant) Jews from his military district, saying they are violating Treasury Department regulations.

17–18 December Gen Hampton's cavalry raids towards Occoquan, Virginia, capturing 150 Union prisoners and 20 wagons.

20 December Gen Grant's advance base at Holly Spring, Mississippi is destroyed by Confederate troops halting his Southern advance.

Burnside made plans to continue the assault the next morning, even planning to lead his troops into the fire. His officers were able to talk him out of this insanity, however, and he had to accept that his first major action had become a disaster. The Union losses totalled 12,700 to only 5300 for Lee's army. This took much of the shine from the Antietam victory, and the year ended with other Union setbacks. Confederates halted General Grant's advance by destroying his advance base at Holly Spring, Mississippi, on 20 December; General Sherman was repulsed outside Vicksburg, Mississippi on 29 December; and the South's twin cavalry heroes, Generals Morgan and Stuart, were

Fredericksburg, Virginia, is a grim picture with its destroyed bridge after the Union attack.

1862

DECEMBER

23 December The Confederate government orders that black slaves serving with Union forces should be dealt with according to state laws. This implies execution.

23 December Confederate President Davis proclaims that Union Gen Benjamin Butler should be considered an outlaw due to his earlier order insulting the women of New Orleans.

25 December Union troops near Vicksburg, Mississippi, destroy railroad tracks leading to Louisiana and Texas.

25–28 December Confederate Gen John Morgan's cavalry completes a 'Christmas Raid' into Kentucky.

26 December Confederate President Davis addresses the Mississippi legislature in Jackson, saying the 'dirty Federal invaders' have insulted women and wantonly destroyed property.

conducting freewheeling raids in Kentucky and Virginia, respectively.

Many in the South recognized that the gains were superficial. The Confederacy did have many outstanding generals and exceptional soldiers, but losses were mounting. And there were not enough Lees and Jacksons. A mood of pessimism was spreading among the war-weary troops, politicians and citizens.

In a letter to President Davis in December, Confederate Senator James Phelan of Mississippi warned:

'The spirit of enlistment is thrice dead. Enthusiasm has expired to a cold pile of damp ashes. Defeats, retreats, sufferings, dangers, magnified by spiritless helplessness and an unchangeable conviction that our army is in the hands of ignorant and feeble commanders, are rapidly producing a sense of settled despair.'

Black soldiers were recruited by the Union and proved to be enthusiastic fighters.

26–31 December Confederate Gen 'Jeb' Stuart leads a raid on Dumfries, Virginia, causing 30 Union casualties and taking some 200 prisoners and other supplies.

28–29 December Confederates repulse Gen Sherman's attack on Chickasaw Bayou at Vicksburg, Mississippi.

31 December The ironclad USS *Monitor* founders and sinks at sea off Cape Hatteras, North Carolina with the loss of 16 lives.

31 December–2 January The Battle of Stones River (or Murfreesboro), Tennessee is a draw, but Confederate forces halt the Union advance on Chattanooga. Casualties: Union, 12,906; Confederate, 11,739

Chapter Three
1863

The Emancipation Proclamation took effect on New Year's Day, and Lincoln promised, 'not one word of it will I ever recall'. He reaffirmed this a week later to General John McClernand, writing that 'broken eggs cannot be mended. I have issued the emancipation proclamation, and I cannot retract it'.

The response was mixed. The day before, working men of Manchester, England, sent the President the type of foreign approval he was seeking: 'Heartily do we congratulate you and your country on this humane and righteous course. We assume that you can not now stop short of a complete uprooting of slavery.' Less welcome was the response from Lincoln's home state, where a resolution of the Illinois Legislature called the proclamation 'a gigantic usurpation' whose result would be 'not only a total subversion of the Federal Union, but a revolution in the social organization of the Southern States ... the present and far-reaching consequences of which to both races cannot be contemplated without the most dismal foreboding of horror and dismay'.

Private reactions were less pessimistic. Union Captain James M. Randall wrote to a friend: 'You ask if I think the Emancipation Proclamation will serve to bring the war to a more speedy close. I answer candidly that I don't believe it will, yet I am heartily in favor of the measure, because I am convinced that its tendency will be to give us a more permanent peace in the end.'

The year's first day also saw the first of several

Left: Lincoln's Emancipation Proclamation was praised in the North. Right: A Confederate assault on Fort Sanders, overlooking Knoxville, Tennessee, failed on 29 November.

On 11 January, 13 Union gunboats led the successful capture of Fort Hindman at Arkansas Post on the Arkansas River.

surprising Confederate naval successes when Galveston, Texas, was retaken by General John Magruder. During this action, two Confederate steamers captured the powerful steamer USS *Harriet Lane* and ran off the Union fleet, killing Commander W. B. Renshaw, whose naval force had won the city just three months earlier.

Then on 11 January, the *Alabama* scored a considerable victory. Operated by a mostly British crew, it was rapidly becoming the scourge of the seas. And now, cruising off Galveston, it sank the USS *Hatteras,* a profound shock to the US Navy. Four days later, the CSS *Florida,* also built in Britain, left Mobile, Alabama, to begin raiding US commercial ships from New York to Brazil. And on 17 January, the blockade of Sabine Pass, Texas, was lifted when two Confederate ships captured two Union ones.

Bogged Down

Back in Virginia, General Burnside was trying to recover from his defeat at Fredericksburg. On 20 January, he began a march to make a circular movement, cross the Rappahannock, and surprise the left flank of General Lee's army. However, his bad luck had not abated: torrential rains and howling winds bogged down his troops in what became known as the 'Mud March'. His tired, waterlogged troops even encountered a sign left across the river for them by the enemy: 'Burnside stuck in the mud'. The *New York Times* correspondent, William Swinton, noted that horses and mules collapsed trying to pull their loads: 'One hundred and fifty dead animals, many of them buried in the liquid muck, were counted in the course of a morning's ride.'

One Union private, Warren Lee Gross, looked for the humorous side:

'The noise of walking was like that of a suction-pump when the water is exhausted. ... Occasionally a boot or shoe would be left in the mud, and it would take an exploring expedition to find it. ... The boys called their shoes "pontoons", "mud-hooks", "soil-excavators", and other names not quite so polite. ... Virginia mud has never been fully comprehended. To fully understand it you must march in it, sleep in it, be encompassed round about by it. Great is mud – Virginia mud.'

1863

JANUARY

1 January Emancipation Proclamation takes effect without freeing any slaves, applying only to those in territories the Union does not control and exempting Union slave states.

1 January Confederate Gen John Magruder surprises the Union garrison at Galveston, Texas and recaptures the city. Most Union ships escape and resume the blockade.

2 January The USS *Passaic* reaches Beaufort Harbor, North Carolina after surviving a gale. Crew members wrote about sinking and placed the message in a bottle thrown overboard.

4 January President Lincoln orders Grant to repeal the expulsion of Jewish merchants from his district and reminds him that Jews are fighting in Union ranks.

8 January The Confederate cavalry of Gen John Marmaduke, joined by Col William Quantrill's Bushwhackers, raid Springfield, Missouri.

Lincoln, feeling equally mired down, did not see the funny side and recalled Burnside. (Today the general's principal legacy is arguably to barbers: his mutton-chop whiskers became known as 'sideburns'.) He was replaced on 26 January by General Joseph Hooker, known as 'Fighting Joe' for his aggressive fighting with the same Army of the Potomac. Just two days before his appointment, Burnside had ordered the dismissal of Hooker, who criticized him for his actions at Antietam, where Hooker was seriously wounded. The President's letter of appointment was also strangely critical of Hooker: 'You are ambitious, which, within reasonable bounds, does good rather than harm; but I think that during General Burnside's command of the army, you have taken counsel of your ambition, and thwarted him as much as you could, in which you did a great wrong to the country and to a most meritorious and honorable brother officer.'

Attempts to Take Vicksburg

On 30 January, General Grant began his monumental campaign to capture Vicksburg, Mississippi, site of the key battery that blocked the Union fleet's free passage on the Mississippi River. Success would cut the Confederacy in half, disrupting its supply lines. Lincoln had earlier pointed at a map and told Admiral David Porter, 'See what a lot of land these fellows hold, of which Vicksburg is the key. ... The war can never be brought to a close until the key is in our pocket.'

Preliminary attacks throughout the previous year had proved futile. Farragut's fleet, which had taken New Orleans, was been beaten back when it reached Vicksburg, 320km (200 miles) up the river. On 24 June, Grant put General Thomas Williams in charge of constructing a canal that would allow ships to avoid the bend that took them close to Vicksburg. Four days later, the fleet dashed upriver under fire, meeting up with the Union's river gunboats on 1 July.

The city was well defended on land approaches by nine forts along 14.5km (9 miles). A river assault on the city by General Sherman then failed. 'We have been to Vicksburg,' he wrote to his wife on 4 January 1863, 'and it was too much for us, and we have backed out'. Now Grant's

US General Joseph Hooker took command of the Army of the Potomac on 26 January.

army was gathered across the river in flat Louisiana, looking up at the imposing heights of the city. As usual, he was matter-of-fact about the job to be done. 'The work of reducing Vicksburg will take time and men,' he informed General Halleck in Washington, 'but can be accomplished.'

11 January Union forces, backed by gunboats, capture Ft Hindman on the Arkansas River, which guards Little Rock.

11 January The CSS *Alabama* sinks the USS *Hatteras* off the coast of Galveston, Texas.

12 January The Confederate Congress meets in Richmond (until 1 May).

14 January Union troops and four gunboats engage the enemy at Bayou Teche, Louisiana.

15 January CSS *Florida* sails from Mobile, Alabama to raid Union ships from New York to Brazil.

21 January The blockade of Sabine Pass, Texas is temporarily lifted when the Confederate ships *Josiah Bell* and *Uncle Ben* capture the Union's *Morning Light* and *Velocity*.

From February to April, he made four abortive attempts to cross the river just north of the city, through woods and bayous. The Mississippi itself was the scene of sporadic engagements. On 14 February, the USS *Queen of the West* was grounded and captured in the Black River 64km (40 miles) below Vicksburg after being battered by the guns of Fort Taylor. Ten days later, repaired by the Confederates, it led three other ships in an attack on the excellent Union gunboat, USS *Indianola,* which surrendered after being run aground.

Again the Southerners began to repair their prize, unaware that an unpleasant surprise was being readied upriver. Admiral David Porter's men constructed a dummy warship out of old boards, using pork barrels on top of each other for smokestacks. The plan was to float this unmanned ship past Confederate batteries to provoke fire, since five of the Vicksburg guns had burst during an earlier barrage. The dummy ship, however, achieved more than this. Not only did the enemy guns come into action, but the Confederates decided to sink both their captured Union vessels, the *Queen of the West* and *Indianola,* to keep them out of Union hands.

US Admiral Andrew Porter commanded the fleet that helped capture Fort Hindman.

On 7 May, General Grant left his supply base at Grand Gulf below Vicksburg, boldly reducing his communications supplies in order to interrupt those of the enemy. One week later, he captured the capital of Jackson, driving out General Joseph Johnston and isolating Vicksburg, 64km (40 miles) away.

Grant would have little further success with Vicksburg as summer approached. His ambitious canal led to disaster after a levee broke on 8 March. The rushing water tore down new dikes and the tools of the workmen, and flooded the soldiers' camps, driving them out. By 19 May, Grant's army had surrounded the city and launched an all-out attack. It was repulsed at every point by the Confederate defenders under the command of General John Pemberton.

A Philadelphia native whose father was a Quaker minister, Pemberton had married a Virginian and taken up the Confederate cause. General Johnston warned him on 18 May that it would be dangerous to be trapped in Vicksburg and that he should preserve the army by withdrawing, but Pemberton was determined to defend the city.

1863

JANUARY

20 January Gen Burnside begins the disastrous 'mud march' in Virginia, in which his troops become bogged down in mud while trying to surprise Gen Lee's forces.

21 January A Union court martial finds Gen Fitz John Porter guilty of failure to obey orders at the Second Battle of Bull Run; he is dishonourably discharged.

23 January Union Gen Burnside dismisses his subordinate Gen Joseph Hooker from military service.

25 January President Lincoln relieves Gen Burnside of command of the Army of the Potomac, replacing him with Gen Hooker.

26 January Gen Burnside's formal Order of Farewell states that his command of the Army of the Potomac 'had not been fruitful in victory'.

Three days later, Grant made a frontal attack, but his 45,000 troops were beaten back by only 18,000 of the 30,000 Confederates in the city. Grant later wrote in his memoirs,

'The attack was gallant, and portions of each of the three corps succeeded in getting up to the very parapets of the enemy and in planting their battle flags upon them; but at no place were we able to enter. ... This last attack only served to increase our casualties without giving any benefit whatever.'

The next day, 23 May, Grant decided to conduct a regular siege – or, as he put it, 'out-camp the enemy'. Four days later, Union troops were forced to begin another siege after an unsuccessful attack on Port Hudson, Louisiana, 40km (25 miles) north of Baton Rouge. Among the soldiers were a number of blacks, and their commander, General Nathaniel Banks, would later write, 'Whatever doubt may have existed before as to the efficiency of organizations of this character, the history of this day proves conclusively to those who

The Union fleet braved shells from Vicksburg, Mississippi on 16 April before passing in the night.

ADMIRAL PORTER'S FLEET RUNNING THE REBEL BLOCKADE OF THE MISSISSIPPI AT VICKSBURG, APRIL 16TH 1863.

29 January The *Princess Royal* is captured by the Union's blockading squadron as it approaches Charleston Harbor with two engines for ironclads, guns, ammunition and medicines.

30 January Gen Grant arrives to take personal command of the army above Vicksburg.

30 January Union troops and the USS *Commodore Perry* sever Confederate supply lines coming down the Perquimans River in North Carolina to Richmond, Virginia.

31 January Confederate gunboats *Palmetto State* and *Chicora* raid Union ships blocking Charleston Harbor, defeating the USS *Mercedita* and USS *Keystone State*.

FEBRUARY

3 February Confederates fail to recapture Ft Donelson, Tennessee.

14 February The USS *Queen of the West* is grounded in the Black River in Louisiana, then abandoned and captured.

were in a condition to observe the conduct of these regiments, that the Government will find in this class of troops effective supporters and defenders'.

Political Difficulties

Meanwhile, activity was lively in the two capital cities. President Lincoln wanted 300,000 more troops, and on 3 March the US Congress passed

the Enrollment Act. The first US conscription act, it required males between the ages of 20 and 45 to enrol for three years of service. Now it was Northererners who complained that this was a 'rich man's war, a poor man's fight' because the act exempted anyone who paid a 'commutation fee' of $300 or who found a substitute to take his place. Substitutes were found and paid by Lincoln, the future President Grover Cleveland, the fathers of the future presidents Theodore and Franklin Roosevelt, and the wealthy J.P. Morgan and Andrew Carnegie.

On that same day, Congress passed a resolution opposing any foreign interference in the war. In part, this was in protest at British companies that were still secretly supplying Confederate warships; the *Georgia* was procured in March 1863. But principally this was a reaction to France's offer of mediation on 9 January, in which the French minister of foreign affairs called the war 'worse than civil, comparable to the most terrible distractions of the ancient republics, and whose disasters multiply in proportion to the resources and valour which each of the belligerent parties develop.'

The USS Queen of the West *ran aground and was captured by Confederates who used it to capture a Union gunboat before sinking the* Queen *to keep it out of the enemy's hands.*

1863

FEBRUARY

24 February Two Confederate ships below Warrenton, Mississippi ground the ram USS *Indianola,* forcing its surrender.

24 February President Lincoln approves the act establishing the Territory of Arizona.

25 February Union forces send a dummy ironclad ship down the Mississippi at Vicksburg, The ship has no crew aboard, but frightened Confederates blow up the captured USS *Indianola.*

28 February Four Union ships shell and destroy the Confederate blockade runner *Rattlesnake* (formerly the CSS *Nashville*) off Ft McAllister, which guards Savannah, Georgia.

MARCH

3 March The first US conscription act, the Enrollment Act, passes. Males aged 20 to 45 must enrol, but can exempt themselves by finding substitutes or paying $300.

3 March The US Congress passes a resolution opposing any foreign interference in the war.

3 March An act of Congress authorizes the award of an honorary brevet rank to officers of the United States Volunteers.

By now, many in the North were tiring of the sacrifice. This was keenly demonstrated on 6 March, only three days after conscription was introduced, when anti-black rioting broke out in Detroit, Michigan – an ominous forewarning of larger riots to come. Then on 17 March, the New Jersey legislature passed a resolution asking the federal government to negotiate a peace with the Confederacy.

For its part, the Confederate Congress had to deal with food shortages on the military and home fronts. The Union blockade was hurting, and on 26 March it passed legislation to establish rules governing the army's impressment of civilian goods, an attempt to end widespread abuses. Prices in Richmond had soared since 1860, the price of 2.2kg (5lb) of sugar increasing from 40 cents to $5.75, and 4.5kg (10lb) of bacon going from $1.25 to $10.

Then on 2 April, Richmond suffered what became known as the 'bread riot', when women paraded through the streets to demand lower prices, chanting 'Bread! Bread! Bread!' (It now sold for $100 a barrel.). The parade flared into a full-scale riot, and citizens broke into shops to loot food, clothing and shoes. Watching this

from the presidential mansion, Davis hurried into the streets, climbing onto a wagon. He was quick to condemn them for stealing jewellery and other non-essentials when it was bread that they needed. Rummaging through his pockets, he pulled out a few bills and coins, tossing them to the crowd with the

The USS Commodore Perry *helped sever enemy supply lines in North Carolina.*

---

3 March Congress adds officers to the Medal of Honor.

3 March Confederate Gen Robert Toombs resigns his commission to return to Georgia as a critic of the Confederacy and the Davis administration.

4–5 March Confederate cavalry rout Union cavalry and capture infantry at Thompson's Station, Tennessee.

6 March Anti-black rioting breaks out in Detroit, Michigan.

8 March Confederate Lt John Mosby's Partisan Rangers raid Fairfax Court House, Virginia and capture Gen Edwin Stoughton in his bed.

8 March A levee breaks on the Mississippi, ruining the canal begun by Union forces on 24 June 1862 to avoid the batteries of Vicksburg.

words 'Here is all I have'. Next, he promised that food would be distributed. Finally, he held up his pocket watch and announced that the militia present would begin firing at the ringleaders if the crowd did not disperse in five minutes. They did, and their leaders were arrested. Davis's personal intervention had stopped the riot, but the discontent would remain.

Here Comes the Cavalry

These were the days when the Confederate cavalry were still unchecked. At the war's beginning, the Union had no answer to superior Southern horsemanship, and the month of March 1863 proved particularly trying. On the 4th and 5th, the Battle of Thompson's Station, Tennessee (also known as Spring Hill or Unionville) brought further defeat for Union troops. The Confederate cavalries under Generals Forrest and W.H. Jackson encountered a strong enemy force, chasing away the Union cavalry and capturing the infantry and its artillery.

Union embarrassment was heightened on 8 March, when the Partisan Rangers of Major John Mosby, known as 'the Gray Ghost', raided

A levee break ruined Union General Ulysses S. Grant's project of cutting a canal on the Mississippi to avoid the guns of Vicksburg.

Fairfax Court House, Virginia, and captured the Union's General Edwin Stoughton in his bed. Mosby himself pulled back the covers from the sleeping man and slapped him on the bottom. Also captured were two captains, 30 privates and 58 horses, provoking the following response from President Lincoln: 'For that I am sorry, for I can make brigadier generals but I can't make horses.'

Towards the end of March, the Confederate cavalries of Generals Morgan and Forrest were on the move again. Morgan sent Colonel Roy Cluke with some of his men to raid Kentucky, and from 22 March until 1 April, the unit engaged at Mount Sterling, Danville, and Dutton Hill. Forrest hit the Tennessee towns of Brentwood and Franklin, both in the region of Nashville, on 25 March.

The Union army was learning from its experiences. Noticing how the enemy's cavalries

1863

MARCH

11 March Union ships fail to disable Ft Pemberton on the Yazoo River near Greenwood, Mississippi.

13 March The Kearny Cross is created for noncommissioned officers and privates who have distinguished themselves in battle. It honours Union Gen Philip Kearny.

14 March Adm Farragut's Union fleet runs past enemy batteries at Port Hudson, Louisiana but receives considerable damage.

15 March Gen Ambrose Burnside is assigned to command the Union's Department of the Ohio.

17 March Grant's Yazoo pass expedition is blocked at Fort Pemberton.

could disrupt operations, they had begun to train their horsemen to be just as skilful. From 17 April to 2 May, Union Colonel Benjamin Grierson's cavalry of 1700 men made a raid from LaGrange, Tennessee to Baton Rouge, Louisiana, in an attempt to divert attention from Grant's crossing of the Mississippi south of Vicksburg. Grierson's men rode 965km (600 miles) in those 16 days, including 122km (76 miles) in the last 28 hours. The raiders included 'Butternut Gucrrillas', nine reconnaissance soldiers dressed in Confederate uniforms (which would have guaranteed their execution if captured). Uncovering an ambush at Union Church, Tennessee, they allowed Grierson to circle safely to Baton Rouge. The raid killed and wounded about 100 Confederates (to 3 raiders killed and 7 wounded) and captured 1000 horses and mules; some 96km (60 miles) of railroad were also destroyed, as were 3000 captured arms.

The opposing cavalries seldom battled. However, one significant fight occurred on 27 April, when the 2000-strong Union cavalry of

The Union fleet passing up the Mississippi River exchanged fire with Fort Hudson.

17 March Cavalries engage at Kelly's Ford, Virginia.

17 March The New Jersey legislature passes a resolution calling for the Federal government to negotiate peace with the Confederacy.

18 March The US Government creates the Provost Marshal Department to police the army and organize conscription.

22 March–1 April Part of Confederate Gen Morgan's cavalry raids Kentucky.

21 March General Sherman rescues Admiral Porter's ironclads, trapped in Steele's Bayou, ending another attempt to reach Vickburg's rear .

Left: Confederate Major John Mosby's cavalry recaptured wagons in northern Virginia.

....

Right: Major John Mosby, the elusive Confederate cavalryman, was known as 'the Gray Ghost'.

crossing mountains and streams. Forrest's cavalry, one-third as large, eventually forced the surrender of Streight's exhausted men. Their victory owed much to a brave girl, Emma Samson. With bullets passing through her skirts, she showed the Confederates a secret ford over Big Black Creek, the only way to cross after the fleeing enemy burned the bridges.

Another Union cavalry raid on 27 April was part of the first movement of the Army of the Potomac under its new commander, General Joseph Hooker. On 12 April, he had written to Lincoln: 'My plans are perfect, and when I start to carry them out, may God have mercy on General Lee, for I shall have none.' Before the battle, he boasted: 'The rebel army is now

Colonel Abel Streight was dispatched to take a steamboat up the Tennessee River to northwestern Alabama (held by the Union). From there, they were to ride across mountainous north Alabama to destroy the railroad line between Atlanta and Chattanooga, the line of supply for General Bragg's troops. General Forrest got wind of this and set off in pursuit, overtaking the Union force. A three-day fight ensued, covering 193km (120 miles) of territory, and

1863

MARCH

25 March Confederate Gen Nathan Bedford Forrest's cavalry raids Brentwood and Franklin, Tennessee.

25 March The US awards its first Medals of Honor to soldiers.

26 March The Confederate Congress legislates for its army's impressment of civilian goods, in an effort to end widespread abuses.

30 March Union Gen Quincy Gillmore's troops rout those of Gen John Pegram in Kentucky, driving them across the Cumberland River.

31 March A Confederate attack on Washington, North Carolina, is halted by Union warships.

APRIL

1 April The Confederate cruiser CSS *Georgia*, built in Scotland, is commissioned off Brest, France.

the legitimate property of the Army of the Potomac. They may as well pack up their haversacks and make for Richmond.'

Lincoln, who had seen several of his pompous generals deflated on the battlefield, was more realistic. 'The hen is the wisest of all the animal creatures,' he said in reference to Hooker's prediction, 'because she never cackles until *after* the egg is laid.'

Hooker had planned to move out on the 12th, but rising rivers blocked the cavalry. About 6000 strong, it was led by General George Stoneman, who was assigned to break up Lee's communications. To accomplish this, Stoneman divided his riders into two columns to cross the Rappahannock and Rapidan, destroying railroad tracks and supply wagons.

A Blow to the Confederates

Lee's position around Fredericksburg nonetheless remained secure, with some 60,000 troops. Hooker, however, had 115,000 men, and he now left 40,000 close to Fredericksburg, taking 75,000 to cross the two rivers upstream and attack Lee's left flank and rear. On 27 April, he was 16km (10 miles) west of Fredericksburg at Chancellorsville

Union ironclads begin to bombard Charleston, South Carolina, and its defences on 10 July but the city where the war began held out for 19 more months before surrendering.

2 April Richmond, Virginia, has a 'bread riot' demanding lower bread prices. It ends when President Davis seems to warn that rioters will be shot by the militia.

2 April The Union's submarine USS *Alligator* sinks while being towed by the USS *Sumter* off Cape Hatteras, North Carolina.

5 April Civilian doctors visiting Camp Douglas in Chicago denounce the prison as an extermination camp. Some 6000 Confederates have died, or 10 per cent of its population.

7 April Eight Union ironclad ships attack Ft Sumter but fail, with three disabled.

8 April The USS *Keokuk* sinks, a victim of the previous day's attack on Ft Sumter.

(not a town but the fine house of the Chancellor family in a 40ha/100 acre clearing). Three days later, he issued a general order saying 'our enemy must either ingloriously fly, or come out from behind his defenses and give us battle on our own ground, where certain destruction awaits him.' Lee, though, read his intentions and also divided his troops, leaving 10,000 at Fredericksburg and sending the rest to protect his flank.

Hooker was advancing through the tangled woods called the Wilderness when General Stonewall Jackson's troops made a surprise attack and drove them back. Lee took advantage of this, boldly dividing his army again. Remaining at Chancellorsville with only 14,000 troops facing Hooker's 73,000 men, he

The Great Seal of the Confederacy highlighted George Washington.

sent the rest with Jackson to attack the Union rear on 1 May. Swooping on General Oliver Howard's troops as they relaxed in camp, the Confederates ran them 3km (2 miles) away.

The successful engagement would, however, prove devastating for the Confederacy. As dusk fell, Jackson went scouting with his staff beyond his pickets near the Union position. When he turned back, his own men mistook him for the enemy and fired. Two of his aides were killed in their saddles, while bullets hit Jackson's right palm, left wrist and left arm, where the bone splintered. Placed under a tree, he was amazed to realize that his wounds were 'from my own men.' He was then

carried to a field hospital, where his left arm was amputated, but at least he had a chance of survival. 'I consider these wounds a blessing,' he said. 'They were given to me for some good and wise purpose, and I would not part with them if I could.' But Lee mourned, 'He has lost his left arm, but I have lost my right.'

General Jeb Stuart now took command of Jackson's men, ordered by Lee to 'Charge! And remember Jackson!' Stuart attacked Hooker's lines on 3 May, singing 'Old Joe Hooker, will you come out of the Wilderness!' as his troops pushed the enemy back to the Rappahannock and Rapidan. Rebel shells also hit the Chancellorsville house, bouncing off a porch pillar that Hooker was leaning against. He mounted his horse and, still dazed, rode off in his own retreat, as the house burned down. Watching the retreat, the correspondent from the *New York Herald* reported: 'On the one hand was a solid column on infantry retreating in double quick from the face of the enemy; on the other was a dense mass of beings who had lost their reasoning faculties, and were flying from a thousand fancied dangers.'

Meanwhile, Union General John Sedgwick

1863

APRIL

12 April–4 May Suffolk, Virginia, is besieged by Confederate troops of Gen James Longstreet.

21 April Union troops capture McMinnville, Tennessee, dispersing about 700 Confederates and taking wagons.

10 April Confederate cavalry attacks Franklin, Tennessee.

17 April Union gunboats begin night runs past the batteries of Vicksburg, Mississipi.

26 April Gen John Marmaduke's Confederate cavalry is repulsed at Cape Girardeau, Missouri.

17 April–2 May Col Benjamin Grierson's Union cavalry raids from LaGrange, Tennessee to Baton Rouge, Louisiana.

Union General George Stoneman (centre) and his cavalry staff take a break in Virginia during their raid in April and May to break up General Robert E. Lee's communications.

advanced on Lee's army. Some of the Confederates left at Fredericksburg moved to counter him and on 4 May fought fiercely at Salem Church to force him back to the Rappahannock. One of the Union's most humiliating defeats ended with Sedgwick's retreat, and he was joined by Hooker, who had earlier pointed at Chancellorsville on a map and boasted, 'If I plant my army there, God Almighty can't drive me out.' The battle became known as 'Lee's masterpiece'. Union casualties totalled 17,278 to the Confederate's 12,821. Nonetheless, the losses hurt the South more than the North.

The wounded Jackson was moved to a small farmhouse, where he caught pneumonia. His condition deteriorated, and on 10 May he died. On his deathbed, he reflected that the victory at Chancellorsville was 'the most successful military movement of my life. But I expect to receive far more credit for it than I deserve.' Lee had not even considered the possibility of his death, saying, 'God will not take him from us now that we need him so much.'

The battle had consequences for the Union too. General Abner Doubleday questioned

27 April–8 May Gen George Stoneman's Union cavalry raids Virginia.

27 April Confederates repulse an attack by a gunboat fleet on Grand Gulf, Mississippi.

27 April–3 May Confederate Gen Forrest's cavalry, with one-third less men, captures Col Abel Streight's cavalry of 2000 men raiding across north Alabama.

28 April The US Army establishes the Invalid Corps, providing meaningful light duty for soldiers unfit for active duty.

30 April A Day of National Humiliation, Fasting, and Prayer, proclaimed by President Lincoln.

30 April The Great Seal of the Confederacy is approved, showing George Washington and the motto 'Deo Vindice' ('God as Our Defender').

Hooker closely about his behaviour during the battle, knowing that he had a drinking problem. Hooker replied: 'Doubleday, I was not hurt by a shell, and I was not drunk. For once I lost confidence in Joe Hooker, and that is all there is to it.' A Union colonel agreed, writing in his diary, 'Hooker was no longer Hooker.' He was relieved of his command on 28 June, and the Army of the Potomac received its last leader, General George Meade.

When Lincoln received news of Chancellorville, he was devastated. 'My God! My God!' he wailed. 'What will the country say?' It said a lot, and much criticism came from the *Chicago Times*, a Copperhead (anti-war) newspaper that downplayed Union victories and exaggerated its defeats. In June, General Burnside issued an order to suppress it, although Lincoln revoked this just three days later.

The President had also overturned a sentence on another critic, the former Ohio Congressman and Peace Democrat Clement Vallandigham. Believing that the South could not be beaten, he called for soldiers on both sides to desert. On 5 May, he was arrested as a traitor on the order of General Burnside, and tried by a military court,

The Confederate victory at Chancellorsville, Virginia, from 1–4 May was called 'Lee's Masterpiece'.

being denied a writ of habeas corpus. He received a sentence of two years in prison, but Lincoln was aware that this would upset Democrats before the next year's election, and set him free, to be banished to the Confederacy through Murfreesboro, Tennessee. There, Vallandigham was subequently so critical of Davis' government that he was banned from the South, and he went to live in Canada until 1864.

Union General William Averell (sitting) lost his command for making critical remarks.

1863

MAY

1 May Gen Grant's troops defeat the enemy at Port Gibson, Mississippi, below Vicksburg.

1 May The Confederate Congress approves the Confederate National Flag, Second Pattern, to replace the First National Confederate flag that was deemed too similar to the US flag.

1 May Confederate cavalry raider Gen John Hunt Morgan receives the CSA Thanks of Congress for his 'varied, heroic and invaluable services'.

1–4 May Gen Lee's Confederates win the Battle of Chancellorsville, Virginia, but Gen 'Stonewall' Jackson is mortally wounded – by his own men. Casualties: Union, 17,278; Confederate, 12,821.

5 May US Congressman Clement L. Vallandigham of Ohio is arrested after opposing the war and urging Union soldiers to desert.

3 May Adm David Porter's fleet and Gen Grant's troops force the evacuation of Grand Gulf, Mississippi.

3 May Union Gen Joseph Hooker relieves Gen William Averell of his command after Averell says the Virginia countryside they occupy is no good for cavalries.

3 May Confederate forces evacuate Grand Gulf, Mississippi below Vicksburg, and Gen Grant arrives, making it a supply base for his troops.

A Fading Optimism

Chancellorsville renewed Southern optimism, and this was reinforced in early June. The French army occupied Mexico City, offering the hope that France would supply the Confederacy with ammunition, food and other vital items. The expedition against Mexico, begun in 1861 with Britain and Spain, violated the Monroe Doctrine, which was hostile to foreign intervention in the Americas. The United States did not, however, object since the object was to protect foreigners there and foreign investments. Britain and Spain dropped out of the affair, so the victory belonged to France. Napoleon III, who was inclined to recognize the Confederacy, was now eager to expand his power across the country.

On 9 June, the Confederates won the largest cavalry battle ever fought in North America. Union General Hooker, then still in command, ordered General Alfred Pleasonton on a reconnaissance mission over the Rappahannock. At that time, Confederate General Jeb Stuart, Lee's 'eyes and ears', was at Brandy Station in Culpeper, Virginia on the Rappahannock, preparing for Lee's upcoming push into

Confederate soldiers lie dead at the stone wall of Marye's Heights above Fredericksburg, killed by Union troops on 3 May, thereby missing the Confederate victory occurring at nearby Chancellorsville.

7 May Gen Grant leaves Grand Gulf, Mississippi, reducing communications with the North, in order to advance east to the state's capital at Jackson.

9 May Confederate President Davis orders Gen Joseph Johnston to take command of forces in Mississippi.

10 May Confederate Gen Jackson dies of his wounds complicated by pneumonia.

10 May Union Gen William Rosecrans reports that he has 8475 cavalry horses but only 1938 mounted men in his 'small cavalry force'.

12 May Union troops under Gen James McPherson win a battle at Raymond, Mississippi a few miles west of Jackson.

13 May Gen McPherson's army reaches Clinton, Mississippi, destroying the railroad and telegraph there.

Pennsylvania. Pleasonton's army of about 11,000 men began to move on 8 June, and the next morning they rode out of the mist, surprising the 10,000 Confederates, who scattered. Rallying, they launched a counterattack, and thus began 12 hours of fighting, in which the cavalry charged with sabres, pistols and rifles. At the end of the day, Confederate infantry reinforcements arrived, and Pleasonton retreated. The Union had lost 936 men, including 486 captured, while the Confederates lost 523. Lee's son, William 'Rooney' Lee, was seriously wounded. He would be captured on 26 June near Hanover, Virginia, while recovering at the home of his wife's relatives, and held until March 1864.

The victory certainly belonged to the Confederates, but two issues dulled its shine. Firstly, it was becoming obvious that Union cavalrymen were now able to fight the enemy on even terms: they had perfected their scouting and

General Robert E. Lee (right) and General Thomas 'Stonewall' Jackson won victory at Chancellorsville, but Jackson was accidentally killed by his own men.

A monument marks the spot where General 'Stonewall' Jackson was mortally wounded.

raiding techniques. Secondly, the battle took place because the troops gathering for Lee's march North had been surprised. The Southern press rounded on Stuart, accusing him of spending too much time presenting grand

1863

MAY

14 May Jackson, Mississippi falls to Gen Grant's forces.

14 May Susan B. Anthony and Elizabeth Cady Stanton found the Women's National Loyal League, seeking an amendment to the US Constitution to abolish slavery.

16 May Battle of Champion Hill (or Baker's Creek), east of Vicksburg, won by Union troops. Casualties: Union, 2441; Confederate, 3851.

17 May Confederates are driven across Mississippi's Big Black River, and 1700 taken as prisoners. The remainder return to Vicksburg.

19 May Gen Grant's assault on Vicksburg is repulsed.

19 May President Lincoln commutes the two-year prison sentence given to US Ohio Congressman Vallandigham of Ohio for opposing the war, banishing him to the Confederacy.

reviews for civilians – as, indeed, he had done just two days before the attack. General Lee may well have regretted his letter to his wife on 8 June: 'I reviewed the cavalry in this section yesterday. It was a splendid sight. The men and horses looked well. They have recuperated since last fall. Stuart was in all his glory.'

To redeem himself, Stuart took off on another showy raid on 24 June around the Union army. This, however, would be to the detriment of Lee and the northern invasion, since Stuart, his 'eyes and ears', was no longer close enough to provide vital reports on the enemy. Still, he did capture more than 400 prisoners and 125 new wagons.

New Disappointments, New Hopes
The summer would bring disappointment for the Confederacy. West Virginia was admitted to the Union on 22 June and officially entered the

Union forces won the Battle of Champion Hill on 16 May.

war eight days later. And in the following month came despair, in two towns far apart in distance and disposition: Gettysburg, Pennsylvania and Vicksburg, Mississippi.

Lee's Army of Northern Virginia was suffering from the loss of Stonewall Jackson and dwindling amounts of troops and supplies.

Political and military leaders understood time was running out to launch a brilliant strike that would ruin Lincoln in the 1864 elections (capitalizing on anti-war sentiment felt in the Congressional elections of 1862) and lead to a peace settlement supported by the British and French.

It was a risky strategy, but Lee had already moved some troops northwest from Fredericksburg four days before the cavalry clash at Brandy Station. General Hooker, still in place, now wanted to rush his Army of the Potomac towards Richmond, but Lincoln understood that a Confederate victory in a Northern state would be more dramatic than the capture of Richmond, so he ordered Hooker to trail Lee and keep enough troops around Washington to defend it. The general responded

27 May A Union assault on Port Hudson, Louisiana, fails, so a siege begins.

23 May Gen Grant decides to lay siege to Vicksburg and starve out its Confederate forces.

22 May Gen Grant's second attempt to take Vicksburg fails.

27 May The Union gunboat USS *Cincinnati* is sunk on the Mississippi River by a large cannon in Vicksburg known as 'Whistling Dick'.

30 May The Confederate Congress designates 'Stonewall' Jackson's brigade as the 'Stonewall Brigade', the only one given an official nickname.

An impressive array of Union wagons are carefully parked in readiness before the Battle of Brandy Station in Virginia on 9 June.

with a demand for more troops, and it was this that finally led Lincoln to remove Hooker – or rather, to accept his resignation. And so, just three days before the Battle of Gettysburg, the command was given to General George Meade.

Meade was famous for his bad temper and unpopular with his subordinates. Grant said, 'This made it unpleasant at times, even in battle, for those around him to approach him even with information.' But he added, 'He was brave and conscientious, and commanded the respect of all who knew him.' Meade was another veteran of the Mexican War, and he rose quickly through the ranks. He was badly wounded at the Battle of White Oak Swamp, Virginia on 30 June 1862, when Lee's men failed to stop McClellan's retreat. He recovered to lead his troops during the defeat at the second Bull Run, Antietam, and the defeat at Chancellorsville. But Meade's men had fought well, and he maintained his reputation as a dependable and competent man. Certainly, his Confederate opposite was only too well aware of the dangers of underestimating him. 'General

1863

JUNE

1 June Union Gen Burnside closes down the *Chicago Times* after it publishes uncomplimentary articles. Lincoln soon overturns the order.

2 June Harriet Tubman, an escaped slave who became a Union scout, leads black soldiers to burn plantations in South Carolina, and sets about 800 slaves free.

6–8 June Union troops repulse Gen Richard Taylor's attack on Gen Grant's base at Milliken's Bend, Louisiana.

7 June The French Army occupies Mexico City, giving rise to Confederate hopes that France will supply food and ammunition to the Confederacy.

9 June Confederates win a cavalry fight at Brandy Station, Virginia, the largest cavalry battle ever fought in America.

Camps were often in shambles after a battle, as seen in Brandy Station, where the largest and first real cavalry battle of the war happened. It made the reputation of the Union cavalry.

Meade will commit no blunder on my front,' noted Lee, 'and if I make one he will make haste to take advantage of it.'

Moving into Pennsylvania on 27 June, Lee issued a warning to his troops to behave properly. Remembering Sherman's tactics in the South, he ordered:

'It must be remembered that we make war only against armed men. The Commanding General, therefore, earnestly exhorts the troops to abstain, with the most scrupulous care, from unnecessary or wanton injury to private property, and he enjoins upon all officers to arrest and bring to summary punishment any soldier disregarding this order.'

As his army paused in Chambersburg, a woman came to Lee's headquarters to ask for bread for the town's hungry population. 'General Lee, I am a Union woman,' she said, 'yet I ask for bread and your autograph.'

With Stuart's Confederate cavalry roaming afar, Lee received no information on the enemy's strength and location for two vital weeks. His frustration was plain: 'I cannot think what has become of Stuart. In absence of reports from him, I am ignorant as to what we have in front

12–24 June Confederate ships raid Union shipping off New England.

14 June At Columbia, Tennessee, Confederate Gen Nathan Bedford Forrest knifes Confederate Lt A. Wills Gould to death after the disgruntled subordinate shoots and nearly kills Forrest.

14 June Gen Richard Ewell's Confederate cavalry captures Winchester, Virginia and its garrison.

17 June The Confederate ironclad CSS *Atlanta* is captured by two Union ironclads in Wassaw Sound on the coast of Georgia.

17 June A cavalry fight occurs at Aldie, Virginia.

of us here. It may be the whole Federal army, it may be only a detachment.' He halted his army's advance west of Gettysburg to await Stuart. Two days before the battle, he told his officers, 'With God's help we expect to take a step or two toward an honourable peace.'

The Battle of Gettysburg

Gettysburg was the war's deadliest battle. It began simply enough, on 1 July, when Confederate soldiers under General Henry Heth went into town after hearing that they could obtain shoes there. They were spotted by General John Buford, the Union's cavalry leader, watching from a hill southwest of the town, and he called for reinforcements. This movement alerted the Southerners, who retreated to their camp before launching an attack. Heth's men defeated the

enemy and killed General John Reynolds, and the Union troops retreated to Seminary Ridge just south of the town. Reinforcements now

US General George Meade (centre) fought at Antietam, Fredericksburg and Chancellorsville.

flooded in on both sides, the Confederates enjoying a three-to-two advantage. They routed General Winfield Scott Hancock's troops, forcing them to Cemetery Ridge, and might have carried the day by attacking them in that position, but General Richard Ewell decided this was too risky.

The next morning, the Union army's line was ranged like a large question mark – straight along the long, low Cemetery Ridge and ending in a curve on Cemetery Hill and Culp's Hill. Just to the south were two unoccupied hills, Round Top and Little Round Top. The Confederates planned to occupy these, but Meade was aware of this and positioned troops to protect them. As evening began, harsh battles broke out in a peach orchard, a wheat field, and a group of boulders that were later known as 'the Devil's Den' in reference to the slaughter that day.

1863

JUNE

19 June Union troops clear Confederates from Middleburg, Virginia, but the 1st Rhode Island Cavalry is annihilated.

20 June In Tennessee, the Union's Army of the Cumberland numbers about 60,000 while the Confederacy's Army of Tennessee has 46,000.

21 June Confederate Gen 'Jeb' Stuart's cavalry withdraws after battling Union cavalry force at Upperville, Virginia.

22 June West Virginia, which had broken away from Virginia, is admitted to the Union as the 35th state.

23 June Confederates capture Union garrison at Brashear City (now Morgan City), Louisiana.

Elsewhere, Union troops repulsed heavy efforts by the enemy to take Cemetery Hill and Culp's Hill.

Confederate Private Jonathan Stevens later recalled, 'The balls were whizzing so thick around us that it looks like a man could hold out a hat and catch it full.' Confederate General Richard Ewell received a bullet in his false leg and remarked, 'It don't hurt a bit to be shot in a wooden leg.' By contrast, Colonel Isaac Avery of the 6th North Carolina Regiment was mortally wounded, and using a twig dipped in his own blood, scratched out a message on a piece of paper: 'Major, tell my father that I died with my face to the enemy.'

The last day of fighting, 3 July, saw Confederate General James Longstreet urging a flanking movement to force the Northerners on the offensive. Lee preferred to assault the enemy's centre directly at Culp's Hill, using the fresh troops of General George Pickett. Longstreet, in overall command of the attack, was violently opposed to the strategy. Said Longstreet, 'I do not want to make this charge. I do not see how it can succeed. I would not make it now but that General Lee has ordered it

Union troops find time to relax in Virginia, the state that saw the most battles during the Civil war. During breaks in campaigns, Union officers often made headquarters in court houses, hotels and private homes.

23–30 June Union Gen William Rosecrans' troops force Gen Braxton Bragg from his position in north Tennessee guarding the route to Chattanooga. (Tullahoma Campaign)

24 June Union troops overcome Confederate defenders at Liberty Gap and Hoover Gap about 16km (10 miles) from Murfreesboro, Tennessee.

25 June Union soldiers explode 1000kg (2200 pounds) of powder under Vicksburg defences, but Confederates repel the attack.

26 June Union troops capture Gen Lee's second eldest son, Gen William Henry Fitzhugh 'Rooney' Lee, at the home of his wife's relatives near Hanover, Virginia.

US General John Buford (far right) was the officer who encountered Confederates moving into Gettysburg. His men blocked their advance until reinforcements arrived.

and is expecting it.' To Pickett, he complained, 'I am being crucified at the thought of the sacrifice of life which this attack will make.'

At the same time, Stuart, newly returned, was to use his cavalry to attack the Union rear.

An artillery duel began at 1 p.m. until ammunition was almost gone on both sides. 'The air was all murderous iron,' noted Union General John Gibbon. And *The Times* of London reported: 'The thundering roar of all the accumulated battles ever fought upon earth rolled into one volume could hardly have rent the skies with fiercer or more unearthly resonance and din.'

Suddenly the battlefield went quiet. 'A deathlike stillness then reigned over the field,' recalled Confederate General A.L. Long, 'and each army remained in breathless expectation of something yet to come still more dreadful.' For his part, Lee believed that his artillery had silenced the enemy's cannon, but most Confederate shells had overshot the Union guns.

Some time after 3 p.m. began Pickett's Charge, the infamous assault on Cemetery Ridge. A line of 15,000 Confederate soldiers marched 1280m (1400yd) across an open field.

1863

JUNE

27 June Confederate navy officers and men are captured off Portland, Maine and sent to Ft Warren on George's Island in Boston Harbor.

27 June Union Gen Hooker sends a dispatch to Gen Henry Halleck in Washington, DC, resigning from the command of the Army of the Potomac.

28 June President Lincoln relieves Gen Hooker of command of the Army of the Potomac, replacing him with Gen George G. Meade.

28 June Confederate attack fails on Ft Butler at Donaldsonville, Louisiana.

29 June George Armstrong Custer becomes the Union's youngest general at the age of 23.

30 June In Hanover, Pennsylvania, Confederate Gen 'Jeb' Stuart's cavalry attacks a Union cavalry unit and escapes when they counterattack.

30 June A Confederate brigade, seeking shoes stored at Gettysburg, skirmishes with a Union cavalry there.

30 June West Virginia officially enters the war on the Union side.

The Battle of Gettysburg in Pennsylvania is acknowledged as the turning point of the war.

Union soldiers remarked on the awesome beauty of the slowly moving line, and waited for them to come within range – then mowed them down. Some soldiers managed to reach the Union line, capturing it briefly before being repulsed. Their broken file marched back, still in a steady step. Pickett, ordered by Lee to use his division to counterattack, replied simply, 'General, I have no division.'

Years after the war, Pickett would grumble about Lee, 'That old man had my division

massacred.' To which Colonel John Mosby countered, 'Well, it made you immortal.'

Stuart's rear attack was also unsuccessful, and the beaten Southerners now streamed past Lee. At the sight, he lowered his head, repeating to himself, 'It's all my fault. My fault.' The Confederates had suffered 28,063 casualties from some 70,000 troops; Union casualties were 23,049 from 85,000.

The Consequences of Gettysburg

That evening, Lee began his retreat but found the Potomac so high from heavy rain that it was impassable. Only on 14 July were all his men across. Like previous leaders of the Army of the Potomac, Meade failed to pursue the retreating Confederates, overestimating Lee's strength and tenacity, much to Lincoln's regret. Reading of Meade's congratulations to his troops, calling for 'greater efforts to drive from our soil every vestige of the presence of the invaders', the president remarked, 'Drive the *invaders* from our soil. My God! Is that all?'

'I am profoundly grateful down to the bottom of my boots for what he did at Gettysburg,' the President later said, 'but I think

General Winfield Scott Hancock and staff. All of these officers were wounded during the Battle of Gettysburg.

JULY

1 July A second Union explosion of powder fails to disrupt Confederate defences at Vicksburg.

1 July The Confederate cavalry of Gen 'Jeb' Stuart shells the town of Carlisle, Pennsylvania and burns the Union cavalry barracks.

2 July Gen John Morgan's Confederate cavalry begins a 24-day raid into Kentucky, Indiana and Ohio.

1–3 July The Battle of Gettysburg, Pennsylvania is a major victory by Gen Meade's Union forces over Gen Lee's Confederates. Casualties: Union, 23,049; Confederate, 28,063

4 July Gen Lee begins his retreat from Gettysburg to Virginia.

4 July Vicksburg surrenders to Gen Grant's forces. He allows 30,000 Confederate troops to leave, in return for a promise not to fight – a promise seldom kept.

4 July Confederates fail to recapture Helena, Arkansas, at a cost of one-fifth of Gen Theophilus Holmes' command.

4 July Former US President Franklin Pierce, speaking in Concord, New Hampshire, says military usurpation in the North 'strikes down the liberties of the people'.

that if I had been General Meade I would have fought another battle.' He put it more bluntly in a letter to General Oliver Howard on 21 July: 'I was deeply mortified by the escape of Lee across the Potomac, because the substantial destruction of his army would have ended the war.'

It would continue for two more years.

Later, reviewing the defeat, Lee said, 'If I had had Stonewall Jackson at Gettysburg, I would have won that fight and a complete victory which would have given us Washington and Baltimore, if not Philadelphia, and would have established the independence of the Confederacy.' And to Longstreet, he confessed in writing, 'Oh, general, had I but followed your advice, instead of pursuing the course that I did, how different all would have been.'

On 8 August, Lee tended his resignation by letter to President Davis: 'I have no complaints to make of any one but myself.' But he was also philosophical, writing, 'We must expect reverses, even defeats. They are sent to teach us wisdom and prudence, to call forth greater energies, and to prevent our falling into greater disasters. Our people have only to be true and united, to bear manfully the misfortunes incident to the war,

On 3 July, the third and last day of fighting at Gettysburg, the South suffered a major defeat.

and all will come right in the end.' His resignation was flatly turned down.

After the war, Lee would find positive things to say about Gettysburg. In 1868, he wrote, 'As it was, victory trembled in the balance for three days, and the battle resulted in the infliction of as great an amount of injury as was received and in frustrating the Federal campaign for the season.'

News of the Confederate defeat at Gettysburg would also clarify the position of the British government. The previous year, Parliament had heard many calls to recognize the Confederate government. On 17 September, the British Foreign Minister Earl Russell said 'we ought ourselves to recognize the Southern states as an independent state'. On 7 October, the Chancellor of the Exchequer, William Gladstone, proclaimed, 'We may anticipate with certainty the success of the Southern states as regards their separation from the North.' After Gettysburg, a member of the government told a London journalist, 'We almost put our foot in it.'

The Capture of Vicksburg

Down in Mississippi, some 1930km (1200 miles) away from the fighting at Gettysburg, Union troops were bunkered down in trenches so close to Vicksburg that hand grenades could be thrown at the Confederates and tossed back before exploding. On 15 June, Confederate General Johnston notified President Davis that Vicksburg was a hopeless case.

Grant's plan was to starve out the trapped Confederates. He approved the digging of mines

1863

JULY

5 July At Bardstown, Kentucky, Union cavalrymen surrender in a livery stable after Confederates exchange fire with them and string ropes across streets to block their escape.

9 July Confederates surrender Port Hudson, Mississippi, their last stronghold on the Mississippi River, after a six-week siege.

9 July Union Gen Sherman's one-week siege of Jackson, Mississippi begins.

10 July Union ironclads under Adm John A. Dahlgren, together with land units, begin to bombard the defences of Charleston, South Carolina. This lasts until the autumn.

12 July Union troops of Gen Jacob Lauman charge the defences at Jackson, Mississippi, but fail with severe losses.

Amputation was a common operation in the field, being the expedient way to guard against the deadly danger of gangrene.

beneath Vicksburg, and on 25 June 998kg (2200lb) of powder was exploded. Union troops rushed through the gap, but were stopped by a second line of Confederates, who had been put in place for such a danger. The blast did dislodge a slave cook, Abraham, who was propelled from a hilltop into Union lines. Iowa troops adopted him and charged fellow soldiers five cents to view the miraculous survivor. Abraham estimated that he had flown ''bout tree mile'. Another mine exploded on 1 July, but the breach created was not large enough to allow troops to pass.

Ultimately, though, General Pemberton's Confederate defenders were doomed from the

13 July Yazoo City, Mississippi is captured by Union forces.

13 July President Lincoln writes Gen Grant acknowledging 'the almost inestimable service you have done the country' and admitting that Grant's Vicksburg strategy, which he had questioned, was correct.

13 July The mutual prisoner exchange agreement is abandoned.

13 July Gen Morgan's Confederate cavalry rides north of Cincinnati, Ohio.

13–14 July Gen Lee's troops withdraw safely over the Potomac River.

13–16 July Reacting to the first drawing of names for the US draft, some 50,000 New Yorkers rioted, killing over a dozen people, mostly blacks.

start. Grant ordered the city to be shelled day and night, and both the trapped soldiers and civilians were slowly starving. To avoid the bombardment, the city's residents constructed about 500 caves, which included furnished rooms with slaves. Union soldiers nicknamed this setup 'Prairie Dog Village'.

The worse problem was the lack of food. Field peas were ground up and mixed with meal to create 'bread'. Mules were butchered and the meat provided to soldiers as rations. The *Chicago Tribune* ran a humorous menu for the survivors in Vicksburg, including 'Mule Tail Soup', 'Mule tongue cold a-la-Bray' and 'Mule beef jered a-la-Mexicana'.

Pemberton, though, was only too well aware of the gravity of the situation. 'I will endeavor to hold out as long as we have anything to eat,' he wrote to General Johnston on 25 May. On 28 June, though, he received an appeal signed by 'Many Soldiers': 'If you can't feed us, you had better surrender us, horrible as the idea is, than suffer this noble army to disgrace themselves by desertion.'

The general was aware of Southern rumours that he would surrender because he was a native

Confederate troops and civilians defied General Ulysses Grant's seige of Vicksburg, Mississippi, for six weeks, with some locals living in caves. The surrender finally came on 4 July.

1863

JULY

15 July The Union's Department of Virginia and North Carolina is created by merging the departments of those two states.

16 July Confederate troops of Gen Joseph Johnson withdraw from Jackson, Mississippi and Gen Sherman's army begin a destructive occupation.

16 July With Union possession of the Mississippi, the steamboat *Imperial* arrives in New Orleans from St Louis, the first complete trip for over two years.

18 July An assault fails by the Union's 54th Massachusetts Regiment on Ft Wagner, which guards Charleston, South Carolina. The regiment is the first comprised of Negro soldiers.

18 July Confederate Gen Joseph Wheeler is given command of all the cavalry of the Army of Mississippi.

26 July Confederate cavalry raider Gen John Morgan and 364 of his men are captured near New Lisbon, Ohio.

Yankee; some even called him a traitor. He gathered his men together and addressed them on the matter:

'You have heard that I was incompetent and a traitor; and that it was my intention to sell Vicksburg. Follow me and you will see the cost at which I will sell Vicksburg. When the last pound of beef, bacon, and flour, the last grain of corn, the last cow and hog and horse and dog shall have been consumed, and the last man shall have perished in the trenches, then, and only then, will I sell Vicksburg'.

On 2 July, the *Vicksburg Citizen* was still feisty:

'The Great Ulysses – the Yankee Generalissimo surnamed Grant – has expressed his intention of dining in Vicksburg on the Fourth of July. ... Ulysses must get into the city before he dines in it. The way to cook a rabbit is "first *catch* the rabbit".'

Two days later, and six weeks after the siege began, Pemberton understood he would have to relinquish the city. He met with Grant

Union Admiral John Dahlgren (centre) took command of the South Atlantic Blockading Squadron on 7 February. He had earlier invented the Dahlgren Gun used by the US Navy.

30 July President Lincoln issues an Order of Retaliation, threatening to execute a Confederate soldier for every US soldier killed in violation of the laws of war.

31 July The Confederacy's Army of Northern Virginia numbers only 41,000, while the Union's Army of the Potomac has more than 75,000.

AUGUST

1 August The US Government opens a large prison at Point Lookout, Maryland where Confederate prisoners had been accommodated in tents.

3 August The Confederate army of Gen Braxton Bragg escapes the larger force of Gen. William Rosecrans in Tennessee by crossing the Cumberland Mountains to Chattanooga.

and agreed to surrender on 4 July in return for paroles for his 31,600 troops. Grant was only too willing to avoid being encumbered with so many prisoners, and on America's Independence Day the Stars and Stripes was raised over the city's court house. The Confederates, released in return for a promise that they would never fight again until properly exchanged, marched out of the city. Grant later wrote admiringly:

'When they passed out of the works they had so long and so gallantly defended, between lines of their late antagonists, not a cheer went up, not a remark was made that would give pain. Really, I believe there was a feeling of sadness just then in the breasts of most of the Union soldiers at seeing the dejection of their late antagonists.'

Opinion in Washington was less understanding. General Halleck sent a critical message to Grant about releasing the prisoners, saying 'the men will immediately be placed in the ranks of the enemy'.

That could not dampen the joy of the victors. 'Surely I will not punish any soldier for being "unco happy" this most glorious anniversary of the birth of a nation,' Sherman wrote to Grant

The Confederate guerrilla leader Colonel William Quantrill and his violent band attacked Lawrence, Kansas, on 21 August, killing some 150 civilian men and boys.

1863

AUGUST

5 August A Confederate electric torpedo severely damages the USS *Commodore Barney* above Dutch Gap, Virginia.

5 August The CSS *Alabama* makes port near Cape Town, South Africa, staying for more than a month.

10 August President Lincoln meets with the abolitionist and former slave Frederick Douglass, who urges full equality for black troops.

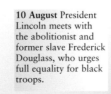

Frederick Douglass

21 August The independent Confederate raider Capt William Quantrill attacks Lawrence, Kansas, burning the town and killing some 150 civilian men and boys.

26–27 August Cavalries clash at Rocky Gap, near White Sulphur Springs, West Virginia.

that day, using the Scottish word 'unco', or 'very'. Even so, he was ready to move on, saying 'Already are my orders out to give one big huzza and sling the knapsack for new fields'.

The Union Encounters Difficulties

The Confederacy was now split and the Mississippi open to the Union. 'The Father of Waters,' said Lincoln, 'again goes unvexed to the sea.'

One irritation remained: Fort Hudson in Louisiana on the river was still holding out. It finally surrendered on 9 July after the troops had eaten all the beef, mules, dogs, and rats available. The campaign had cost Union forces some 3000 men, as well as 60 cannon, 5000 small arms, and two steamers. The Confederates' casualties exceeded 7200.

Two months later, on 4 September, the Union almost lost its hero, when Grant fell from his horse in New Orleans as it shied from a locomotive in the street. He was taken to a hotel attended by several doctors. 'My leg was swollen from the knee to the thigh,' he recalled, 'and the swelling, almost to the point of bursting, extended along the body up to the armpit. The pain was

Union troops stormed Charleston's Fort Wagner on 18 July but were driven back.

almost beyond endurance.' He lay in the hotel for more than a week without being able to turn himself in bed. He was then carried on a litter to a steamer and taken back to Vicksburg, where he was unable to move for some time afterwards.

Despite Union successes at Gettysburg and Vicksburg, everything was not well on the home front. Reports circulated of the carnage at Gettysburg, and on 11 July, only eight days after the battle, trouble flared in New York. The first names were drawn for the draft, under the new conscription law, which was mistakenly linked by many people to the recent Emancipation Proclamation. Conscripts felt that they were being drafted to free slaves, and two days after the draw, a riot broke out in New York City.

A mob made up primarily of Irish-American protesters, whose low-paying jobs were often taken by blacks, attacked a draft office and burned the building, helped by angry firemen who did nothing. For four days, a mob of up to 50,000 people went on a rampage, targeting blacks. Estimates of the number of blacks killed vary from one dozen to one hundred, including a crippled coachman who was hanged, his fingers and toes hacked off and his body

SEPTEMBER

29 August The Confederate submarine *H. L. Hunley*, sinks in Charleston Harbor during practice dives.

2 September Confederates under Gen Edmund Kirby Smith occupy Lexington, Kentucky.

2 September Union Gen Ambrose Burnside captures Knoxville, Tennessee and establishes headquarters there.

4 September The CSS *Florida* enters the harbour of Brest, France, where authorities detain her for a few days.

4 September Gen Grant is thrown by his horse in New Orleans. He is unable to walk or mount his horse without assistance until late October.

6 September Confederates abandon Ft Wagner on Morris Island in Charleston Harbor after almost two months of Union bombardments.

burned. Others were thrown into rivers, and hundreds fled to New Jersey. The rioters also burned a black orphanage and church, and attacked the homes of Republican leaders and Horace Greeley, who had strongly advocated abolition in his *New York Tribune.*

The police were joined by some 20,000 soldiers from the Army of the Potomac just back from Gettysburg, to battle the mob through streets and even on rooftops. At least 82 rioters were killed or executed. The city was finally circled by 43 regiments and peace restored. The draft selections began again on 19 August. Across the Union, it raised about 150,000 new soldiers, about three-quarters of them paid substitutes.

Other Northern cities experienced discord, as well. One newspaper in Pennsylvania ran the headline, 'Willing to fight for Uncle Sam but not for Uncle Sambo.'

On 26 July, Union troops finally captured the cavalry raider General John Morgan and 364 of his men near New Lisbon, Ohio. Morgan had begun raiding Kentucky, Indiana and Ohio on 2 July, and the troops of General Edward Hobson set off in pursuit. After his capture, Morgan was

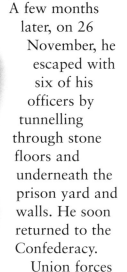

President Lincoln said of Union General Ulysses S. Grant, 'I can't spare this man – he fights!'

imprisoned in the Ohio State Penitentiary in Columbus. A few months later, on 26 November, he escaped with six of his officers by tunnelling through stone floors and underneath the prison yard and walls. He soon returned to the Confederacy.

Union forces had yet to catch up with the more ruthless Confederate raider, Colonel William Quantrill. A Ohio native, he

had once been against slavery, but he became a Confederate guerrilla 'bushwhacker' in Kansas and Missouri. On 21 August, he led his 450 violent men in an attack on the anti-slavery town of Lawrence, Kansas, killing about 150 mostly unarmed civilian men and boys, and forcing their female relatives to watch. They also burned buildings, destroying property valued at $1.5 million, before disappearing into woods.

Union General Thomas Ewing, Jnr retaliated. Settlers who might be supplying Confederate guerrillas were driven from their homes in four Missouri border counties, making refugees of about 10,000 people. They were then set upon by Union guerrilla Jayhawkers, who also burned their empty homes. In the fall, General Sterling Price led 12,000 Confederates into the state to take advantage of the situation, but was repulsed by a Union force under General Samuel Curtis, who chased them into Arkansas.

Quantrill now changed tactics. On 4 October, dressed in Union uniforms, his men captured and killed some 100 Union cavalrymen travelling to Fort Smith, Arkansas. On 6 October, he used the same trick to kill 65 Union soldiers at Baxter Springs, Kansas. He went to Texas to continue

---

1863

SEPTEMBER

8 September The Davis Guards, a mostly Irish Confederate regiment, successfully defend Ft Grisby, Texas, on the Gulf of Mexico, from four Union gunboats.

8 September Three Union gunboats attack Confederates at Sabine Pass, Texas, but two are captured and the third retreats.

8 September Union Adm John Dahlgren orders a night boat attack to capture Ft Sumter in Charleston Harbor, but it fails.

9 September Union troops capture Cumberland Gap, Tennessee and its Confederate garrison.

9 September Gen Bragg's Confederate army evacuates Chattanooga, Tennessee, which is occupied by Union forces under Gen William Rosecrans.

10 September Confederates evacuate Little Rock, Arkansas, which is then occupied by Union troops under Gen Frederick Steele.

13 September An engagement of cavalries occurs at Culpeper, Virginia.

raiding, soon parting ways with a psychotic member of his band, William 'Bloody Bill' Anderson, who was known to carry Union scalps braided into a necklace around his horse's neck. In one attack, he ambushed a train carrying 24 unarmed Union soldiers on leave, and murdered them, then killed more than 120 members of a posse sent to pursue his band.

After the war, two of Quantrill's men, Frank and Jesse James, became outlaws protected by families in Kansas who harboured memories of the Union guerrilla atrocities.

Interest shifted in the fall to Chattanooga, Tennessee. General William Rosecrans's Army of the Cumberland occupied the city after forcing Confederates under General Braxton Bragg to evacuate it on 9 September. The Union general then ordered a pursuit, misjudging that the fleeing enemy was in disarray. President Davis, recognizing that he could ill afford another defeat, ordered General Longstreet's troops to be shifted from Lee's army to Bragg's. On 19 September, the emboldened Bragg attacked his pursuers 16km (10 miles) south of Chattanooga in thick forest near Chickamauga Creek in Georgia, even before his reinforcements arrived.

Confederate soldiers struck a typical pose at Culpeper, Virginia in September. The war was the first recorded by photographers. Mathew Brady worked tirelessly on the Union side.

19 September Calvaries clash at Rockville, Maryland.

19–20 September Confederates under Gen Bragg win the Battle of Chickamauga, Georgia, forcing Gen Rosecrans' army to retreat to Chattanooga. Casualties: Union, 16,170; Confederate, 18,454.

27 September Confederate Col Joseph Shelby leads a cavalry raid into Missouri. (It lasts until 28 October.)

OCTOBER

4 October Col William Quantrill's Confederate guerrillas, disguised in US uniforms, capture then and kill some 100 Union cavalry on the way to Fort Smith, Arkansas.

Neither side carried the day, but that night Longstreet arrived and the next morning the nervous Rosecrans realized that he was outnumbered by some 60,000 men to 50,000. When Longstreet's army launched a frontal attack, Rosecrans could not see some of his own troops, who were hidden by the forest. Sending a whole division to fill a gap that did not exist, he created a real one, which the Confederates broke through for hand-to-hand combat that swept away nearly half of the Union army.

Union Captain Isaac Cusac with the 21st Ohio Infantry recalled the fearful battle: 'The major gave orders to fix bayonets, which was promptly obeyed, but when the order was given to "forward march", not a man moved.' Confederate General Henry Benning had two horses killed under him during the battle, and Johnny Klem, the 12-year-old drummer with the 22nd Massachusetts Regiment, shot and killed a Confederate colonel who attempted to capture him. 'I did not like to stand and be shot at without shooting back,' said Klem, already

A folding table in camp was a luxury, enjoyed here by members of a New York infantry unit.

1863

OCTOBER

5 October The Confederate submarine CSS *David* damages the USS *New Ironsides* with a spar torpedo off Charleston, South Carolina.

6 October Col William Quantrill's raiders, wearing Union uniforms, surprise and kill 65 Union soldiers at Baxter Springs, Kansas.

10 October At Blue Springs, Tennessee, Gen James Shackelford's Union cavalry attacks Gen John S. Williams's force, which withdraws to Virginia.

13 October Confederates under Gen Joseph Shelby are defeated by Union troops of Gen E.B. Brown at Arrow Rock, Missouri.

known as 'the Drummer Boy of Shiloh' and now earning himself the nickname 'the Drummer Boy of Chickamauga'.

Rosecrans retreated, though he was able to move back to Chattanooga in an orderly fashion thanks to General George Thomas and his men at the rear, who held the line for the rest of the day. The Confederate assaults against them were relentless, which earned Thomas the nickname of 'the Rock of Chickamauga'. The Southerners were able to claim victory at Chickamauga, but their casualties were higher – 18,454 to the Union's 16,170. Morevover, 10 Confederate generals had been killed or wounded, including General Benjamin Hardin Helm – actually a close friend of President Lincoln, whose wife was his sister-in-law.

Lincoln was advised of the defeat on 16 October by US Assistant Secretary of War Charles A. Dana, who said of Rosecrans, 'The incapacity of the commander is astonishing, and it often seems difficult to believe him of sound mind. His imbecility appears to be contagious.'

The July draft riot in New York City happened only 10 days after the Battle of Gettysburg.

15 October The Confederate submarine *H. L. Hunley* sinks for the second time in Charleston Harbor, killing its owner and a crew of seven.

16 October President Lincoln assigns Gen Grant to command all armies in the West.

19 October Confederate Gen 'Jeb' Stuart's cavalry routs the troops of Gen Hugh Kilpatrick at Buckland Mills, Virginia, calling the action 'the Buckland Races'.

19 October Union General William Rosecrans is relieved of his command as a result of his defeat at Chickamauga, Georgia. Gen George Thomas replaces him.

20 October Confederates attack Union forces at Philadelphia, Tennessee, capturing 300–400 prisoners and 38 wagons.

21 October Union Gens Grant, Rosecrans and Hooker meet in Nashville, Tennessee to plan the assault on Chattanooga.

As Union troops retreated from Chickamauga, Snodgrass Hill was held by US General George Thomas, earning him the nickname of 'the Rock of Chickamauga'.

1863

OCTOBER

28 October The battle of Wauhatchie, Tennessee frightens some 200 mules that stampede toward Confederates. Believing it to be a cavalry attack, some troops panic and flee.

28 October The Great Northwestern Sanitary Commission Fair in Chicago auctions President Lincoln's copy of the Emancipation Proclamation for $3000 to raise funds for this relief organization.

28 October Union Gen Quincy Gillmore announces The Gillmore Medal for his enlisted men who distinguished themselves in operations before Charleston from July to September 1863.

NOVEMBER

2 November Confederate Gen Henry Allen is elected Louisiana's governor. He was wounded at the Battle of Baton Rouge on 5 August 1862, and his left leg amputated.

2 November Union troops secure a position on the Mexican border at Brazos Santiago, Texas.

That same day, Lincoln relieved Rosecrans of his command. Five days later the President told his secretary, John Hay, that Rosecrans 'is confused and stunned, like a duck hit on the head, ever since Chickamauga.'

Bragg's Confederates now moved after the enemy in Chattanooga, bottling up Union forces in that city while General Joseph Wheeler's cavalry broke their supply lines. Indeed, President Davis was confident enough to visit his troops there on 10 October.

Decisive Action

'Hold Chattanooga at all hazards,' ordered Grant from Louisville on 19 October. 'I will be there as soon as possible.' He arrived four days later as the newly appointed commander of the new Military Division of the Mississippi – and the atmosphere changed. He replaced Rosecrans with General George Thomas as commander of the Army of the Cumberland. The Northern force then broke the siege, re-establishing a supply line on 26 October and bringing in supplies by steamboat.

The Confederate victory at Chickamauga on 19 and 20 September raised Southern spirits.

Newspaper vendors deliver the developments during the war

6 November Union troops move up the Rio Grande to occupy Brownsville, Texas.

6 November The Western Sanitary Commission informs President Lincoln that hundreds of former slaves would 'gladly return to slavery, to avoid the hardships of freedom'.

7 November In an unusual bayonet attack at dusk, Union troops overcome the enemy at Rappahannock Bridge, Virginia.

10 November US Secretary of War Edwin Stanton orders the Signal Corps to transfer all its telegraph equipment to the Military Telegraph Service.

13 November The Confederate commissioner to Europe, Col A. Dudley Mann, meets with Pope Pius IX at the Vatican, presenting a letter from President Davis.

Grant's next step was to push the Confederates off Missionary Ridge on the eastern side of the city, a position that overlooked the Union army below, as did Lookout Mountain on the southwest, some 610m (2000ft) high. The Confederates now miscalculated. Bragg was too confident of his 10km (6 mile) defensive position and weakened his force on the crest of Missionary Ridge by sending Longstreet, with several divisions and 35 cannon, to West Virginia to aid the fight against the Union forces of General Burnside.

Not surprisingly, the Confederates were in trouble when Sherman arrived with fresh troops on 23 November. Grant ordered his army to dress in military parade uniforms, and when the enemy moved off a forward hill for a better view, the Northerners attacked and established Grant's headquarters there. Sherman then crossed the Tennessee River to assault the north of Missionary Ridge. Finally, at 4 a.m. on 24 November, General Hooker's men successfully attacked Lookout Mountain. The early fog and heavy rain gave the fight the nickname of the 'Battle above the Clouds'.

Bragg then compounded his mistake. Unwisely splitting his forces, he sent half to the bottom of Missionary Ridge, with instructions to fire when the enemy came within 180m (200yd) and then retreat. The next morning, 25 November, the fateful battle began. Confederates were holding off Sherman's men, so Grant ordered Thomas to assault the base of

The Battle of Chickamauga in Georgia, was won by Confederate General Braxton Bragg's troops.

1863

NOVEMBER

17 November Union troops take Aransas Pass, Texas, east of Mustang Island, off Corpus Christi Bay.

18 November Confederate forces of Gen James Longstreet push a Union cavalry back into Knoxville, Tennessee, and begin a siege of the town.

19 November President Lincoln delivers his Gettysburg Address during the dedication of the military cemetery at the battlefield of this Pennsylvania town.

19 November At Matagorda Bay, Texas, Union forces attack Ft Esperanza, which the Confederates partially destroy and evacuate.

23–25 November Gen Grant's army scales heights overlooking Chattanooga, Tennessee, routing Confederates under Gen Bragg and breaking their siege of the city. Casualties: Union, 5824; Confederate, 6667.

Confederate prisoners waited dejectedly after Union forces won the Battle of Chattanooga, Tennessee, on 25 November. The key fight for Lookout Mountain was called 'the Battle above the Clouds'.

24 November Union Gen Meade's forces advance to attack Gen Lee's army at Mine Run, a brook in Virginia.

26 November Gen Sherman and Hooker pursue the enemy's retreat from Chattanooga for some distance, with Hooker encountering severe resistance.

26 November Confederate cavalry raider Gen John Morgan and six of his officers escape by digging out of the Ohio State Penitentiary in Columbus.

29 November Gen Meade decides to call off his attack on Gen Lee at Mine Run after seeing the large Confederate force.

29 November Union troops in Ft Sanders overlooking Knoxville, Tennessee repulse a Confederate attack.

DECEMBER

4 December Freedman's Village, for 1100 freed slaves, is dedicated by the US Government at Arlington, Virginia, on the grounds of Robert E. Lee's former home.

the ridge to draw the enemy in that direction. Many of Bragg's men now decided to fight rather than retreat as ordered, and they were overwhelmed.

The Union troops in the centre were those of General Thomas. Defeated at Chickamauga, they had something to prove, and they now ignored their orders and fought straight up the steep slope. 'Who ordered those men up the hill?' queried Grant. Said corps commander General Gordon Granger, 'No one. They started without orders. When those fellows get started, all hell can't stop them.' Grant's response was simple: 'It will be all right if it turns out all right.'

It did. Thomas' men routed the enemy. Confederate Private Sam Watkins recalled, 'I was trying to stand aside to get out of their way, but the more I tried to get out of their way, the more in their way I got.'

Bragg now retreated into Georgia and the loss of Chattanooga was a fatal one for the Southerners, who took 6667 casualties compared to the Union's 5824. Their defeat also opened up Union supply and communication lines, which allowed Sherman to launch his campaign against Atlanta. President Davis,

The Confederate position on Missionary Ridge looked down on the enemy from a great height at Chattanooga, but General Ulysses Grant's troops took the hill in a pitched battle.

1863

DECEMBER

5 December The Union army controls Tennessee after Confederates withdraw from their siege of Knoxville.

7 December President Lincoln asks people to assemble at their places of worship and thank God for the Chattanooga victory.

7 December Confederate President Davis addresses his Congress, bitterly denouncing the enemy as 'hardened by crime'.

7 December Confederates disguised as passengers seize the US steamer *Chesapeake* off Cape Cod, Massachusetts and sail it to Nova Scotia, Canada.

7 December President Lincoln issues a Proclamation of Amnesty and Reconstruction, offering pardons to anyone in the Confederacy taking an oath of loyalty to the United States.

8 December President Lincoln's message to Congress notes that some 100,000 former slaves are now in US military service.

assessing the defeat, warned, 'We are now in the darkest hour of our political existence.'

The Gettysburg Address

Six days before the battle for Missionary Ridge, Lincoln was at Gettysburg dedicating the military cemetery there. It was an event his wife had begged him to skip because their son, Tad, was sick. Edward Everett, a former US secretary of state and Massachusetts governor, spoke for two hours. Lincoln, who had been asked simply to say 'a few appropriate remarks', spoke for less than three minutes. When he sat down he muttered, 'I failed, I failed, and that is about all that can be said about it.' The *Chicago Times* condemned his speech as 'silly, flat, and dishwatery utterances.' It has since become the best-known speech in American history, under the title of the Gettysburg Address:

Fourscore and seven years ago our fathers brought forth on this continent a new nation, conceived in Liberty, and dedicated to the proposition that all men are created equal.

Now we are engaged in a great civil war, testing whether that nation, or any nation, so conceived and so dedicated, can long endure.

We are met on a great battle-field of that war. We have come to dedicate a portion of that field, as a final resting-place for those who here gave their lives that that nation might live. It is altogether fitting and proper that we should do this.

But, in a larger sense, we can not dedicate – we can not consecrate – we can not hallow – this ground. The brave men, living and dead, who struggled here, have consecrated it, far above our poor power to add or detract. The world will little note, nor long remember, what we say here, but it can never forget what they did here. It is for us the living, rather, to be dedicated here to the unfinished work which they who fought here have thus far so nobly advanced. It is rather for us to be here dedicated to the great task remaining before us – that from these honored dead we take increased devotion to that cause for which they gave the last full measure of devotion – that we here highly resolve that these dead shall not have died in vain – that this nation, under God, shall have a new birth of freedom – and that government of the people, by the people, for the people, shall not perish from the earth.

At Gettysburg, Lincoln sat left of the man in top hat and sash. His famous address was so short, no photographer could record it.

11 December A letter arrives in Richmond from Pope Pius IX addressed to the 'Illustrious and Honorable Jefferson Davis, President of the Confederate States of America'.

12 December The Confederate government ends its policy of allowing Northern food supplies for Union prisoners.

13 December Georgia establishes the Georgia State Line militia, whose members are exempt from the Confederate draft.

15 December Gen James Longstreet's troops fail to capture three Union cavalry brigades at Bean's Station, Tennessee, resulting in Longstreet relieving three generals of their commands.

17 December Congress awards Gen Grant a gold medal, the only one presented during the war, and gives him an official Thanks of Congress.

Chapter Four
1864

This was the last full year of the deadly war and this was the year
that was to demonstrate the crushing power of the Union armies
led by generals Grant and Sherman, who both received
promotions in March.

Lincoln called Grant to Washington and hosted a reception for him at the White House, the type of formal occasion that made the general uncomfortable. One congressman attending the reception watched the blushing and sweating general and recalled, 'For once, at least, the President of the United States was not the chief figure in the picture. The little, scared-looking man who stood on a crimson-covered sofa was the idol of the hour.'

Left: US General William T. Sherman (leaning on rear of cannon) consults with his staff during the siege of Atlanta.
Right: A crow's nest signal station was needed but risky.

On the next day, 9 March, Grant received the newly created rank of lieutenant general, a title previously held only by George Washington and Winfield Scott. This made him general-in-chief of all US armies, replacing General Halleck, who had been unable to coordinate military movements successfully from his Washington base. In reality, Grant considered it more important to lead the Army of the Potomac, and he continued to rely upon General Meade to keep an eye on the big picture.

Sherman was also elevated, given his chief's former command of the Military Division of the Mississippi. This meant that he was now head of the army's main operations in the West.

The South made changes too. On 24 February, General Bragg became military

adviser to President Davis. Bragg had resigned after Chattanooga, though blaming others for his defeat, and had been replaced by General Joseph Johnston.

Actions Thwarted

The first two months of the year had brought dramatic events. Union officers made a spectacular escape from Libby Prison, a former cotton warehouse on the James River in Richmond. They dug a tunnel, which proved to be too short when tried on 7 February. But after two more days of digging, 107 officers escaped through it, led by Colonel Thomas Rose, who had been captured at Chickamauga. Surfacing from the 18m (60ft) tunnel, they ran through the streets of Richmond, but Rose and 47 others were recaptured, while two drowned crossing streams. Rose would later be exchanged and go on to fight in Tennessee at the battles of Franklin and Nashville.

So it was about time that the Confederacy officially opened what would become the war's most infamous

prison – Andersonville, near Americus, Georgia. Officially named Camp Sumter, it was constructed quickly, to relieve Richmond by housing Union prisoners incarcerated in the city's Libby and Belle Isle prisons. Opened on 27 February, it was soon host to a large and ever-increasing number of

prisoners, which eventually totalled some 32,899. This overcrowding, combined with poor sanitation and inadequate food, resulted in a high death rate.

Shortly after the escape from Libby Prison, on 17 February, the Confederate

Only Union officers were held at Libby Prison on the James River in Richmond.

1864

JANUARY

1 January Confederate Gen William 'Extra Billy' Smith, who fought at Gettysburg, becomes governor of Virginia.

2 January Confederate Gen Patrick Cleburne advocates that certain slaves be freed in order to fight as Confederate troops, but this is rejected.

19 January Arkansas, a Confederate state with slaves, approves a new constitution that is anti-slavery.

30 January Union Gen William Rosecrans is given command of the Department of the Missouri.

submarine CSS *H. L. Hunley* (officially a semi-submersible) became the first in the world to sink a ship in combat. The USS *Housatonic* went down at the entrance to Charleston Harbor, but the action also sunk the submarine and killed all eight of its crew.

It must be said, the submarine was a simple affair, and two previous crews had also been killed testing it. It was hand-propelled, and the crew submerged armed with watches and a lighted candle. The flame would go out when oxygen became critical, and the vessel returned to the surface when any of the crew said 'Up'.

The *Hunley* would eventually be raised, on 8 August 2000, to be placed in the old Charleston navy base. The remains of the crew were buried on 17 April in Charleston's Magnolia Cemetery.

The Confederate Navy remained active in the spring of 1864. The CSS *Alabama* made a fateful voyage to Europe around South Africa's Cape of Good Hope. On 27 April, it captured and burned the last of its prizes, the *Tycoon*, and one of the *Tycoon's* crew even signed up to serve on the *Alabama*. By now, though, the Confederate ship was worn out, and its Commander Raphael Semmes said, 'We are like

The Battle of Olustee, or Ocean Pond, Florida occurred on 20 February and was a Confederate victory. Union casualties numbered 1,861 and the Confederates lost 934.

a crippled hunter limping home from a long chase.' His crew had captured a total of 65 US ships on the high seas, burning 52 of them, converting one into an auxiliary cruiser, bonding nine, and releasing one without a bond.

Elsewhere, on 5 May the ram CSS *Albemarle* battled seven blockade ships to a draw in the mouth of the Roanoke River. The next day, a Confederate torpedo destroyed the USS *Commodore* in the James River.

FEBRUARY

1–3 February Confederate force fails to recapture New Bern, North Carolina.

2 February Confederate boats capture and destroy USS *Underwriter* in the Neuse River, North Carolina.

3 February Gen Sherman's Union army leaves Vicksburg, Mississippi on the Meridian Campaign.

5 February Gen Sherman's force skirmishes with Confederates in Mississippi at Clinton and Jackson.

6 February Gen Sherman occupies Jackson, Mississippi for the third time, destroying the city and burning citizens' belongings in the streets.

Union General Ulysses S. Grant (sitting far left) and his staff often disagreed with General-in-Chief Henry Halleck in Washington, but Grant took over his duties on 9 March.

The Confederate Soldiers Rally

After helping take Chattanooga, General Sherman returned to Vicksburg. From there, he set out on 3 February with some 20,000 infantry, his purpose to follow the Southern Mississippi Railroad to Meridian, destroying it along the way. Other potential targets were the line east of Meridian to Selma, Alabama, where a cannon foundry and arsenal were located, and the line that ran down to Mobile, Alabama, the Confederacy's only remaining port on the Gulf of Mexico.

Sherman ordered General William Sooy Smith to move his infantry and cavalry from Memphis to meet his force at Meridian by the 10th. Smith started well, marching through Mississipi and destroying millions of bushels of corn and up to 3000 bales of cotton. On 20 February, however, he met the Confederate cavalry of General Nathan Bedford Forrest. Acting on the principle 'get there first with the most', his forces were still holding their own. Indeed, General Johnston named Forrest as the war's greatest soldier, and General Sherman called him 'that devil Forrest', saying the Confederate had to be 'hunted down and killed if it costs 10,000 lives and bankrupts the Federal treasury'. Forrest was the only Confederate cavalry leader never defeated until a week before the war ended.

Forrest's small force met Smith's troops at West Point. Despite having just 2500 men to counter Smith's army, which included infantry and 20 cannon as well as 7000 cavalry troops, Forrest blocked Smith's progress at a bridge. The Northerner now decided to retrace his steps back to Okolona, but Forrest followed with attacks that continued all the way back to

1864

FEBRUARY

7 February Gen Truman Seymour's Union troops, half of them black, land and capture Jacksonville, Florida, having left Hilton Head, South Carolina the previous day.

9 February Union Col Thomas Rose leads 107 other Union officers in an escape from Libby Prison in Richmond, Virginia. Rose and 47 others are recaptured.

9–14 February Union troops advance into the interior of Florida.

10 February A total of 109 commissioned Union officers escape from Richmond's Libby Prison through a 18m (60ft) tunnel.

11 February Union troops leave Memphis and march into Mississippi, destroying millions of bushels of corn and 2000–3000 bales of cotton.

The US Army created an Invalid Corps in 1863 for soldiers disabled or otherwise unfit for combat. They served as support personnel. Its name was changed to Veteran Reserve Corps on 18 March.

Memphis, turning the retirement into a rout. In the action, Forrest lost the younger of his seven brothers, whom he had treated almost as a son.

Meanwhile, Sherman, wreaking damage wherever possible on the march through Mississippi, arrived in Meridian on 14 March. He waited until the end of the month for General Smith to arrive, then gave up and returned to Vicksburg. He next sent 10,000 troops to join the army of General Nathaniel Banks for a campaign up the Red River into Louisiana to capture Shreveport. This was directed at the perceived French threat in Mexico; Lincoln wanted US troops based in Texas near the border.

By 12 March, Banks' own 17,000 troops were on the move with Admiral Porter's flotilla of 13 ironclads and seven gunboats from New Orleans, 'the most formidable force that had ever been collected in western waters'. Two days later, they had captured the Confederate artillery garrison at the partially completed Fort De Russy, Louisiana. Other engagements followed, but Union progress was

14 February Gen Sherman's Union army occupies Meridian, Mississippi after marching 242km (150 miles) in 11 days, and destroys buildings, railroads and supplies.

17 February In Charleston Harbor, the Confederate *Hunley* becomes the world's first submarine to sink a ship, the USS *Housatonic*. It, too, sinks, killing all eight crew.

19 February Union Gen Sherman receives the official Thanks of Congress for his Chattanooga campaign.

20 February The Battle of the Olustee, Florida, is fought among swamps and won by Confederate forces, halting the Union attempts to take Florida.

21 February Gen Nathan Bedford Forrest's Confederates rout a larger Union force at West Point, Mississippi.

Mary E. Walker was the US Army's only woman surgeon.

slowed by Grant, who wanted Sherman's troops back for the Atlanta campaign. The river level then fell, and the sluggish ships heading for Alexandria had to endure Confederate firepower lined along the banks, which put two out of service.

As Porter reached Alexandria on 25 April, the river was so low that the gunboats needed an extra 1.2m (4ft) of water to pass. Faced with the possibility of having to destroy his fleet to keep it out of enemy hands, Porter instead put 3000 men to work, to build a dam out of trees, rocks and four barges. The structure collapsed after four gunboats passed over, but was rebuilt to allow the remaining ships to escape to the Mississippi River. Confederates subsequently destroyed five near Alexandria between 1 May and 8 May. Back on land, Banks' troops were harassed by 8000 Confederates led by General Richard Taylor. It took until 26 May to complete the retreat, thus ending one of the Union's most humiliating campaigns.

Controversy

Meanwhile, General Forrest's victory at Okolona invigorated his new troops, and in mid-March he headed northwards. By the 24th, he had captured Union City, Tennessee, and its garrison. The next day, he raided Paducah, Kentucky and captured Union horses. But he was heading for an engagement that would damage his reputation.

On 12 April, his 1500 troops arrived at Fort Pillow, Tennessee, 64km (40 miles) north of Memphis. Along with the gunboat USS *New Era*, the fort protected Union navigation on the Mississippi. Its troops consisted of 295 whites and 262 blacks under Major Lionel Booth. The Confederates surrounded the fort, and a sniper soon killed Major Booth. Forrest now demanded its surrender from Major William Bradford, who had taken command. He asked for an hour's consideration, but Forrest knew Union reinforcements were on the way and gave him 20 minutes. Bradford's response was to call off negotiations.

The Southerners now easily overran the fort, driving the defenders down the riverbank into the hands of more Confederate troops. Reports of what happened next differ. The Union account describes how the soldiers surrendered immediately, only to be massacred by the enemy, who yelled, 'No quarter! Kill the damned niggers! Shoot them down!' The Confederate version insists that the defenders fought to the last. The only agreement is that Union total losses were 231 killed and 100 seriously wounded, while the Confederate losses were 14 killed and 86 wounded.

'The river was dyed with the blood of the slaughtered for 200 yards [180m],' reported Forest. 'It is hoped that these facts will demonstrate to the Northern people that Negro soldiers cannot cope with Southerners.'

1864

FEBRUARY

22 February Gen Forrest's troops continue to rout Union cavalry under William Sooy Smith, at Okolona, Mississippi.

23 February In Richmond, 400 Union prisoners are moved from Belle Isle to Libby Prison to await transfer to the new facility at Andersonville, Georgia.

24 February Gen Braxton Bragg goes to Richmond to become a military adviser to Confederate President Davis.

27 February The Confederacy's prison at Andersonville, Georgia opens for Union prisoners of war.

MARCH

2 March Documents are found near Richmond, Virginia, on the body of Union Col Ulric Dahlgren, detailing plans to burn Richmond and assassinate Confederate President Davis.

The North was inflamed by news of the incident, and by reports claiming that black soldiers were buried alive and that tents containing the Union wounded were set alight. US Secretary of War Stanton asked Sherman to investigate 'the alleged butchery of our troops', and Grant wired Sherman, 'If our men have been murdered after capture, retaliation must be resorted to promptly.'

President Lincoln disagreed: 'To take the life of one of their prisoners on the assumption that they murder ours, when it is short of certainty that they do murder ours, might be too serious, too cruel a mistake.' Frederick Douglass, the son of a slave, visited him on 12 April to ask for revenge, but the President ruled against it. 'I shall never forget the benignant expression of his face,' Douglass wrote later, 'the tearful look of his eye, the quiver in his voice, when he deprecated a resort to retaliatory measures.'

In his defence, Forrest said:

'I regard captured Negroes as I do other captured property and not as captured soldiers. ... It is not the policy or the interest of the South to destroy the Negro, on the contrary to preserve and protect him, and all who have

The Battle of Fort Pillow on 12 April was known in the North as a 'massacre', saying the Confederates under General Nathan Bedford Forrest killed Negro soldiers who had surrendered.

5 March Gen Sherman's Union army returns to Vicksburg after completing the Meridian Campaign.

4 March The USS *Pequot* captures the Confederate blockade runner, the *Don*, off Beaufort, North Carolina.

8 March About 100 Copperheads (Northerners sympathizing with the Confederacy) kill five Union soldiers on furlough in Charleston, Illinois.

9 March Gen Sherman is put in command of the Union armies in the West.

9 March Maj Gen Grant is promoted to Lieutenant General.

12 March President Lincoln appoints Gen Grant as General in Chief of all Union armies, replacing Gen Henry Halleck.

surrendered to us have received kind and humane treatment.'

And Sherman recalled in his memoirs:

'No doubt Forrest's men acted like a set of barbarians, shooting down the helpless negro garrison after the fort was in their possession; but I am told that Forrest personally disclaims any active participation in the assault, and that he stopped the firing as soon as he could. He had a desperate set of fellows under him.'

The Battle of the Wilderness

In May, Grant and Sherman were on the move again. On the 3rd, Grant took 118,000 men of the Army of the Potomac across the Rapidan River in Virginia. This would be the Union's sixth 'On to Richmond' campaign, and this time it would not be abandoned, ending only when the Confederate capital fell, a full 11 months later.

The next day, Sherman moved out of Chattanooga, determined to force the Confederates of General Johnston back to Atlanta before taking the city, known as the Gate City of the South. Sherman considered Johnston one of the South's most able soldiers,

making it clear that 'No officer or soldier who served under me will question the generalship of Joseph E. Johnston'. But with twice the number of soldiers, he knew that his main concern was to keep railroad lines open, to

Union soldiers rest after crossing a river during the Battle of the Wilderness.

1864

MARCH

12 March A Union flotilla of 13 ironclads and seven gunboats begins a journey up the Red River in Louisiana, seeking to capture Shreveport.

14 March Union troops of Gen Nathaniel Banks capture Ft De Russy, Louisiana during their Red River expedition.

14 March Confederate Gen Edmund Kirby Smith orders the burning of 150,000 bales of cotton valued at $60 million, to keep it from Union troops in Louisiana.

18 March The US Army renames its Invalid Corps as the Veteran Reserve Corps.

18 March Union forces occupy Alexandria, Louisiana without opposition.

20 March Gen George Stoneman begins his Union cavalry raid from Tennessee into southwestern Virginia and North Carolina (until 23 April).

bring supplies from Chattanooga and beyond. The only danger came from Forrest's cavalry, so he sent out General Samuel Sturgis to 'whip Forrest' in Tennessee. Sturgis tried to keep up with the elusive Confederate, even following him into Mississippi, but finally reported back that Forrest was 'too great a plunderer to fight anything like an equal force'.

As for the Confederates, Lee did not oppose the river crossing but waited with his 18,000 troops in the protective Wilderness woods. Hard, close fighting began there on 5 May. That evening, General Burnside's army joined Grant's, but the Confederates were still waiting for their reinforcements the next morning, when a powerful Union assault began. The Southerners scattered, allowing the Union troops to advance about 1.6km (1 mile), almost into Lee's field headquarters.

As the Confederates retreated, they were delighted to meet General Longstreet's army, which had been marching for two nights and a day to join the battle. As a Texas brigade rushed forward, Lee rode to join them, but the soldiers halted him with the cry, 'Go back! Lee to the rear! We won't go on unless you go back!'

Colonel William Oates, of the 15th Alabama Regiment, watched Lee and later observed, 'I thought he at that moment the grandest specimen of manhood I ever beheld. He looked as though he ought to have been, and was, the monarch of the world.'

The Battle of the Wilderness, the first direct confrontation between Lee and Grant, was well underway. The men were fighting over much of the same ground as the Battle of Chancellorsville, fought just one year earlier, and the woods were still littered with bones and the debris of battle. The Wilderness was familiar to the Southerners, and the larger size of the Union army made it difficult for the soldiers to coordinate where visibility was less than 46m (50yd).

The Confederates now had some 60,000 troops. 'Face the fire and go in where it is hottest,' ordered Confederate General Ambrose Hill. And Longstreet told his men, 'Hit hard when you start, but don't start until you have everything.' They checked the Union lines, and by standing together on an unfinished railway line hidden by underbrush, pushed them back. Over in the opposing army, General Meade

Union officers enjoy a leisurely dinner at their camp at Brandy Station, Virginia.

21 March About 250 Confederate soldiers are surprised and captured at Henderson's Hill, Louisiana.

24 March Confederate troops of Gen Nathan Bedford Forrest capture Union City, Tennessee and its garrison.

25 March Gen Forrest's Confederates raid Paducah, Kentucky.

asked Grant to consider a manoeuvre. 'Oh!' said the general. 'I never manoeuvre.'

Even as the battle was going his way, Longstreet was mistakenly shot by his own men, amid the confusion of battle smoke and brush

Union troops occupied breastworks on the north bank of the Rapidan in the Battle of the Wilderness.

fires in the woods. He was badly wounded, and the Confederates then also fatally shot their General Micah Jenkins. Officers began using compasses to lead their men. Longstreet had taken a ball through his throat and into his shoulder, and hours were lost as his men were left without direction while he received medical attention. By then, the enemy was no longer in retreat but well entrenched, having constructed log breastworks to shelter behind. Both sides made great efforts to rescue the wounded from the burning brush fires. In the Union camp was their famous nurse, Clara Barton. 'While our soldiers fight, I can stand and feed and nurse them,' she said during the battle. 'My place is anywhere between the bullet and the battlefield.'

On the morning of the 7th, the battlefield scene was gloomy: both sides were dug in and the dead littered the woods. Union Captain Thomas Barker refused to take his men in another charge, even 'if Jesus Christ himself should

A bugler was a key messenger during a battle, such as the Battle of the Wilderness.

1864

APRIL

7 April A cavalry engagement occurs at Wilson's Plantation in Louisiana.

2 April Union Gen Wilson's cavalry captures Selma, Alabama as Gen Forrest's Confederate cavalry flees.

8 April The Union flotilla's journey up the Red River, which began on 12 March, is halted by Confederates at Sabine Crossroads, Louisiana, and forced to retreat.

8 April The US Senate, by a vote of 38 to 6, passes the 13th Amendment to the Constitution, which would abolish slavery.

9 April Union forces under Gen Nathaniel Banks during their Red River campaign, repulse a Confederate attack at Pleasant Hill, Louisiana.

order it!' Jerome Stillson, correspondent for the *New York Tribune*, wired his editor: 'We've had a most bitterly contested battle – really *worse* than Gettysburg inasmuch as the bullet has been more destructive than artillery.' The Union had lost 17,666 casualties and the Confederates only 7750. Grant was beginning to earn his nickname of 'the butcher' for throwing masses of men at the enemy, calculating that Southerners could not keep up the attrition even if they won the battles.

Told about the Army of the Potomac fighting hard in the standoff battle, President Lincoln recalled: 'When my wife had her first baby, the doctor from time to time reported to me that everything was going on as well as could be expected under the circumstances. That satisfied me *he* was doing his best, but still I felt anxious to hear the first squall. It came at last, and I felt mightily relieved. I feel very much so about our army operations at this moment.'

'An Abattoir'

The battle over, Lee realized that his army would be unable to throw the invaders back to the Rapidan. For his part, Grant understood

The wounded being retrieved in the Battle of the Wilderness.

....

that he would have to fight all the way to Richmond. His larger force had again been fought to a standstill, and some reports said Grant retired to his tent weeping. But he had no intention of withdrawing. Instead, he surprised even his own men by sending General Meade army past Lee's right side, to an area between the Army of Northern Virginia and its capital. Spotsylvania Court House, some 19km (12 miles) away, was a crossroads town.

Lee was surprised by the move and sped south, both Union and Confederate troops reaching the town on the same day, 8 May. Lee's troops built fieldworks; Grant, insisting that he would 'fight it out on this line if it takes all

summer', made an initial attack on the Confederate left flank, which failed. On 10 May, he used heavy artillery to bombard the enemy before attacking near its centre, an inverted V-shaped defensive line called 'the Mule Shoe'. It was breached and about 1000 prisoners taken.

---

10 April Confederate troops south of the Tennessee–Georgia line capture Mary Edwards Walker, the US Army's only woman surgeon. She is released after four months.

12 April Confederate Gen Nathan Bedford Forrest's troops capture Ft Pillow, Tennessee, on the Mississippi River, massacring black soldiers.

12 April The Confederate cavalry led by Thomas Green successfully attack a Union gunboat expedition at Blair's Landing, Louisiana. Green himself is killed.

14 April The Manhattan Fair in New York raises some $1 million for the Sanitary Commission, a relief organization for the US Army.

17 April Gen Grant halts all prisoner exchanges.

However, Grant informed Washington, 'The enemy hold our front in very strong force, and evince a strong determination to interpose between us and Richmond to the last.'

Two days later, 12 May, Grant once more attacked the centre. The Southerners were forced back about 800m (875yd), the Union troops settling into the trenches they had overrun. This battle was the beginning of trench warfare in its modern sense. As at the Wilderness, Lee attempted to lead the counterattack himself, but once more had to move to the rear when his troops complained. Devastating hand-to-hand fighting occurred in the cramped northwest section, later called 'the Bloody Angle', where the carnage continued for nearly 20 hours before the exhausted Confederates withdrew, just after midnight.

'Rank after rank was riddled by shot and shell and bayonet thrusts, and finally sank, a mass of torn and mutilated corpses,' wrote Union General Horace Porter of that day. 'Trees over a foot and half [45cm] in diameter were cut completely in two by the incessant musketry. … We had not only shot down an army, we had shot down a forest.'

The Dahlgren gun, a powerful weapon on Union warships, was invented before the war by US Ordinance Officer (later Admiral) John Dahlgren. It was nicknamed 'the soda-water bottle' because of its shape.

The weather became rainy over the next few days, and Grant attempted a few times to flank the enemy without success. He then went back to another frontal attack on 18 May, causing immense casualties on both sides. It was Lee who took the offensive on the following day, attacking Grant's right, but neither army could make headway. Almost all the wounded lay behind Confederate lines but Grant, as he had done at Vicksburg, refused to ask for a truce to allow them to receive medical attention and for the dead to be buried. As before, his policy of 'relentless

1864

APRIL

18 April President Lincoln speaks at the Sanitary Fair in Baltimore, saying wartime retaliation is a mistake.

19 April The Confederate ram CSS *Albemarle* sinks the gunboat USS *Southfield* and forces other Union ships to withdraw from Plymouth, North Carolina.

20 April Confederates capture Plymouth, North Carolina.

20 April Gen Wilson's Union cavalry captures Macon, Georgia.

21 April Dr Mary E. Walker, the US Army's first woman assistant surgeon, arrives in Richmond after her capture. The *Richmond Whig* describes her as 'quite ugly'.

22 April The US Congress passes an act that adds the motto 'In God We Trust' to coins.

Members of the Union Army Quartermaster's Department built steamers on the Tennessee River at Chattanooga in 1864.

25 April Confederate troops under Gen Edmund Kirby Smith capture 211 wagons of Union Gen Frederick Steele at Marks's Mills, Arkansas.

27 April The CSS *Alabama* captures its last ship, the *Tycoon*, while sailing to Europe from the Cape of Good Hope.

30 April Confederate President Davis' 5-year-old son, Joe, falls from a balcony of the Confederate White House. He dies the following day.

MAY

1 May The Union forces 'available and present for duty' number 662,345, with 117,000 in hospitals or unfit for duty.

1–8 May Confederate cavalry destroy five Union boats in action around Alexandria, Louisiana.

hammering' meant that his casualties were the heaviest, but these he could afford. The Union lost about 17,500; the Confederacy some 10,000.

Confederate Private Alexander Hunter said of the opposing general:

'At this time the privates of the rank and file had not much belief in Grant's generalship. His mad charges in which he lost thousands, his repeated attacks and repulses, until the vicinity of Spotsylvania resembled a great abbatoir, where, instead of cattle being slaughtered, precious humanity gave up their lives, was not their idea of a master of the art of war.'

Another confrontation between the Army of the Potomac and the Army of Northern Virginia loomed, both forces racing south. Grant wanted to get around Lee's army, and Lee was not fighting defensively. He warned an aide: 'We must destroy this army of Grant's before he get to the James. If he gets there, it will become a siege, and then it will be a mere question of time.'

The Confederate ram CSS Albemarle *fought valiantly against the Union's blockade ships.*

Small Victories, Big Losses

Nor was Grant the only problem for the Confederates. Union armies were advancing deeper into Virginia. General Sheridan and about 10,000 troops began a raid towards Richmond, disrupting the lines of communication between 9 May and 24 May. Also on 9 May, General Custer's arm of Sheridan's army began a two-day assault that destroyed Confederate food supplies as well as more than 100 railroad cars, two locomotives, and 16km (10 miles) of track at Beaver Dam Station.

Hearing of this, General Jeb Stuart set out with a Confederate cavalry of about 4500, taking up positions at Yellow Tavern at 8 a.m. to block Sheridan's advance to the capital city. The Northerners arrived at about 11 a.m. and launched a major attack at 4 p.m. Stuart, aware that his far left was weak, rode off towards it. Custer attacked at this point and drove the Confederates back, but they soon rallied and counterattacked. This involved mounted fighting with sabres – the exception in eastern Virginia, as Sheridan later recalled, because of the dense woods and the practice of barricading.

Seated on his horse, Stuart was firing at the

1864

MAY

3 May Gen Grant crosses the Rapidan River in Virginia with 100,000 men to move towards Richmond.

3 May Union forces of Gen Frederick Steele end their retreat to Little Rock, Arkansas.

4 May Gen Sherman's Union force leaves Chattanooga, Tennessee, on the march towards Atlanta, Georgia.

US artillery shook Atlanta daily.

5 May The Confederate ram, CSS *Albemarle*, battles seven blockade ships to a draw in the mouth of the Roanoke River.

5 May The Confederate cruiser CSS *Georgia* is commissioned. It was built in Dumbarton, Scotland in 1862 and purchased by the Confederacy in March 1863.

The CSS Albemarle *was the last Confederate ram, sunk by a small launch on 27 October by a torpedo attached to a spar.*

In the Battle of Spotsylvania, Virginia, Union General Grant had the largest casualties as he failed to defeat General Lee's troops.

retreating enemy when a shot from less than 14m (15yd) away hit his abdomen. He died the next day in Richmond. His last words were, 'I am going fast now. I am resigned. God's will be done.' His loss to the South was immense. Lee said, 'I can scarcely think about him without weeping.'

Elsewhere in Virginia, Confederates were able to block the enemy's incursions. General Beauregard's army met General Butler's force on 12 May at the Battle of Fort Darling on Drewry's Bluff. Fighting continued until the 16th, when Butler's troops were attacked in a dense fog. The fighting was confused, and Butler finally withdrew under a heavy rainstorm to Bermuda Hundred. Beauregard gave chase and by the next morning had built earthworks that had Butler's army trapped. On the 20th, the Confederates captured the enemy's advance rifle pits at Ware Bottom Church, but lost them after a counterattack. Still, Butler remained 'bottled up', as Grant put it.

5–7 May The Battle of the Wilderness in Virginia is inconclusive between Gens Grant and Lee. Casualties: Union, 17,666; Confederate, 7750.

6 May A Confederate torpedo destroys the USS *Commodore* in the James River in Virginia.

6 May Confederates accidentally kill their own Gen Micah Jenkins and seriously wound Gen James Longstreet at the Wilderness in Virginia.

7 May The Union's Division of West Mississippi, sometimes called the Trans-Mississippi Department, is created.

8 May A cavalry skirmish at Todd's Tavern, Virginia is inconclusive.

8–19 May The Battle of Spotsylvania, Virginia, directed by Gens Grant and Lee, is inconclusive. Casualties: Union, 17,500; Confederate about 10,000.

General Jubal Early's Confederate army was enjoying similar success. The Union general Franz Sigel, was moving up the Shenandoah Valley, with 6500 men, infantry and cavalry. The advance was delayed by the Confederate cavalry of General John Imboden, who was then reinforced by the troops of J. C. Breckinridge at New Market. Among the Southerners were 247 cadets from the Virginia Military Institute (VMI), Stonewall Jackson's old school. On 15 May, the enemies clashed. Breckinridge attacked early in the morning, and by 4 p.m. Sigel called for a general retreat in the heavy rain. He had lost 831 men to the Confederates' 577, which included 10 cadets from the Virginia Military Institute killed and 47 wounded. Sigel was relieved of his command four days later.

Deeper South in Georgia, General Johnston's Confederates repulsed the troops of Sherman at Resaca, fighting from 13 May to 15 May before

Union Generals George Armstrong Custer and Alfred Pleasonton were distinguished in many battles and both also fought Indians.

withdrawing. They then also blocked the progress of General Joseph Hooker, part of Sherman's army, at New Hope Church (Dallas), fighting from 25 May to 27 May. However such successes were mere obstacles that could only delay, not prevent, Sherman's inexorable advance towards Atlanta.

Political Considerations

The Union generals were keeping a close watch on the political scene, this being a presidential year. General Sheridan later remembered:

'I deemed it necessary to be very cautious; and the fact that the Presidential election was impending made me doubly so, the authorities at Washington having impressed upon me that the defeat of my army might be followed by the overthrow of the party in power, which event, it was believed, would at least retard the progress of the war, if, indeed, it did not lead to the complete abandonment of all coercive measures.'

On 31 May, radical Republicans nominated General John C Frémont to run against the man who would be nominated as their own party's official candidate – Lincoln, they assumed. On 7 June, the Republican Party, calling itself the National Union Party, met in Baltimore and re-nominated Lincoln. For Vice President, they chose Andrew Johnson, a War

1864

MAY

9 May Gen George Crook's Union force defeats the small cavalry command of Gen Albert Jenkins at Cloyd's Mountain, Virginia, and Jenkins is mortally wounded.

9 May Union Gen Philip Sheridan advances towards Richmond to disrupt the Confederates' lines of communication.

9–10 May The forces of Union Gen George Armstrong Custer destroy more than 100 railroad cars, two locomotives, and 16km (10 miles) of track at Beaver Dam Station, Virginia.

10 May The infamous Confederate raider Capt William Quantrill is fatally wounded by Union troops in Kentucky as he travels to assassinate President Lincoln.

10 May At Crockett's Cove, Virginia, Gen John Morgan's cavalry and infantry repulse the Union troops of Gen William Averell, who retreats to West Virginia.

Democrat who was the military governor of Tennessee. The Democrats were supposed to meet in Chicago on 4 July, but the victories at Gettysburg and Vicksburg undermined their electoral platform – a call for peace. The meeting was rescheduled for 29 August (just four days before Sherman took Atlanta), and General George McClellan was nominated. Having been removed from his command by Lincoln, he described the president as 'the original gorilla'.

No other country had ever held such an election while a civil war raged. Despite the recent impressive victories, President Lincoln was doubtful that the country still wanted his leadership:

'I have seen enough to satisfy me that I am a failure, not only in the opinion of the people in rebellion, but of many distinguished politicians of my own party. But time will show whether I am right or they are right and I am content to abide its decision.'

The New York newspapers thought another candidate should be sought. 'Mr. Lincoln is already beaten,' wrote Horace Greeley in his *New York Tribune*. 'He cannot be elected. And

General Grant leans over a pew outside Massaponax Church, Virginia, to study a map held by General George Meade on 21 May, two days before facing General Lee at the North Anna River.

11 May The Battle of Yellow Tavern, Virginia results in the withdrawal of the Confederate cavalry and the mortal wounding of its leader, Gen 'Jeb' Stuart.

12 May Gen Sherman's Union army breaks through Snake Creek Gap near Dalton, Georgia. Confederates have held them off since 7 May.

12 May Confederate Gen 'Jeb' Stuart dies in Richmond, Virginia from wounds suffered at the battle of Yellow Tavern, Virginia.

13 May Pvt William Henry Christman of the 67th Pennsylvania Infantry is the first military man interred at Arlington National Cemetery, Virginia.

13 May Adm David Porter's squadron escapes low water in the Red River in Louisiana after dams are quickly built to let him retreat from Alexandria.

War-torn flags symbolized gallentry, as this one for a Pennsylvania infantry unit.

13–15 May Gen Sherman's Union troops are repulsed by Gen Johnston's at Resaca, Georgia, but the Confederates withdraw after hearing news of Union reinforcements.

we must have another ticket to save us from overthrow.' And James Gordon Bennett in the *New York Herald*, thought everyone should be replaced: 'Lincoln has proved a failure. McClellan has proved a failure. Frémont has proved a failure; let us have a new candidate.'

By August, Lincoln was becoming more depressed. Of his generals, he said 'I have no reason to believe that Grant prefers my election to that of McClellan.' And of his own chances, 'I am going to be beaten, and unless some great change takes place, *badly* beaten.' Indeed, on the 23rd, he sent this memorandum to his cabinet members:

'This morning, as for some time past, it seems exceedingly probable that this administration will not be re-elected. Then it will be my duty to so co-operate with the President elect, and to save the Union between the election and the inauguration; as he will have secured his election on such ground that he can not possibly save it afterwards.'

Later he was more bullish, attacking the Democrats, who had made McClellan sign onto a peace platform: 'There is no program offered by any wing of the Democratic party, but that

must result in the permanent destruction of the Union.' Now he felt certain 'if I live' to be re-elected, but was less sure he deserved the honour: 'I am now inspired with the hope that our disturbed country further requires the valuable services of your humble servant.'

Finally, he had poignant thoughts about his future:

'I hope, however, that I may never have another four years of such anxiety, tribulation, and abuse. My only ambition is and has been to put down the rebellion and restore peace, after which I want to resign my office, go abroad, take some rest, study foreign governments, see something of foreign life, and in my old age die in peace with all of the good of God's creatures.'

The election campaign itself would prove ill-mannered. Democrats said

The Battle of Resaca, Georgia, was another Union victory for General Sherman.

1864

MAY

12–16 May Confederates under Gen Beauregard repulse Gen Benjamin Butler's force at the Battle of Ft Darling on Drewry's Bluff, Virginia.

14–15 May Gen Sherman's Union army battles Confederates under Gen Joseph Johnston at Resaca, Georgia, 29km (18 miles) south of Dalton, forcing Johnston to withdraw.

15 May Gen Jubal Early's Confederates defeat Gen Franz Sigel's army at New Market, Virginia to end Union plans of sweeping the enemy from Virginia's Shenandoah Valley.

18 May In the last action in the Trans-Mississippi region, Confederate cavalry under Gen St John Liddell clash with Adm David Porter's fleet at Yellow Bayou, Louisiana.

Republicans were 'Negro-loving'; the Republicans condemned Democrats as traitors for seeking peace. Indeed, the Confederate Vice President Alexander Stephens called McClellan's nomination 'the first ray of real light since the war began'.

During that summer, Congress was equally active. By a vote of 95 to 66, the House of Representatives defeated the 13th Amendment to the Constitution, which would have abolished slavery. But Congress did finally pass the bill, signed by Lincoln on 28 June, to repeal the Fugitive Slave Law of 1850. On 30 June, Congress passed the Internal Revenue Act, increasing taxes to pay for the war. And on 2 July, it passed a severe Reconstruction plan for the South, though Lincoln vetoed it.

Holding On

Things were not looking good for the Union on the battlefield. Grant crossed the James River on 14 June to take Petersburg, but Lee's army was quick to meet him. General Beauregard was defending the area with just 5400 men, and reinforcements were quick to come. The number of men increased to 41,499; even so,

Union General Franz Sigel had served in the German Army before moving to America.

Grant's force outnumbered them, totalling 63,797. After fighting from 15 June to 18 June, Grant abandoned his idea of capturing Petersburg and settled into a siege, a tactic that had worked so well in Vicksburg. The fighting had cost the deaths of 1688 Union men, with a further 8513 wounded and 1185 captured or missing; the Confederate totals are unknown.

Sherman would also hit problems that month on his Atlanta march, being repulsed by Johnston's army at Kennesaw Mountain on 27 June. This time the Confederates had the larger army, 17,733 against 16,225 men. Attacking uphill against Confederate positions that were well entrenched behind rocks, the Union forces accomplished little in three assaults, and took heavy losses. Sherman suffered 2051 casualties, Johnston only 442. But this would be the Confederate general's last stand against the invaders. From now on, he would prefer to withdraw, hitting out occasionally, a tactic that earned him the nickname of 'Retreating Joe' and the eventual loss of his command.

20 May The Battle of Ware Bottom Church, Virginia, keeps Gen Butler's Union troops bottled up at Bermuda Hundred next to the earthworks of Gen Beauregard's force.

25 May Five volunteers from the Union gunboat USS *Wyalusing* fail to destroy the Confederate ram CSS *Albemarle* with a torpedo in Albemarle Sound, North Carolina.

25–27 May Confederates under Gen Joseph Johnston repulse Gen Joseph Hooker's troops at New Hope Church, Georgia.

26 May Gen Nathaniel Banks' Union army reaches Donaldsonville, Louisiana, completing their retreat from Alexandria.

31 May Radical Republicans nominate Gen John C Frémont to run against their own party's President Lincoln.

Better news reached Washington from England. The feared CSS *Alabama* was sunk by the USS *Kearsarge* off Cherbourg, France on 19 June. During the battle the Confederates lost nine killed, 21 wounded, while the Union vessel only had three wounded. When the *Alabama* sank, 12 of the crew drowned. Some were rescued by the enemy, but Commander Semmes and others were rescued by an English yacht and escaped. The Southern crew went to London and were feted as heroes. Semmes

toured Europe and returned home to be promoted to rear admiral and take command of the Confederacy's James River squadron.

The *New York Times* of 6 July gave over its entire front page and much of page 4 to the news, saying: 'The pirate Alabama has at last

....

Neatly spaced Union tents awaited the Battle of Cold Harbor, Virginia, on 3 June.

gone to the bottom of the sea.' Noted Admiral Farragut in a letter to his son, 'I would sooner have fought that fight than any ever fought on the ocean.'

On July 2, General Jubal Early's Confederate cavalry headed for Washington, raiding though Maryland on the way. On 9 July, at Monocracy, General Lew Wallace's troops, outnumbered two to one, engaged them enough to slow the advance and allow reinforcements to reach the capital. Early's men reached the edge of Washington on

1864

MAY

31 May–3 June At the Battle of Cold Harbor, Virginia, Gen Lee's Confederates defeat Gen Grant's troops, which sustain far greater losses.

JUNE

5 June Union Gen David Hunter's men rout Confederates at Piedmont, Virginia.

6 June Gen Hunter's Union force takes Staunton, Virginia, unopposed.

7 June The Republican Party (National Union Party) Convention in Baltimore, Maryland, renominates President Lincoln as its candidate and nominates Andrew Johnson for Vice President.

10 July and fired on Fort Stevens. Visiting at the time was President Lincoln, who twice exposed his tall form on the parapet to snipers. On one of these occasions, Captain Oliver Wendell Holmes, Jnr failed to recognize Lincoln and yelled, 'Get down, you damn fool, before you get shot!' The President looked bemused but quickly obeyed. The Confederates, having probed the city's strengthened defences, decided to withdraw.

Sherman in Georgia was doing better against Johnston's dodging tactics. On 5 October, the Union's food supply depot at Allatoona was surrounded by Confederates led by General Samuel French. The garrison had just 860 men, but they fought well to defend it. Sherman, 21km (13 miles) away, had his signal officer send a wigwag message saying 'Sherman is moving in force. Hold out' and another repeating, 'General Sherman says hold fast. We are coming.' This was later quoted in newspapers as 'Hold the fort, for I am coming' and turned into a popular and inspiring hymn, 'Hold the Fort'.

After sighting these messages, French withdrew his troops before Sherman arrived. He had lost 799 men from more than 2000, while Union losses were 707 from 1944.

Black Union soldiers bury the bones of men killed at the Battle of Cold Harbor. This was General Robert E. Lee's last major victory and one of General Ulysses S. Grant's greatest blunders.

9 June Confederate Gen John Morgan's last cavalry raid into Kentucky is surprised at Mt Sterling, and several men are captured.

10 June The Confederate Congress increases the military age limits to between 17 and 50.

10 June Gen Morgan's Confederate cavalry captures Cynthiana, Kentucky and its garrison.

10 June Gen Samuel Sturgis' invasion of Mississippi is defeated by half as many Confederates under Gen Nathan Bedford Forrest, at Brice's Cross Roads, outside Guntown, Mississippi.

11–12 June The cavalry Battle of Trevilian Station, Virginia is won by Confederates under Gen Wade Hampton over the force of Gen Philip Sheridan.

12 June Gen John Morgan's Confederate cavalry battles a Union force four times larger in Cynthiana, Kentucky. But with ammunition running out, it is driven from the state.

The Confederacy Takes the Offensive

President Davis had enough of Johnston's retreating, and on 17 July relieved him as commander of the Army of Tennessee. The replacement was General John B. Hood, who had criticized Johnston's cautious strategy. The outgoing general returned the compliment. After handing over command, he telegraphed Secretary of War James Seddon and made a couple of points. First, that he had slowed down Sherman's more much powerful army, and that the contrast between the two forces was starker even than the contrast between Lee's army and Grant's. Second, that in reference to Hood: 'Confident language by a military commander is not usually regarded as evidence of competence.'

Certainly, the young Hood had impressed no one. At West Point, he had finished in the bottom fifth of his class, but he led his Texan brigade well at Second Bull Run and Antietam. His left arm was crippled from a shot taken at Gettysburg, and he lost his right leg at Chickamauga. Davis needed a proven fighter

Pontoon bridges, such as this one over the James River, were essential for rapid troop movements.

1864

JUNE

14 June Gen Grant crosses the James River intending to capture Petersburg, Virginia.

14 June Confederate Gen Leonidas Polk is killed by an artillery shot near Kenesaw Mountain, Georgia.

15 June Part of the grounds of Robert E. Lee's home at Arlington, Virginia are appropriated for a military cemetery by Gen Montgomery Meigs, in command of the garrison there.

15 June The US House of Representatives, by a vote of 95 to 66, defeats the 13th Amendment to the Constitution abolishing slavery.

15–18 June At Petersburg, Virginia, Gen Lee's forces repulse those of Gen Grant, who begins a siege of the city.

General Grant's troops crossed the James River on 14 June heading for Petersburg, Virginia.

and, true to form, Hood went on the offensive just two days after his appointment.

The part of Sherman's army targeted by Hood was General George Thomas' Army of the Cumberland. It was attacked on 20 July as it was crossing Peach Tree Creek. The attack was timed for 1 p.m. but was delayed by three hours due to a confusion on taking positions. Hood blamed Genreal William Hardee, and Hardee blamed Hood. Once across, Thomas, who had stood fast as 'the Rock of Chickamauga', rushed his artillery forward and joined them to direct their fire. The assault now descended into stalemate, for which Hood blamed Hardee, claiming that his troops did nothing but 'lay down' behind breastworks. He had lost 2500 killed or wounded of his 18,832 men; Thomas' losses were some 1600 killed or wounded from 20,139.

16 June President Lincoln addresses the Sanitary Fair in Philadephia, Pennsylvania, asking for more soldiers for victory, even 'if it takes three years more'.

17–18 June At Lynchburg, Virginia, the Confederate troops of Gen John Breckinridge repulse Gen David Hunter's men, who retreat to West Virginia.

19 June The USS *Kearsarge* sinks the CSS *Alabama* off Cherbourg, France.

27 June Gen Johnston's Confederates repulse Gen Sherman's forces at Kennesaw Mountain, Georgia.

28 June President Lincoln approves the bill passed by Congress to repeal the Fugitive Slave Law of 1850.

This level of attrition did not stop Hood from again attacking the enemy two days later outside Atlanta, an engagement known as the Battle of Atlanta. Heavy fighting led to nothing, and both sides returned to their original lines. Hood's desperate and costly assaults led to about 8000 casualties compared to Thomas' total of only 3722. The Union did, however, suffer a major loss when General James McPherson was killed. 'The country has lost one of its best soldiers,' said Grant, 'and I have lost my best friend.'

Above: Union supplies grew on the landing at City Point, Virginia, during their siege of Petersburg.

Left: Officers of the USS Kearsarge *won fame when their ship sank the dreaded CSS* Alabama.

1864

JUNE

30 June The US Congress passes the Internal Revenue Act, increasing taxes to finance the war.

JULY

2 July The US Congress passes the Wade–Davis bill for a Reconstruction program. This is more severe than the proposals of President Lincoln, and he vetoes it.

2–13 July Gen Jubal Early's Confederates raid Maryland with the intention of reaching Washington, DC.

3 July Confederates repulse a Union attack on Ft Johnson on James Island in Charleston Harbor.

The invaders now set about cutting off Hood's communications and supplies. To protect his railroad link, the Confederate general made yet a third attack on 28 July at Ezra Church, losing another 2500 men to no effect. The Confederates now moved into Atlanta and waited behind its impressive defences for a Union attack. Instead, Sherman laid siege on 25 August, beginning a constant bombardment of the vital railroad town. Sherman justified this by saying Atlanta was a 'fortified town', having magazines, arsenals, foundries and public stores.

The siege of Petersburg, Virginia by Union troops began in June and lasted a year.

The Battle of Allatoona Pass in Georgia on 5 October was a failed Confederate attempt to capture General Sherman's supply depot. Sherman's message was misquoted as 'Hold the fort'.

'Let us destroy Atlanta and make it a desolation,' Sherman told General Oliver Howard. Earlier in the month, he had telegraphed General Halleck: 'One thing is certain, whether we get inside of Atlanta or not, it will be a used-up community when we are done with it.'

Six days later, General Hardee led his Confederates in a final desperate attack at Jonesboro against Union entrenchments, to stop Sherman's men from tearing up the Montgomery & Atlanta Railroad south of the city. The assault failed and ended any hope the South had of saving Atlanta.

By Land and Sea

Meanwhile, at the siege of Petersburg, General Ambrose Burnside was now in command of the 9th Crops of Grant's Army. He now came up with an audacious plan, to blast a giant hole in the enemy's defences and pour troops through. This would be done by digging a tunnel underneath the fortifications and filling it with four tons of black powder, then covering up the beginning of the tunnel with tamped-down dirt and lighting the powder with a 29m (98ft) fuse.

1864

JULY

9–22 July Gen Lovell Rousseau begins his Union cavalry raid from Decatur, Alabama to Marietta, Georgia.

10–11 July President Lincoln visits Ft Stevens in Washington, DC, when it comes under fire from Confederates under Gen Jubal Early.

12 July Gen Early's Confederates withdraw from the outskirts of Washington, DC, after learning that its defences have been reinforced.

14 July Union troops repulse a Confederate attack by Confederates at Harrisburg, Mississippi near Tupelo, but they burn Harrisburg and begin a retreat to Memphis, Tennessee.

Deserters told the Union troops that the Confederates thought all of Petersburg was being mined and that they were 'resting upon a slumbering volcano'.

The first lighting failed, so volunteers had to enter the tunnel and relight the fuse. The blast shot timbers and dirt 30m (100ft) into the air, burying a regiment of the defenders. The Union troops now attacked. The initial plan had been to use black soldiers to attack through the gaping hole, but General Meade belatedly decided this would be politically dangerous. Straws were now drawn and General James Ledlie's men, who had not trained for this assignment, charged into the tunnel instead of around the crater. (Ledlie himself stayed back, drinking rum in a shelter.) Riflemen at the rim of the crater now had the luxury of a trapped quarry, and cannon were also brought to the slaughter. The Confederates then counterattacked, meeting and killing many of the black division, who had advanced, avoiding the tunnel. The Union lost 3798 men, the Confederates about 1500 casualties.

'It was a stupendous failure,' Grant would write about the Battle of the Crater. 'It was the

General Grant called the Petersburg mine assault a 'stupendous failure'. On 30 July, the enemy picked off Union troops rushing through a crater they had created by explosives.

17 July Confederate President Davis replaces Gen Joseph Johnston with Gen John B. Hood as commander of the Army of Tennessee, which faces Gen Sherman's force in Georgia.

17 July Gen Lovell Rousseau's Union cavalry arrives at Opelika, Alabama and destroys the railroad track that connects Montgomery, Alabama with Columbus, Georgia.

18 July Christopher Memminger is replaced by George Trenholm as Secretary of the Treasury for the Confederacy.

20 July At the Battle of Peachtree Creek near Atlanta, an attack by Confederate Gen Hood's force fails on the army of Gen George Thomas.

22 July Gen Hood's Confederates again attack Gen Sherman's troops outside Atlanta without success.

saddest affair I have witnessed in the war.' He dismissed Ledlie and gave extended leave to Burnside, who resigned within a few months, leaving the army for good.

Good news was still coming from the US Navy, which was now bearing down on Mobile, Alabama, the last unconquered port on the Gulf. For the Battle of Mobile Bay on 5 August, Admiral David Farragut had four ironclads and 14 wooden ships. He was facing Admiral

This artwork depicts the death of Union General James McPherson (on horse) at the Battle of Atlanta on 22 July.

The strong Confederate works around Atlanta kept the Union army from assaulting it directly. The Battle of Atlanta actually comprised several battles around the city in late July.

1864

JULY

24 July Confederate Gen Jubal Early's cavalry defeats Union forces at Kernstown, Virginia.

26-31 July Gen George Stoneman leads his Union cavalry in a raid in Georgia from Decatur to Macon.

29 July Union troops wreck railroad tracks between Jonesboro and Griffin in Georgia.

28 July A second attack by Gen Hood on Gen Sherman's force fails at Ezra Church, Georgia near Atlanta.

Franklin Buchanan, who had captained the *Virginia* against the *Monitor*. Now he had only three small, wooden ships and one ironclad, but it was the largest one afloat, the CSS *Tennessee*. The bay's entrance was defended by Fort Morgan on an eastern peninsula and Fort Gaines on Dauphin Island to the west; its waters were filled with mines (underwater torpedoes).

Farragut directed his fleet from his flagship, the *Hartford,* where he instructed his sailors to lash him to the mast, to counter his vertigo. Within minutes his lead ironclad, the *Tecumseh,* struck a mine and sank, carrying down most of its crew. 'Sunk by a torpedo!' said Captain James Alden, watching from the USS *Brooklyn.* 'Assassination in its worst form!' The tragedy halted the fleet until Farragut issued his famous command, 'Damn the torpedoes! Full speed ahead!'

The fleet cruised past the forts and into the bay, bumping a few mines that did not explode. They quickly captured or drove away the wooden ships. Buchanan was aboard the *Tennessee,* which tried to ram the enemy, swapped shots with them and then took refuge close to Fort Morgan. As Union crews stopped for breakfast, Buchanan brought his ship out to

renew the battle, but it was surrounded, rammed and fired upon. Its funnel was shot away and her rudder chains broken, making her drift helplessly. Buchanan was seriously wounded, and was taken with his crew to the Union naval base at Pensacola, Florida. The next day, a combined Union army and navy force took Fort Gaines and, after a three-day siege, Fort Morgan on 23 August.

Sherman Takes Atlanta
Atlanta was evacuated on 1 September by General Hood. When the news reached the Northerners, General George Thomas 'snapped his fingers, whistled, and almost danced', Sherman recalled. His troops marched in and much of the city burned, fires set by both sides. 'Atlanta is ours and fairly won,' Sherman telegraphed to Lincoln. And Private William Miller of the 75th Indiana Infantry, recorded in his diary: 'The arsenal contained some small-arms and about four thousand pikes and sabers for cutting up Yankees, and now we are here for the sacrifice and the butchers are not at home.'

Confederate General John B. Hood had the impossible task of stopping the assault on Atlanta.

30 July Union Gen Ambrose Burnside conducts a large mine explosion under the defences of Petersburg, Virginia, but the subsequent tunnel attack fails.

30 July Confederate forces demand a ransom of $500,000 from Chambersburg, Pennsylvania and burn down the business district when it is not paid.

30 July Gen George Stoneman reaches Macon, Georgia with his Union cavalry. He is captured during action at Hillsboro while circling toward Andersonville to liberate prisoners.

AUGUST

3 August Confederates surprise the cavalry of Gen Horace Capron near Jug Tavern, Georgia. Some of his troops drown when a bridge collapses at Mulberry Creek.

5 August Adm David Farragut's Union fleet wins the Battle of Mobile Bay, Alabama. He supposedly says, 'Damn the torpedoes! Full speed ahead!'

6 August The CSS *Tallahassee* leaves Wilmington, North Carolina, to begin a successful three-week interruption of US shipping.

Union Admiral David Farragut (right) and Captain Percival Drayton take a break aboard the USS Hartford *in Mobile Bay.*

On 7 September, Sherman ordered all citizens to evacuate Atlanta. Immediately, Mayor James Calhoun complained, noting that nothing like this had happened in US history and asking what the helpless people had done to be driven from their homes, 'to wander as strangers, outcasts and exiles, and to subsist on charity'.

Sherman was unsympathetic, writing to the mayor:

'You might as well appeal against the thunderstorm as against the terrible hardships of war. ... War is cruelty and you cannot refine it; and those who brought war into our country deserve all the curses and maledictions a people can pour out. ... We don't want your negroes or your horses, or your houses or your land, or anything you have; but we do want and will have a just obedience to the laws of the United States.'

An Atlanta lady also questioned the order, but Sherman sidestepped the issue. Southern soldiers, he told her, were the bravest in the world, because they had fought against

1864

AUGUST

8 August Ft Gaines on Dauphin Island at the head of Mobile Bay in Alabama, is surrendered with 900 men to Union Gen Gordon Granger.

17 August Confederates under Gen Jubal Early push the army of Union Gen Philip Sheridan across the Potomac River.

21 August Confederate Gen Nathan Bedford Forrest's army attacks Memphis, Tennessee, and withdraws.

23 August President Lincoln send his cabinet members a memo stating that 'it seems exceedingly probable that this Administration will not be re-elected'.

23 August Ft Morgan, guarding Mobile Bay, Alabama, is surrendered by Confederate Gen Richard Page to Gen Gordon Granger.

The Battle of Mobile Bay, Alabama, on 5 August saw Admiral David Farragut's Union fleet close the last major port on the Gulf of Mexico east of Texas. 'Damn the torpedoes!' he called. 'Full speed ahead!'

four or five times their number. But he then added a warning: 'You can beat us in fighting, but we can outmanoeuvre you. Your generals do not work half enough. We work day and night, and spare no labour, nor pains, to carry out our plans.'

If his actions and motives were somewhat confused, William Tecumseh Sherman was himself something of an enigma. He loved Southerners and the South one moment, and hated them the next. Born the son of an Ohio Supreme Court justice and orphaned early, he was raised by US Senator and cabinet member Thomas Ewing, whose daughter he later married. Sherman graduated from West Point and then served in Florida and at Fort Moultrie in Charleston Harbor, developing many friends in that city. He took part in the Mexican War and then left the army to try banking, law and real estate. Eventually he became superintendent of the Louisiana State Seminary of Learning and Military Academy near Alexandria, which later became Louisiana State University (LSU). He liked the position but felt uncomfortable at the break-up of the Union – his brother John was a US senator –

25 August Gen Sherman begins the siege of Atlanta.

29 August The Democratic National Convention meeting in Chicago nominates Gen George McClellan as its presidential candidate.

31 August President Lincoln addresses the 148th Ohio Regiment in Washington, DC, telling them the war is an attempt 'to overwhelm and destroy the national existence'.

31 August An attack by Confederates under Gen William Hardee fails at the Battle of Jonesboro, Georgia, ending any chance of the Confederates defending Atlanta.

SEPTEMBER

1 September Gen Hood's Confederates evacuate Atlanta, Georgia, but torch the city.

Officers keep watch at Fort Gaines, guarding Mobile Bay from the west on Dauphin Island, Alabama. With Fort Morgan on the east, the Confederates had a formidable defence.

1864

SEPTEMBER

2 September Gen Sherman's troops occupy Atlanta, Georgia, but much of the city has been destroyed.

4 September Confederate cavalry raider Gen John Morgan surprised and killed by Union troops at Greeneville, Tennessee.

7 September Gen Sherman orders civilians to evacuate Atlanta.

8 September Gen George McClellan accepts the Democratic nomination as the party's presidential candidate, stating that the nation must be reunited.

and so he resigned to return to Missouri. On 14 May 1861, he accepted an appointment as colonel to the 13th Infantry, which fought well at the disastrous First Battle of Bull Run, earning him a promotion to brigadier general.

Sherman was an intense person who occasionally showed emotional and even mental instability. After Bull Run, he seems to have suffered a mild nervous breakdown while commanding troops in Kentucky. This led some officers, including McClellan, to label him crazy. He carried on, proving to be one of the Union's most direct speaking and acting generals, and his troops admired and trusted him. He had a reputation of toughness, even brutality, but at the end of the war he offered such benevolent terms of surrender to General Johnston that President Andrew Johnson had to have them renegotiated.

In Richmond, President Davis was trying to remain optimistic despite the loss of Atlanta. 'Let no one despond,' he urged. 'The first effect of disaster is always to spread a deeper

Barracks No. 1 at Fort Morgan, Alabama, took a pounding during the Battle of Mobile Bay.

16 September Confederate Gen Wade Hampton captures 2500 US Army cattle 9.6km (6 miles) from Gen Grant's headquarters in Virginia.

16, 18 September Confederate troops fail to take Ft Gibson in Indian Territory (now Oklahoma).

17 September Gen John C. Frémont withdraws as a Republican presidential candidate to avoid splitting his party.

19 September Despite higher casualties, Gen Philip Sheridan's Union forces defeat those of Gen Jubal Early in Winchester, Virginia. Casualties: Union, 5018; Confederate, 3921.

19 September Confederate Gen Sterling Price's army, with several cavalry divisions added, raids Missouri, continuing through October.

Union General William Emory's 19th Corps helped win the Battle of Winchester, Virginia, on 19 September.

gloom than is due to the occasion.' His citizens, however, were in deep gloom. 'Atlanta is gone,' wrote Mary Chesnut in her diary. 'That agony is over. There is no hope but we will try to have no fear.'

Almost at the same time, Davis received word that the South's beloved cavalry leader, General John Morgan, had been killed on 4 September. Some nine months after escaping from prison in Ohio, he was surprised and surrounded in a house in Greeneville, Tennessee, and he was shot dead as he tried to escape. He had just returned from a raid in Kentucky with 2000 cavalrymen, half of them marching because they lacked horses.

On Through the Fall

September was an active month for cavalries. On his Shenandoah Valley Campaign, Union General Sheridan received information from a spy (a Quaker schoolteacher): a Confederate division and 12 cannon had been shifted from General Early's army. He therefore launched an attack on 19 September, at Winchester, Virginia.

1864

SEPTEMBER				OCTOBER

21 September Confederate Gen Nathan Bedford Forrest begins his cavalry raid to middle Tennessee.

22 September Union Gen Sheridan's troops win over Gen Early's at Fisher's Hill, Virginia.

23–24 September Gen Forrest's Confederate cavalry captures the Union garrison at Athens, Alabama.

27 September Union forces of Gen Thomas Ewing repulse the troops of Gen Sterling Price at Fort Davidson, Missouri, but then evacuate and blow it up.

1 October Confederate Gen Joseph Wheeler's cavalry begins a week-long raid into Tennessee to disrupt the communication and supply lines of Gen William Rosecrans.

The battle went to his superior force, although he took more casualties – 5018 to 3921. They clashed again four days later at Fisher's Hill, and Sheridan's men were again victorious. This time it was the fading Confederates who took the greatest losses, 1235 to only 528.

But events were not going all the Union way. A day earlier, General Forrest's cavalry raided middle Tennessee. Then, on 24 September, he captured the Union garrison at Athens in north Alabama, and began to tear up railroad tracks in Tennessee. But Union troops were massing, from Sherman's forces in Atlanta, and from Memphis, Chattanooga, and Nashville, as well as further north, until there was a total of 30,000 troops chasing the Confederate's small cavalry. 'I do not think we shall ever have a better chance than this,' said General George Thomas. The wily Forrest, however, used a ferry to escape over the Tennessee River on 6 October. He had killed and wounded many of the enemy, caused an immense amount of damage to the railroad, and stolen guns and stores.

....

Union soldiers were hardly in danger as they waited out the siege of Atlanta.

2 October Confederates repulse a Union attack on Saltville, Virginia, the Confederacy's main source of salt.

2 October Confederate Gen Joseph Wheeler's cavalry captures a large Union wagon train at Anderson's Cross Roads, Tennessee.

2 October Gen George Armstrong Custer is given command of the US 3rd Cavalry Division.

3 October Gen Wheeler's Confederate cavalry captures McMinnville, Tennessee.

3 October The Confederate army of Gen John Bell Hood captures Big Shanty and Acworth in Georgia.

7 October Troops of Union Gen George Crook defeat part of Gen Wheeler's cavalry at the Duck River near Farmington, Tennessee.

7 October The Confederate cruiser CSS *Florida* is captured by the USS *Wachusett* off Bahîla, Brazil.

A depot in Atlanta is in ruins after General Sherman's Union troops blew it up as they left the city.

By October, the South was running out of warships. The USS *Wachusett* captured the CSS *Florida* in the harbour of Bahia, Brazil on 7 October (violating international law). The Confederate ship, which had captured or destroyed 37 US vessels, was towed all the way back to Hampton Roads and sunk there.

Then on 27 October, a small Union launch, with a crew of 14 led by Lieutenant William Cushing, used a torpedo on a spar to sink the last Confederate ram, the CSS *Albemarle,* in the Roanoke River in Virginia. The explosion also sank the launch, and two of the crew were drowned and 11 captured; Cushing himself and another sailor swam to safety.

Lincoln Returned

On 8 November, Lincoln won his presidential election, taking 55 per cent of the total popular votes, winning 2.2 million to McClellan's 1.8 million. He was the first President to be re-elected since Andrew Jackson in 1832. (General Frémont, the radical Republican candidate, had dropped out on 17 September to avoid splitting his party.) The Republicans also gained large majorities in Congress, overturning the

1864

OCTOBER

11 October The Butler Medal is announced by Union Gen Benjamin Butler for black soldiers' in his command at New Market Heights on 9 September 1864.

12 October US Supreme Court Chief Justice Roger Taney, a Confederate sympathizer, dies.

13 October Maryland, a slave-holding Union state, adopts a new constitution that abolishes slavery.

15 October Union prisoners begin to arrive at Camp Lawton near Millen, Georgia, a new prison twice the size as Andersonville, from where they are transferred. In total, more than 10,000 are moved.

Democrats' majority there after 60 years.

His return to the White House was cheered – and jeered. A telegram from Grant told him that the election passing off quietly 'is a victory worth more to the country than a battle won.' But the *New York Daily News* on 11 November editorialized: 'Let Mr. Lincoln be *President* for the next term; hitherto he has been a dictator.'

His own comments were humble, saying, 'It is no pleasure to me to triumph over anyone.' He told supporters who came to serenade him on 10 November that 'it adds nothing to my satisfaction that any other man may be disappointed or pained by the result.' The election, he said, 'has demonstrated that a people's government can sustain a national

election in the midst of a great civil war. Until now, it has not been known to the world that this was a possibility. It shows, also, how sound and how strong we still are.' Finally, he became philosophical: 'Human nature will not change. In any future great national trial, compared with the men of this, we shall have as weak and as strong; as silly and as wise; as bad and as good.'

In the Battle of Franklin, Tennessee, Confederate General John B. Hood made a rash frontal assault that cost him a quarter of his men.

Union soldiers relax in front of an abandoned and gutted home that was caught in the crossfire on the outskirts of Atlanta.

16 October Gen Nathan Bedford Forrest begins his raid into Tennessee. It lasts until 10 November.

19 October Gen Sheridan defeats Gen Early at Cedar Creek, Virginia, virtually ending Confederate resistance in the Shenandoah Valley.

19 October The CSS *Shenandoah,* bought in England in September as the *Sea King,* is commissioned off the Madeira Islands.

20 October President Lincoln proclaims the last Thursday in November as Thanksgiving Day, an annual US holiday.

22 October Confederate Gen John Bell Hood begins his campaign into Tennessee.

Sherman on the March

On 16 November, exactly a week after Lincoln's re-election, Sherman began his successful but infamous march through Georgia, travelling with some 62,000 troops about 435km (270 miles) to the sea. He destroyed railroads and supplies, while also allowing his soldiers to steal crops and to loot and burn private homes across an area 96km (60 miles) wide. (Officially, his men were ordered not to enter homes except as authorized foragers.) One beautiful home that was destroyed was the plantation belonging to Confederate General Howell Cobb. Sherman spent one night there, on 22 November, and his troops left it in ruins the following day. Later that day, they captured Georgia's capital at Milledgeville, and held a mock legislative session there, passing a bill to rejoin the Union. Then they trashed the state library.

Sherman had made the decision to stop worrying about his northern supply and communication lines. The opinion in Washington, which heard nothing from him for a month, was that this decision was foolhardy and dangerous. 'I know what hole he went in at,' Lincoln would tell people, 'but I can't tell

Union soldiers suffered in the cold in their outer lines around Nashville. The battle saw Confederate General John Bell Hood's army crushed by General George Thomas' Union troops.

1864

OCTOBER

23 October Gen Alfred Pleasonton's Union troops battle Confederates under Gen Sterling Price at the Big Blue River in Missouri, forcing the invaders to retreat.

25 October Gen Pleasonton, pursuing Confederate Gen Price, overtakes the rearguard of Gen John Marmaduke's cavalry and captures nearly 1000 prisoners, including Gens Marmaduke and William Cabell.

27 October The CSS *Albemarle,* the last Confederate ram, is sunk by a small launch's torpedo in the Roanoke River in Virginia.

NOVEMBER

4 November Confederate raiders capture three Union gunboats on the Tennessee River near Johnsonville, Tennessee, driving back the Union fleet's coordinated attack from north and south.

8 November President Lincoln wins re-election over former general George McClellan, the Democrats' candidate. Andrew Johnson is his Vice President.

you what hole he'll come out of.' Even Grant agreed, saying that Sherman was like a ground mole disappearing under a lawn. 'You can here and there trace his track, but you are not quite certain where he will come out till you see his head.'

The general also introduced a new, disturbing element into warfare: the belief that a war can be won by terrorizing the civilians who support it. If locals burned bridges or were hostile, his army commanders were to 'order and enforce a devastation more or less relentless, according to the measure of such hostility'. An editorial in the *Macon Telegraph* on 30 November called him 'The desolator of our homes, the destroyer of our property, the Attila of the west.' Indeed, Sherman seemed to delight in that image, writing to his wife that the Southerners 'regard us as the Romans did the Goths, and the parallel is not unjust.' Again, he declared, 'I want to make a raid that will make the South feel the terrible character of our people.'

Perhaps the best summary of the march was given by Major Thomas Osborne, Sherman's chief of artillery: 'We burned all cotton, took all provisions, forage, wagons, mules, horses, cattle,

Union prisoners await their meagre daily rations at Andersonville Prison (Camp Sumter) in Georgia. Its Swiss-born commander, Major Henry Wirz, was the only man executed for war crimes.

16 November Gen Sherman begins his march through Georgia, destroying railroads, supplies and private homes over an area 97km (60 miles) wide.

16 November Gen Hood's Confederate army crosses the Tennessee River.

21 November Gen Hugh Kilpatrick's Union cavalry skirmishes with the Georgia state troops of Gen Howell Cobb at Griswoldville, driving them back into Macon.

21 November Confederate Gen John Henry Winder is put in charge of all war prisoners east of the Mississippi River.

22 November Union Gen Sherman spends the night in Georgia in the plantation home of Confederate Gen Howell Cobb, which his troops then destroy.

23 November A Union powder boat explodes 132kg (290lb) of powder 908m (830yds) from Ft Fisher, North Carolina but has no significant effect on the enemy.

Nashville's important sights included its Capitol, military tents and railway depot.

1864

NOVEMBER

23 November Gen Sherman's troops capture and ravage Milledgeville, the capital of Georgia.

25 November Eight Confederate agents from Canada start 19 fires in New York City.

25–26 November Gen Joseph Wheeler's Confederate cavalry attack Gen Sherman's army at Griswoldville, Georgia, but is forced to withdraw.

29 November Gen Hood's Confederates encircle Gen John Schofield's army at Spring Hill, Tennessee, but allow the Union troops to escape to Franklin.

30 November The Battle of Franklin, Tennessee, is decisively won by Union Gen John Schofield's army over Gen John Hood's Confederates. Casualties: Union, 2326; Confederate, 6252

30 November An engagement occurs at Honey Hill, or Grahamville, South Carolina, and Union troops withdraw.

hogs and poultry and the many other things which a country furnishes and which may be made available for the support of an army. In fact, as we have left the country I do not see how the people can live for the next two years.'

Along the way, the Confederate cavalry of General Joseph Wheeler tried to impede the thundering Northerners, but their punches were ineffective. An engagement at Griswoldville on November 25 and 26 was typical of the useless hit-and-run attacks, Wheeler's men inflicting three casualties and capturing 18 before withdrawing.

Richmond was hearing of more agony in Tennessee, where the Battle of Franklin took place on 30 November. Trying to inspire his Army of Tennessee, General Hood marched his men into that state after the fall of Atlanta. His plan was to cut off Sherman's supply line (which Sherman had broken himself) and then to march all the way to Virginia to attack the rear of Grant's army.

At Franklin, 24km (15 miles) south of Nashville, Hood virtually repeated Pickett's disastrous charge at Gettysburg. Finding the combined Union armies of Generals John Schofield and George Thomas entrenched behind formidable fieldworks, he ordered his men to attack over 3km (2 miles) of open

Union troops explore Fort McAllister at Savannah after capturing it on 13 December.

DECEMBER

1–14 December The Confederate army of Gen Hood gathers in front of Nashville, Tennessee.

1 December Union Gen George Stoneman begins his cavalry raid from eastern Tennessee into southwestern Virginia (until 2 January 1865).

6 December President Lincoln gives his annual message to Congress, noting that the power of the Executive 'would be greatly diminished by the cessation of actual war'.

6 December President Lincoln appoints Salmon Chase, a Radical Republican, as Chief Justice of the Supreme Court after Chase resigns as Secretary of the Treasury.

6–9 December At Deveaux's Neck, South Carolina, Confederates trade shots with Union forces felling trees to create an opening to fire on the Charleston & Savannah Railroad.

ground – without artillery support, which was still too far to the rear. Hood's subordinates argued against this plan, but to no effect, and the Southerners were easily mowed down. They lost 6252 men that day to the Union's 2326.

Despite this defeat, Hood ordered his tired troops to follow the withdrawing Northerners 121km (75 miles) to Nashville, where he would encounter an even larger Union army. Finding the city turned into a fortress, Hood stopped in the hills south of Nashville and instructed his men to dig defensive trenches in the freezing temperatures. General Thomas watched all this but was not ready to move, even after he received the order to attack from Grant, then based in Virginia. Finally, just as Grant had decided to travel south and take over the troops himself, Thomas turned his men loose on the enemy, chasing them 3km (2 miles) away before routing them entirely in driving rain. Fought on 15–16 December, this decisive battle was the last major battle in the West and virtually obliterated the Army of Tennessee, which retreated into

General Sherman's Union troops remove ammunition in wheelbarrows from captured Fort McAllister.

1864

DECEMBER

7–27 December A Union campaign fails to capture Ft Fisher on the North Carolina coast.

13 December Adm David Farragut is acclaimed a war hero as he arrives in New York City after his Gulf of Mexico victories.

13 December Gen Sherman's Union army captures Ft McAllister guarding Savannah, Georgia.

15–16 December Gen Hood's Confederate force is defeated at Nashville, Tennessee, after attacking Gen George Thomas' troops. Casualties: Union, 3061; Confederate nearly 6000

18 December Union Gen Grant writes Gen Sherman to express the opinion that, if the Confederacy is lost, Gen Lee 'wants Richmond to be the last place surrendered'.

20 December Confederates withdraw from Savannah, Georgia as Gen Sherman's force nears.

Mississippi. In January, Hood was relieved of his command – at his own request.

Four days after Nashville, the Confederates were withdrawing from Savannah, Georgia as Sherman's force approached. On the 22nd, he took the city, ending his march to the sea. He wrote his wife: 'Like one who has walked a narrow plank, I look back and wonder if I really did it.' So did General Wheeler, who congratulated his Confederate troops, praising them because 'you retarded his advance and defeated his cavalry daily, preventing his spreading over and devastating the country.'

On 22 December, Sherman sent a telegram to the President: "I beg to present to you, as a Christmas gift, the city of Savannah, with one hundred and fifty heavy guns and plenty of ammunition, and also about twenty-five thousand (25,000) bales of cotton.'

Lincoln's reply came immediately: 'Many, many thanks for your Christmas gift, the capture of Savannah.' There was also a question: 'But what next?'

Union troops camped in front of Fort Harrison, Virginia, where General Grant ordered a surprise attack.

21 December Confederate Flag Officer W.W. Hunter destroys his navy's remaining Savannah Squadron to prevent Gen Sherman's troops from capturing it.

22 December Gen Sherman takes Savannah, ending his destructive march through Georgia, and telegrams President Lincoln that he presents the city to him as a 'Christmas gift'.

24–25 December The Union's joint army and navy assault on Ft Fisher at Wilmington, North Carolina, is unsuccessful.

26 December President Lincoln writes to thank Gen Sherman for the Christmas gift of Savannah, asking, 'But what next?'

28 December Gen Grant's troops capture Ft Harrison on the outer defences of Richmond, Virginia.

Chapter Five
1865

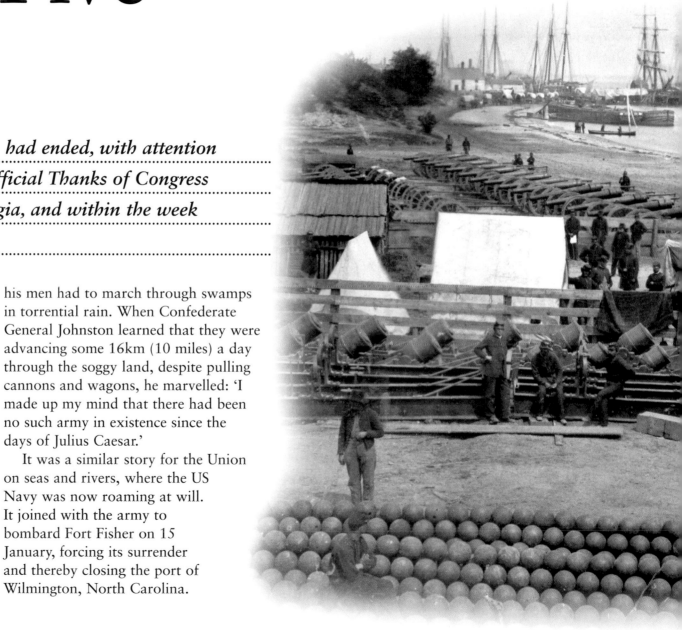

The last year of the war began as 1864 had ended, with attention centred on Sherman. He received the official Thanks of Congress on 10 January for his triumph in Georgia, and within the week was heading northwards.

South Carolina had begun the war, and his troops punished it even more savagely than they had Georgia, burning seemingly every house in their path. Sherman admitted that his army 'is burning with an insatiable desire to wreak vengeance upon South Carolina. I almost tremble for her fate.'

Sherman made a feint towards Charleston, then headed for the state's capital of Columbia. The winter was one of the coldest for years, and

Left: Union soldiers celebrate the news of the capture of Fort Fisher in North Carolina.
Right: General Grant's headquarters at City Point, Virginia, was visited by Lincoln.

his men had to march through swamps in torrential rain. When Confederate General Johnston learned that they were advancing some 16km (10 miles) a day through the soggy land, despite pulling cannons and wagons, he marvelled: 'I made up my mind that there had been no such army in existence since the days of Julius Caesar.'

It was a similar story for the Union on seas and rivers, where the US Navy was now roaming at will. It joined with the army to bombard Fort Fisher on 15 January, forcing its surrender and thereby closing the port of Wilmington, North Carolina.

This was the last open Confederate port, and one of the most successful for enabling ships to run the Union blockades. Wilmington itself fell a week later.

On 23 January, the South's James River Squadron under Flag Officer John Mitchell tried to sail 56km (35 miles) down the James River to bombard General Grant's headquarters at City

Charleston lay in ruins when Union troops entered it on 18 February.

Point, Virginia. The squadron consisted of three ironclads, seven gunboats and two torpedo boats, but failed in its mission when the ironclad CSS *Drewry* and wooden CSS *Scorpion* ran aground; the first was fired upon and exploded, and the other captured.

The Confederacy Considers Defeat

It was now becoming clear that the fight to uphold slavery was a fight for a lost cause. On 11 January, the Missouri legislature passed a resolution to abolish slavery in that Union state. On the same day, Robert E. Lee, who had always argued for its abolition, made a statement outlining his support for gradual emancipation. On the last day of the month, the US Congress finally passed the 13th Amendment to the Constitution, prohibiting slavery by a vote of 119 to 56. It then sent this to the states for ratification.

The South was now virtually assured of defeat. The two sides began to exchange messages and Lincoln's adviser Francis Preston Blair Sr paid a secret visit to Richmond on 16 January. Finally an official meeting was called, for 3 February at Hampton Roads, Virginia. Two

1865

JANUARY

6 January The Confederate ram, the CSS *Stonewall*, built in France, sails from Denmark. (The war ends before it sees action.)

10 January Union Gen Sherman is given the official Thanks of Congress for his operations in Georgia.

11 January Gen Lee publicly declares that he supports a plan of gradual emancipation.

11 January Missouri passes a resolution that abolishes slavery in the Union state.

15 January A joint US Army and Navy operation captures Ft Fisher to close the port of Wilmington, North Carolina, the last open Confederate port.

Fort Fisher

days before attending, Lincoln telegraphed Grant: 'Let nothing which is transpiring change, hinder, or delay your military movements or plans.'

Lincoln was accompanied by his secretary of state, William Seward. President Davis sent three commissioners: Vice President Stephens; Robert Hunter of Virginia, the president pro tem of the Confederate Senate; and Judge John Campbell of Alabama, formerly of the US Supreme Court. In the meeting, held aboard a steamer, the Confederates insisted on independence, but Lincoln insisted that the war would end only if the Southern states abolished slavery and returned to the Union. It is said that Lincoln took a piece of paper and wrote on it only one word, 'Union', before giving it to the Southerners to add their terms.

On 6 February, three days later, President Davis spoke in Richmond about the Confederate failure, saying:

'Let us then unite our hands and our hearts, lock our shields together, and we may well believe that before another summer solstice falls upon us, it will be the enemy that will be asking us for conferences and occasions in which to make known our demands.'

Charleston was devastated after four years of bombardment, yet as General Sherman's army approached it, General Henry Halleck wrote to him, 'I hope that by some accident the place may be destroyed...'

16 January President Lincoln's adviser, Francis Preston Blair Sr, enters secret peace negotiations with Confederate President Davis in Richmond. Nothing is resolved.

23–24 January A Confederate fleet tries to sail up the James River to attack Gen Grant's headquarters at City Point, Virginia, but fails when its heaviest ironclad runs aground.

30 January The Confederate ironclad ram, the CSS *Stonewall*, is commissioned in Denmark, having been built in France.

31 January The US Congress passes the 13th Amendment to the Constitution that would prohibit slavery. It goes to the states for ratification.

31 January The Confederate prison population at Camp Chase in Columbus, Ohio, peaks at 9423.

31 January Gen Sherman's Union army numbers some 100,000, compared to Confederate Johnston's force of more than 40,000.

Not surprisingly his judgement and leadership came under sustained attack. He had always been unpopular with some Confederate officials, including his vice president, and now the governor of Georgia even threatened to secede from the Confederacy. Secretary of War James Seddon, also the target of many attacks, resigned and was replaced on 4 February by General John Breckinridge. Of more import, the Confederate Congress wanted General Lee to replace the President as commander of all armies. Davis resisted, but on 23 January the act was forced through, and he had no choice but to sign. He officially appointed Lee as General-in-Chief on 6 February.

South Carolina's condition was so dire that Lee immediately brought General Joseph Johnson out of retirement to command his old Army of Tennessee, as well as other Confederate troops in the state. He was given the assignment of stopping Sherman – a tall order since the Union army outnumbered his by some 80,000 to 20,000. Johnson decided to establish his headquarters at Raleigh, North Carolina, knowing that the Northern force in South Carolina could now be delayed only by heavy rain.

President Lincoln made his second inaugural speech on 4 March 1865. In this short speech, he said, 'Let us strive on to finish the work we are in, to bind the nation's wounds, to care for him who shall have borne the battle...'

1865

FEBRUARY

1 February Gen Sherman's army begins a destructive march through South Carolina and North Carolina.

3 February President Lincoln rejects a peace request by Confederate Vice President Alexander Stephens during a meeting at Hampton Roads, Virginia.

4 February President Davis appoints Gen John C. Breckinridge as Secretary of War.

5 February President Lincoln proposes compensation of $400 million to the Confederate states if they stop fighting and ratify the 13th Amendment, but his cabinet rejects this.

6 February Confederate President Davis appoints Gen Lee as commander of all Confederate forces.

6 February Confederate Gen John Pegram is killed at Hatcher's Run, Virginia. (Two months later, his younger brother, Col William Pegram, is mortally wounded at Five Forks.)

The Appomattox River played an important part in General Ulysses S. Grant's Appomattox campaign. Here the two armies met and clashed at a bridge over the river in the waning days of the war.

The state capital, Columbia, was taken on 17 February. The Confederate troops had evacuated, and as the enemy approached, Mayor T.J. Goodwyn sent a message to Sherman asking that the citizens receive 'the treatment accorded by the usages of civilized warfare. I therefore respectfully request that you will send a sufficient guard in advance of the army, to maintain order in the city and protect the persons and property of the citizens.'

This fell on deaf ears. In fact, before he had even entered the city, Sherman sent a telegram to General Halleck in Washington, saying, 'I look upon Columbia as quite as bad as Charleston, and I doubt if we shall spare the public buildings there as we did at Milledgeville [Georgia's capital]'.

The city soon raged with fires. The Confederates blamed drunken Union soldiers, Sherman insisted the retreating Southerners had purposely caused the damage. In his official report, he charged the conflagration to General Wade Hampton, later explaining, 'I did so pointedly, to shake the faith of his people in him, for he was in my opinion boastful, and professed to be the special champion of South Carolina.' A

9 February Union Gen Philip Sheridan is given the official Thanks of Congress for his Shenandoah Valley campaign.

9 February The Confederate Vice President Alexander Stephens leaves Richmond, Virginia to retire to his home in Georgia.

11 February Gen Lee proclaims amnesty for all Confederate soldiers absent without leave if they report for duty within 20 days.

17–18 February Charleston is evacuated as the Union's army and navy approach.

17 February Gen Sherman's troops occupy Columbia, South Carolina. Much of the city is burned – it remains unclear whether Union or Confederate forces are to blame.

17 February Molly Bean, who disguised herself as a man and fought for two years with the 47th North Carolina, is captured by Union troops outside Richmond.

year after the war, Hampton said of Columbia that Sherman had 'burned it to the ground, deliberately, systematically and atrociously'.

Union General Henry Slocum recalled seeing the flames from his camp miles away:

'Nearly all the public buildings, several churches, an orphan asylum, and many of the residences were destroyed. The city was filled with helpless women and children and invalids, many of whom were rendered houseless and homeless in a single night. No sadder scene was presented during the war. The suffering of so many helpless and innocent persons could not but move the hardest heart.'

Slocum also added a more rueful note: 'A drunken soldier with a musket in one hand and a match in the other is not a pleasant visitor to have about the house on a dark, windy night, particularly when for a series of years you have urged him to come, so that you might have an opportunity of performing a surgical operation on him.'

On 25 February, the South Carolina diarist Mary Boykin Chesnut recorded her thoughts about the capital falling: 'Shame – disgrace – misery. … The grand smash has come.'

With Columbia taken, Charleston was

Union forces won the Battle of Bentonville, North Carolina.

evacuated, even as the Union army and navy bore down upon it. Northerners rightly blamed the city for beginning the war and wanted appropriate revenge – plus a little more. General Halleck wrote to Sherman:

'Should you capture Charleston, I hope that by some accident the place may be destroyed; and if a little salt should be sown upon its site, it may prevent the growth of future crops of nullification and secession.'

Sherman replied:

'I will bear in mind your suggestion as to Charleston, and don't think "salt" will be necessary. … The whole army is burning with an insatiable desire to wreck vengeance on South Carolina. I almost tremble at her

1865

FEBRUARY

18 February The Union's South Carolina 21st Colored Infantry takes possession of Castle Pinckney in Charleston Harbor.

18 February The CSS *Shenandoah* leaves Melbourne, Australia, to continue raiding US commercial ships in the Pacific Ocean.

22 February Union forces capture Wilmington, North Carolina.

22 February An engagement occurs at Douglas Landing in Pine Bluff, Arkansas.

22 February Union Gen Hugh Kilpatrick reports to Gen Sherman that 18 of his men were murdered in North Carolina by Gen Wade Hampton's cavalry.

23 February The Confederate Senate defeats a bill that would put 200,000 blacks in the Confederate army.

fate, but feel that she deserves all that seems in store for her. Many and many a person in Georgia asked me why we did not go to South Carolina, and when I answered that I was en route for that state, the invariable reply was, "Well, if you will make those people feel the severities of war, we will pardon you for your desolation of Georgia." '

There was precious little left to ruin in Charleston, which had endured four years of bombardment. In Charleston Harbor, Fort Sumter and Castle Pinckney were also evacuated. The former was occupied on 18 February by a few troops of Lieutenant Colonel A.G. Bennett, who raised the Stars and Stripes; the latter by South Carolina's 21st Colored Infantry. Bennett now took just 22 men with him to the city to demand its surrender, and there he encountered fires set by retreating troops. The mayor surrendered, and also accepted his offer to put out the fires. Union reinforcements now arrived and helped to save the arsenal and railway depots. Charleston was thus spared the ravages of the vengeful Sherman, who was then still in Columbia.

After a few days of destroying railroads in

Five Forks, Virginia, saw the last major battle of the war, as General Philip Sheridan's Union army defeated General George Pickett's forces. This victory helped conclude the war.

MARCH

27 February Gen Sheridan's Union cavalry begins its raid into northern Virginia (lasting until 25 March).

2 March President Lincoln rejects Gen Lee's request for negotiations.

2 March At Waynesboro, Virginia, Gen Sheridan's cavalry captures the remainder of Gen Jubal Early's army, capturing 1600 Confederates and 11 guns.

3 March The US Congress creates the Freedmen's Bureau to aid former slaves.

4 March President Lincoln is inaugurated for his second term and calls for 'malice toward none; with charity for all'.

4 March The Confederate Congress approves the Confederate National Flag, Third Pattern, to replace the Second Pattern, which resembles a white truce flag.

Richmond was destroyed by Union shells and by the departing Confederates setting fires.

the Columbia area, Sherman marched off for North Carolina, to link up with General John Schofield's army of 30,000 and then proceed north to join Grant. Marching over swamps and swollen rivers, he reached Fayetteville on 11 March, destroying the arsenals there. The Confederates were also gathering together as many troops as possible, including the remains of the Army of Tennessee, which had been resting in Mississippi since their Nashville defeat.

On 2 March at Waynesboro, Virginia, General Custer's cavalry of 4840 men, part of General Sheridan's army, captured most of General Jubal Early's remaining Confederate army, reduced now to just 1600 men. Early, two other generals, and 20 other men escaped, but General Lee relieved Early of his command on 30 March. This would be the end of

Sheridan's long Shenandoah Valley Campaign, begun the previous year on 7 August. During this time, he had stripped the valley of crops and could report, 'A crow would have had to carry its rations if it had flown across the valley.' Indeed, Sheridan's 45,000 men had stolen 4000 cattle, killed 3000 sheep, and destroyed more than 70 mills and 2000 barns filled with wheat, hay and farming implements. For this campaign of destruction, Sheridan was given the Thanks of Congress.

Peace Anticipated

The day of Early's defeat, Lincoln rejected a request from Lee for negotiations to end the war. Two days later, on 4 March, the President was inaugurated for his second term. The former slave, Frederick Douglass, was there and worried: 'I felt then there was murder in the air, and I kept close to his carriage on the way to the Capitol, for I felt that I might see him fall that day. It was a vague presentiment.'

Lincoln knew the war was won but anticipated problems during peacetime. In his short inaugural speech, he said that neither side had expected the war to be of such magnitude

1865

MARCH

12–14 March Gen Sherman's troops occupy Fayetteville, North Carolina, destroying the arsenal and machinery formerly at Harper's Ferry Arsenal.

13 March Confederate President Davis signs a bill that permits slaves to enlist, thereby earning their freedom.

15 March Gen Sherman's army has an engagement with Gen William Hardee's Confederate troops at Averysboro, North Carolina, but continues onwards.

17 March Actor John Wilkes Booth's plot to kidnap President Lincoln fails when the President does not visit the Campbell Hospital in Washington as expected.

19–21 March The Battle of Bentonville, North Carolina is won by Gen Sherman's army over Gen Johnston's Confederates.

21 March Gen Lee forwards President Davis a dispatch from Gen Johnston that his small force cannot hinder Sherman. 'I can do no more than annoy him.'

or duration and that God had given both the North and South 'this terrible war as the woe due to those by whom the offense [of slavery] came'. He concluded with ringing words:

'With malice toward none, with charity for all, with firmness in the right as God gives us to see the right, let us strive on to finish the work we are in, to bind up the nation's wounds, to care for him who shall have borne the battle and for his widow and his orphan – to do all which may achieve and cherish a just and lasting peace among ourselves and with all nations.'

After the speech, Lincoln said, 'I am a tired man. Sometimes I think I am the tiredest man on earth.' He told others that he believed this speech would

'... wear as well as – perhaps better than – anything I have produced; but I believe it is not immediately popular. Men are not flattered by being shown that there has been a difference of

The Confederate navy destroyed its James River Squadron on Richmond's harbour to keep the ships from the enemy.

24 March President Lincoln arrives at Gen Grant's headquarters at City Point, Virginia for a three-week stay, conferring with Grant, Gen Sherman and others.

24 March The Confederate ironclad ram, the CSS *Stonewall*, sails from Ferrol, Spain to raise the blockade of one or more Southern ports. (However, the war ends before its arrival.)

25 March The Battle of Ft Stedman, Virginia is won by Union forces. Casualties: Union, 2080; Confederate some 4500.

26 March Siege of Mobile, Alabama begins.

27 March Union troops begin a siege of Spanish Fort, Alabama, across the bay from Mobile.

27–28 March President Lincoln confers with Gens Grant and Sherman at City Point, Virginia, suggesting that generous terms of surrender be offered to the Confederacy.

purpose between the Almighty and them. ... It is a truth which I thought needed to be told.'

Charles Francis Adams, Jr, the general and historian, called the speech 'the historical keynote of this war. ... Not a prince or minister in all Europe could have risen to such an equality with the occasion.'

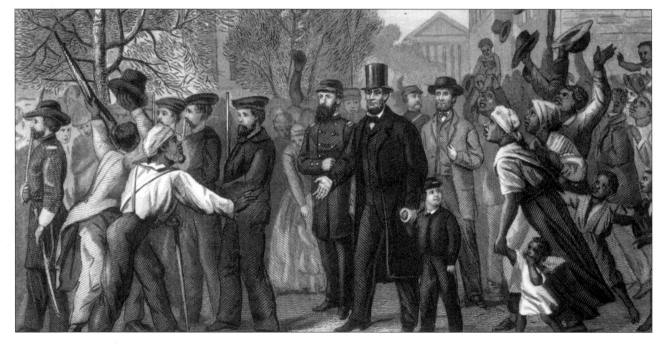

Final Resistance

Down in Richmond, a final desperate measure was signed by President Davis on 13 March: slaves would be enlisted into the Confederate army. The Senate had voted on 23 February to enlist 20,000 blacks. Lee had backed this measure for some time, saying 'We must decide whether the Negroes shall fight for us or against us.'

At this time, Sherman's army was well into North Carolina, brushing off Johnston's feeble defensive attempts. A sharp engagement did take place on 15 March at Averasboro, where General William Hardee's Confederates tried to block the advance, losing 865 men to Sherman's 678. Then came the largest confrontation of the march, at Bentonville, where Johnston gathered together the 20,000 men left in his army, including the troops of Beauregard, Bragg, Hardee, Hill and Hampton. It was a final desperate attempt, but three days of fighting, from the 19th to the 21st, came to naught. The Confederates had to retreat, having lost 2606 men to Sherman's 1646. On the last charge, Hardee's 16-year-old son, who had become a soldier on that very day, was killed.

Retreating from Bentonville, Johnston sent a dispatch to President Davis with an ominous message about Sherman: 'I can do no more than annoy him'.

President Lincoln and his son, Tad, walked through the captured Confederate capital on 5 April.

1865

MARCH	APRIL
30 March Gen Lee dismisses Gen Jubal Early from his command, saying Early retains his full confidence but not that of the public.	**1 April** Union Gen Sheridan's army wins the last major battle of the war over Gen George Pickett's men at Five Forks, Virginia.

1–9 April Union forces win the battle of Blakely, Alabama near Mobile.

2 April Confederate Gen Nathan Bedford Forrest is defeated at Selma, Alabama, and 2700 of his troops are taken prisoner, though Forrest escapes.

2 April Gen Lee withdraws from Petersburg, Virginia, ending the Union siege that began on 19 June 1864.

2 April While attending St Paul's Episcopal Church in Richmond, President Davis receives a telegram from Gen Lee announcing the need to evacuate the city.

Meanwhile, in Washington on 17 March, five masked conspirators waited to carry out their plan – to kidnap Lincoln and then ransom him for Confederate prisoners. The Maryland actor John Wilkes Booth, a Southern sympathizer, waited with four others for Lincoln to visit the Campbell Hospital, the Soldier's Home. But the President's plans changed, and he did not appear.

A week later, Lincoln arrived at Grant's headquarters at City Point, Virginia, where he spent three weeks conferring with his generals. Sherman, taking a break, joined them. 'Must more blood be shed?' the President asked. When informed that more battles would indeed be needed to conquer Lee, he shook his head and said, 'My God, my God. Can't you spare more effusions of blood? We've had so much of it.' In the ensuing conversations, Lincoln urged that generous terms of surrender be offered to the Confederates.

On 1 April, General Sheridan's army, back in Virginia from the Shenandoah Valley Campaign, fought the last major battle of the war at Five Forks, where five dirt roads met. Attacked on the previous day by the Confederates of Generals Pickett and Fitzhugh Lee, they now brought their overwhelming numbers to surround the enemy and drive them from their entrenchments. The Southerners lost a particularly large number of prisoners, about 5200 from a total of 19,000 men.

Union troops were also crushing the last resistance in Alabama. On 2 April, the cavalry

....

The siege of Petersburg lasted over nine months before General Lee withdrew on 2 April.

Richmond's centre is still called 'the Burnt District'.

2–3 April Confederates evacuate Richmond. They destroy the James River Squadron to keep it from falling into Union hands.

3 April Midshipmen from the Confederate Naval Academy escort their government's archives and treasury bullion from Richmond southwards.

3 April Union troops capture Petersburg and Richmond, Virginia.

3 April Union Gen John Croxton's brigade captures Tuscaloosa, Alabama and burns part of the University of Alabama.

5 April Union troops of Gen Henry Davies charge through a swamp at Amelia Springs, or Jetersville, Virginia to rout a Confederate wagon train.

5 April President Lincoln takes a triumphant tour of Richmond.

5 April Confederate President Davis issues a proclamation to his people, saying they should 'meet the foe with fresh defiance, and with unconquered and unconquerable hearts'.

of General James Wilson defeated the shrinking cavalry of General Nathan Bedford Forrest at Selma, a large munitions centre, and took 2700 prisoners. This was Forrest's only defeat during the war, and he escaped capture. On 12 April, General Edward Canby's army marched into the port city of Mobile, which had been evacuated the previous night. The 4500 Confederates withdrew to Montgomery, where they surrendered on 4 May.

The heart of the Confederacy was also dying. The 10-month siege laid by Lee's army at Petersburg, Virginia ended when he withdrew on 2 April, a day after a final, unsuccessful attack at Five Forks. Shells had struck his headquarters, and some 60,000 of his troops had already deserted. Seeing more Union troops get into position, Lee noted calmly, 'This is a bad business, colonel.' The Petersburg campaign cost 42,000 Union casualties and 28,000 Confederates.

News of the withdrawal was conveyed by telegram to President Davis as he attended St

Paul's Episcopal Church in Richmond. Members of the congregation saw his face turn pale as he read Lee's assessment: 'I see no prospect of doing more than holding our position here till night.' Davis stood up and walked down the aisle, followed by some of the congregation – causing the minister to come to the altar rail and beg them to finish the service.

The President called his cabinet together to relay the news, and by the late afternoon, General Breckinridge arrived to say that they must evacuate the city that night. At 11 p.m., a train pulled out with Davis and his cabinet on a 225km (140 mile) trip to Danville.

Safe there the next afternoon, the President issued a rousing proclamation:

'Animated by that confidence in your spirit and fortitude which never yet failed me,

General Grant (centre) met with his staff before joining General Lee for the historic surrender.

1865

APRIL

6 April The Battle of Sayler's Creek, Virginia is won by Union forces. Gen Lee's son, Gen Custis Lee, is captured.

8 April Gen George Custer captures four trainloads of Confederate supplies at Appomattox Station.

9 April Gen Lee surrenders his Army of Northern Virginia to Gen Grant at the village of Appomattox Court House, Virginia.

9 April Gen Edward Canby's Union force captures Spanish Fort on Mobile Bay, taking 500 prisoners and 50 guns.

10 April Gen Lee issues General Order Number Nine, his farewell to his Army of Northern Virginia.

10 April Washington, DC celebrates the Union victory. A crowd assembles at the White House, and President Lincoln orders the band to play 'Dixie'.

Generals Lee and Grant had an informal conversation before signing the surrender agreement. This was held in Appomattox Court House, Virginia, where Wilmer McLean, a retired grocer had made his home.

I announce to you, fellow-countrymen, that it is my purpose to maintain your cause with my whole heart and soul. ... I will never consent to abandon to the enemy one foot of soil of any of the States of the Confederacy. ... Let us not despond, my countrymen, but meet the foe with fresh defiance, with unconquered and unconquerable hearts.'

Back in Richmond, the city was rocked by explosions – and not by the enemy. The Confederate navy under Admiral Raphael Semmes chose to destroy the James River Squadron, scuttling its ironclads in the river. Departing troops burned vital supplies, even tobacco warehouses, and fires engulfed the city. (To this day, the business district of Richmond is known as the 'Burnt District'.) Former slaves cheered as the first Union troops arrived, General Godfrey Weitzel's Massachusetts men. Locals and Union troops looted throughout the city, and drunken riots ensued.

Lee's wife, unable to travel because of severe arthritis, was still in the city, and a black Union soldier was posted outside her house for protection. She complained that the black soldier was 'perhaps an insult', so a white soldier replaced him.

On 3 April, President Lincoln and Grant arrived in Petersburg and shook hands. The President thanked him profusely, his face beaming. With them was Lincoln's oldest son, Robert Todd Lincoln, who was on Grant's staff. The next day, Lincoln travelled by barge to Richmond, to make a triumphant tour. 'Thank God I have lived to see this,' he said. 'It seems to me that I have been dreaming a horrid nightmare for four years, and now the nightmare is over.'

11 April President Lincoln appears in an upper window of the White House and, in his last public address, calls for conciliation in reconstruction.

12 April Mobile, Alabama surrenders to Union troops after being evacuated the previous day by Gen Dabney Maury's troops.

12 April Gen James Wilson's cavalry captures Montgomery, Alabama.

13 April Confederate Gen Joseph Johnston in North Carolina requests an armistice.

13 April Confederate President Davis and his cabinet meet in Greensboro, North Carolina and decide, against Davis' wishes, to try to negotiate a peace.

13 April Union Gen Sherman occupies Raleigh, North Carolina.

Lee Surrenders

Lee had pulled his troops from Richmond, planning to link up with General Johnston's army. Grant, however, pursued him, determined to stand between the two Confederates forces. Approaching Danville, Lee found the way blocked by Sheridan's army, so he turned towards Lynchburg. On 3 April, he reached Amelia Court House, where he had ordered rations to be stored. But the nearly starving troops found the storehouse empty, since his request had never reached commissary officials.

Lee's exhausted and haggard soldiers, many shoeless, now fought their last battle, at Sayler's Creek. There, Union cavalry attacked the rear and edges of the Confederates, who were moving southwest to Rice Station, where supplies could be had by rail from Lynchburg. On 6 April, the Northerners made a full attack. The weakened Confederates put up a valiant fight, even fighting hand-to-hand, but were overrun. Six of Lee's generals were captured, including his eldest son Custis Lee, and one-

Despite the obvious hostility of the crowd, he walked through the streets for about 1.6km (1 mile) with his eldest son, Robert Todd Lincoln. Former slaves came up to the President, removing their hats, bowing and blessing him. Some even fell to their knees, calling him the Messiah. With acute embarrassment, Lincoln asked them to rise, telling them, 'You must kneel to God only and thank Him for your freedom.' Lincoln then went to the Confederate White House, now General Weitzel's headquarters, and sat in Jefferson Davis's chair, smiling.

1865

13 April Washington, DC, has a 'grand illumination' of the city to celebrate Gen Lee's surrender.

13 April The US Army begins reducing its numbers.

14 April President Lincoln meets with his cabinet and urges a generous conciliation for the South.

14 April The original US flag is raised over Ft Sumter by Gen Robert Anderson, who had surrendered the fort when the war began.

14 April President Lincoln is fatally shot by actor John Wilkes Booth in Ford's Theater in Washington, DC. He dies early the next morning.

14 April US Secretary of State William Seward is stabbed by a co-conspirator of John Wilkes Booth.

third of army was lost, about 8000 men having been killed, wounded or captured.

The day after the battle, General Sheridan sent Grant a message saying, 'If the thing is pressed, I think Lee will surrender.' Grant relayed this to Lincoln, who responded, 'Let the thing be pressed.'

In the late afternoon of that same day, Grant sent Lee a message saying, 'The result of last week must convince you of the hopelessness of further resistance.' He added that he regarded it as 'my duty to shift from myself the responsibility of any further effusion of blood, by asking of you the surrender of that portion of the Confederate States Army known as the Army of Northern Virginia.'

Lee held council with his generals. General Henry Wise, whom he had promoted at Sayler's Creek to a major general, urged him to surrender, but Lee became angry, asking what would the country think if he did not fight on. 'Country be damned!' retorted Wise. 'There is no country. There has been no country for a year or more. You are the country to these men.'

General Edward Alexander then suggested that Lee should not surrender but instead

disband the army, allowing the men to 'scatter like rabbits and partridges in the bushes' and reassemble somewhere to continue the fight. But Lee answered that it was essential to consider the effect of this on the country as a whole, which was already demoralized by four years of war. If disbanded, the army would become 'mere bands of marauders'. 'And, as for myself,' he concluded, 'you young fellows might go to bushwhacking, but the only dignified course for me would be to go to General Grant and surrender myself and take the consequences of my acts.'

A crowd within Fort Sumter awaits the raising of the American flag on 14 April.

15 April Vice President Andrew Johnson takes the oath of office as President.

16 April A Union cavalry under Col Oscar LaGrange takes Ft Tyler in West Point, Georgia, the war's last battle east of the Mississippi.

18 April Confederate Gen Joseph Johnston surrenders his army to Gen Sherman at Durham Station, North Carolina.

19 April President Lincoln's funeral procession is held on Pennsylvania Avenue in Washington, DC.

19 April Confederate President Davis reaches Charlotte, North Carolina, where he learns of President Lincoln's assassination.

President Lincoln was shot by John Wilkes Booth in Ford's Theatre, watched by his wife (centre) and Major Henry Rathbone and his fiancée, Clara Harris.

1865

APRIL

20 April Confederate Col John Mosley, refusing to surrender, disbands his Partisan Rangers at Millwood, Virginia.

20 April Union Gen James Wilson captures Macon, Georgia, which surrenders under protest, citing provisions of an armistice agreed on by Gen Sherman and Confederate Gen Johnston.

23 April Confederate President Davis petitions the US government for peace and to allow Confederate states to re-enter the Union on the same terms as before, but this is rejected.

24 April Confederates burn the CSS *Webb* to avoid capture below New Orleans after it failed to escape into the Gulf of Mexico.

26 April Gen Johnston surrenders his Confederate army.

26 April John Wilkes Booth, Lincoln's assassin, is surrounded in a tobacco barn and fatally shot near Bowling Green, Virginia.

Still, Lee took one last punch at 'those people', ordering General John Gordon to attack the next morning. His troops pushed the Union cavalry back and reached the Union breastworks at the crest of a hill, capturing two guns, but the enemy closed in on all sides, and Gordon fell back to the tiny village of Appomattox Court House.

'There is nothing left for me to do,' Lee told his officers, 'but to go and see General Grant, and I would rather die a thousand deaths.' Just before noon, he sent a note to the Union general, and then dispatched a colonel to locate an appropriate building in the village where the surrender could be formalized. The first person encountered by the colonel was Wilmer McLean, a Virginian who had moved there to avoid the war, after his house had been shelled at the first major battle at Bull Run. He was now talked into providing a parlour for the surrender.

Lee was first to arrive at the McLean house, dressed in a magnificent grey uniform with an engraved sword at his side. Grant arrived half an hour later, without a sword and wearing a private's soiled shirt and pants and boots that were splattered with mud. Recalled Grant, 'I must have contrasted very strangely with a man so handsomely dressed, six feet high and of faultless form.' They shook hands with their staffs in the room. The two generals had served together during the Mexican War, and began to talk of those old days. 'Our conversation grew so pleasant,' Grant wrote in his memoirs, 'that I almost forgot the object of our meeting.'

Twelve days before Lee's surrender, Lincoln had sent messages to Grant, Sherman and Admiral Porter, saying, 'I want no one punished. Treat them liberally all around. We want those people to return to their allegiance to the Union and submit to the laws.' Grant now offered Lee generous terms. The 28,000 officers and men of the Army of Northern Virginia would be paroled, and allowed to return home without being disturbed by US authorities if they agreed to stop fighting. Officers could keep their side arms and horses. Grant also supplied Lee's starving men with rations and stopped his own men from any boisterous celebrations of the Confederates' defeat, reminding his troops that the Southerners were 'our countrymen again'.

John Wilkes Booth was an actor who had sympathized with the Southern cause.

26 April The Confederate Congress meets for the last time, in Charlotte, North Carolina.

26 April The Confederate Army of Tennessee surrenders at Greensboro, North Carolina.

27 April The steamship *Sultana* sinks in the Mississippi River near Memphis, killing some 1700 passengers, most of them Union soldiers returning from Confederate prisons.

27 April The body of John Wilkes Booth is returned to Washington on the USS *Montauk*.

27 April George Trenholm resigns as Secretary of the Treasury for the Confederacy, citing ill health.

29 April At Yorkville (now York), South Carolina, Confederate President Davis and his four remaining cabinet members plan a retreat to Texas to re-establish the Confederacy there.

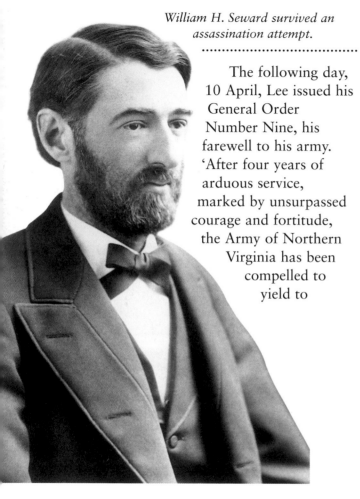

William H. Seward survived an assassination attempt.

....

The following day, 10 April, Lee issued his General Order Number Nine, his farewell to his army. 'After four years of arduous service, marked by unsurpassed courage and fortitude, the Army of Northern Virginia has been compelled to yield to

overwhelming numbers and resources.' Explaining that he wanted to 'avoid the useless sacrifice of those whose past services have endeared them to their countrymen,' he concluded: 'With an increasing admiration of your constancy and devotion to your country, and a grateful remembrance of your kind and generous consideration of myself, I bid you an affectionate farewell.'

The surrender was greeted in the North by joyful celebrations. At a White House reception on 10 April, Lincoln was in fine spirits and even requested the playing of "Dixie". Considering it 'one of the best tunes I have ever heard', he added, 'Since we've conquered the rebel army, we've also conquered 'Dixie'. Two days later, The New York World editorialized: 'The campaign has made General Grant what he never was before – a great general in the estimation of the whole army.'

Despite everything, Jefferson Davis was not pleased by the decision to stop fighting. 'Even after that disaster,' he wrote to his wife, Varina, on 23 April, 'if the men who "straggled," say thirty or forty thousand in number, had come back with their arms and with the disposition to

fight, we might have repaired the damage; but panic has seized the country.'

On 14 April came the fourth anniversary of the surrender of Fort Sumter. Its commander on that day, Major (now General) Robert Anderson, raised the same tattered flag back on its pole in a ceremony attended by Northern dignitaries and about 4000 former slaves.

A Tragic Revenge

That same evening in Washington, Good Friday, President Lincoln and his wife headed for Ford's Theatre to see the British comedy *Our American Cousin*. General Grant and his wife had been invited to join them in the presidential box, but had given their excuses since they were travelling to Philadelphia. Taking their place were Major Henry Rathbone and his fiancée, Clara Harris.

Also in the theatre was the actor John Wilkes Booth, now intent on assassinating the President. As Lincoln's bodyguards became engrossed by the play, Booth slipped into the box with derringer and dagger. He fired a bullet into the back of Lincoln's head, slashed the major with his dagger, and leaped onto the

1865

MAY

2 May President Johnson offers a $100,000 reward for the capture of former Confederate President Davis.

4 May Confederate Gen Richard Taylor surrenders his army to Gen Edward Canby at Citronelle, Alabama.

4 May Confederate President Davis, in retreat at Washington, Georgia, performs his last official act, appointing Capt Micajah Clark as the Confederacy's acting treasurer.

4 May President Lincoln is buried in Oak Ridge Cemetery outside Springfield, Illinois.

10 May Former Confederate President Davis is captured at Irwinsville, Georgia, while fleeing.

10 May The trial begins of John Wilkes Booth's co-conspirators in the assassination of President Lincoln. (It lasts about six weeks.)

10 May President Johnson declares the official end of armed resistance to the federal government.

stage, breaking his ankle. 'Sic semper tyrannis!' he yelled, quoting the state motto of Virginia, which means 'thus be it ever to tyrants'. Before anyone could react, Booth was out of the building and riding away on a horse held by other conspirators.

Six men carried the unconscious Lincoln across the street to a boarding house and laid him gently on a bed, but doctors knew that the wound was mortal. He died at 7.22 a.m. the next morning, the first American president to be assassinated.

Across town, Booth's accomplice, Lewis Powell, stabbed and seriously wounded Secretary of State William Seward. Another conspirator was too fearful to carry out his assignment, the killing of Vice President Andrew Johnson. Washington fell into a panic, suspecting a Confederate conspiracy perhaps ordered by the uncaptured Jefferson Davis. At Harper's Ferry, the nurse Sarah Blund wrote her family, 'The soldiers here are enraged and talk of nothing now but revenge and retaliation.' And in the South, young Sarah Morgan Dawson wrote in her diary: 'I abhor this, and call it foul murder, unworthy of our cause – and God grant

President Lincoln's funeral procession was held on 19th April on Pennsylvania Avenue in Washington, DC.

11 May The Confederate Vice President Alexander Stephens is arrested in Georgia (and will serve five months in Ft Warren on George's Island in Boston Harbor).

11 May Confederate troops in Arkansas surrender at Chalk Bluff.

11 May Confederate troops in Florida surrender in Tallahassee.

26 May Confederate Gen Edmund Kirby Smith surrenders the last Confederate force, the Trans-Mississippi Department, to Gen Edward Canby at Galveston, Texas.

13 May In the last battle of the war, Confederate troops under Col John S. Ford defeat Union forces at Palmetto Ranch near Brownsville, Texas.

19 May The CSS *Stonewall* is given up to Cuban officials in Havana.

19 May Camp Ford, the largest Confederate prison west of the Mississippi, is closed at Tyler, Texas.

it was only the temporary insanity of a desperate man who committed this crime. Let not his blood be visited on this nation, Lord!'

Nothing more transpired, however, allowing the nation to grieve. Lincoln's coffin lay in state in the East Room of the White House, before being carried down Pennsylvania Avenue to the Capitol on 19 April. That same day, Davis reached Charlotte, North Carolina, where he learned of the assassination. 'I am sorry. We have lost our best friend in the court of the enemy.' Confederate Senator Clement C. Clay was more emotional, crying, 'Then God help us! If that is true, it is the worst blow that has yet been struck the South.'

Harper's Weekly summed up the nation's mood: 'Beaten on every field of recognized warfare, treason outdid its very self, and killed our President.'

On 26 April came two events: the Confederate cabinet met for the last time in Charlotte and John Wilkes Booth was trapped in a tobacco barn in Bowling Green, Virginia, and fatally shot.

Lincoln's body lay in the rotunda of the Capitol, viewed by thousands each hour. Finally,

It took two days for the Grand Armies of the Republic to parade down Pennsylvania Avenue in the Grand Review.

1865

MAY

22 May Former Confederate President Davis is imprisoned at Ft Monroe on Chesapeake Bay, Virginia. (He will be released without trial on 13 May 1867.)

23 May The US Army of the Potomac is formally disbanded.

23–24 May About 150,000 US soldiers parade through the streets of Washington, DC in the victorious army's Grand Review.

29 May President Johnson presents his proclamation of amnesty and pardon for Southerners, which is more lenient than Congress desires.

JUNE

2 June Confederates surrender their last seaport at Galveston, Texas.

6 June President Johnson offers amnesty to all Confederate prisoners of war prepared to swear that they never fought voluntarily.

it was carried by train to his hometown of Springfield, Illinois. His funeral was held on 4 May in Oak Ridge Cemetery, conducted by the Rev Matthew Simpson, a bishop of the Methodist Episcopal Church. 'Look over all his speeches; listen to his utterances,' he said. 'He never spoke unkindly of any man. Even the rebels received no word of anger from him. … But the great act of the mighty chieftain, on which his fame shall rest long after his frame shall moulder away, is that of giving freedom to a race.'

The new President, Andrew Johnson, offered a $100,000 reward on 2 May for the capture of Jefferson Davis. Two days later, Davis was hiding in Washington, Georgia, stubbornly performing what would be his last official duty, the appointment of Micajah Clark as the Confederacy's acting treasurer. On 10 May, he was captured near Irwinville, Georgia; the next day, the Confederacy's vice president, Alexander Stephens, was arrested in Georgia. Stevens would serve only five months in Fort Warren in Boston Harbor, but Davis was imprisoned for

Reviewing the parade were President Johnson and Generals Grant, Sherman and Meade.

13 June Robert E. Lee applies for amnesty – and is refused by President Johnson.

23 June Gen Stand Watie, Native-American leader of a Cherokee cavalry, becomes the last Confederate general to surrender, to Col Asa Matthews.

28 June The Confederate cruiser CSS *Shenandoah* in the North Pacific fires the last shot of the war, capturing 11 ships of the US whaling fleet there.

JULY

5 July The Camp Chase Prison at Columbus, Ohio, is closed. A total of 2229 Confederate prisoners have died there.

7 July Four of the eight co-conspirators in the assassination of President Lincoln are hanged.

18 July Adm Louis Goldsborough arrives in Flushing, the Netherlands, to assume command of the US Navy's reinstated European Squadron.

31 July The US Navy reactives its East India Squadron.

two years, sometimes held in shackles, at Fort Monroe on Chesapeake Bay, Virginia.

Despite the gloom of Lincoln's death, the US military held a victorious Grand Review in May. It took two days, the 23rd and 24th, for some 150,000 soldiers to parade through the streets of Washington – to tumultuous cheering and bands playing 'The Star-Spangled Banner.'

After Lee's surrender, the Confederacy suffered its death throes. In the last true but meaningless battle, Confederate troops of Colonel John S. Ford defeated a Union force on 13 May at Palmetto Ranch near Browsville, Texas. On 23 June, the Confederate Cherokee leader General Stand Watie became the last officer to surrender; and on 28 June, the CSS *Shenandoah* fired the war's last shot while capturing 11 US whaling vessels in the North Pacific. Only on 6 November was the last Confederate flag lowered by the *Shenandoah* as it arrived in Liverpool, England.

Four of the eight co-conspirators in Lincoln's assassination were tried, and were hanged on 7

The cruiser CSS Shenandoah *fired the war's last shot on 28 June in the North Pacific.*

1865

AUGUST				SEPTEMBER	NOVEMBER

2 August Lt James Waddell, commanding the CSS *Shenandoah* in the Pacific, hears from an English ship that the war is over and sails for Liverpool, England.

12 August The US Navy reactivates its Brazil Squadron.

17 August The Andersonville National Cemetery is dedicated beside the prison at Andersonville, Georgia. The US flag is raised by nurse Clara Barton.

30 August The fleeing former Confederate Secretary of State Judah Benjamin reaches England and resumes his legal career.

31 August Robert E. Lee is named president of Washington College (now Washington and Lee University) with an annual salary of $1,500 a year.

5 September All Southern ports are reopened to foreign trade.

6 November The last official Confederate flag is lowered on the CSS *Shenandoah* as it arrives in Liverpool, England.

July. Radical congressmen also called for mass executions of those who had led the rebellion, but Lincoln's spirit of forgiveness prevailed. The only Confederate hanged for war crimes was the commander of Andersonville Prison, Swiss-born Major Henry Wirz, who had allowed the prisoners to suffer intolerable conditions. He was executed on 10 November in Washington as the crowd chanted, 'Andersonville, Andersonville, Andersonville…'

Robert E. Lee was allowed to settle into a peaceful life. After having his application for amnesty turned down by President Johnson, he

Members of the Washington Signal Corps gather in Georgetown, Virginia, at the war's end.

became president of Washington College in Virginia (renamed Washington and Lee after his death), and urged his fellow Southerners to become loyal Americans.

For its part, the US Congress looked to the future, forming a Joint Committee on Reconstruction on 4 December. And the year came to an appropriate close: the states ratified the 13th Amendment to the Constitution, abolishing slavery.

Maj Henry Wirz being executed

10 November Maj Henry Wirz, commander of the Andersonville, Georgia Confederate prison, is hanged in Washington, DC, the only Confederate to be executed as a war criminal.

24 November Mississippi is the first Southern state to establish 'Black Codes' restricting the rights of the freed slaves.

DECEMBER

1 December President Johnson restores the writ of habeas corpus suspended by Lincoln.

4 December The US Navy reactivates its West India Squadron.

13 December The US Congress forms a Joint Committee on Reconstruction.

6 December The 13th Amendment to the US Constitution abolishing slavery is ratified.

Chapter Six
Aftermath

The war was over, but the fighting continued in the political arena. The South had to be 'reconstructed' in the North's image, and it would not be easy to bring the old Confederate states back into the Union as equals. The ruined economy had to be restored, and the devastated Southern cities rebuilt.

President Lincoln had foreseen the difficulties. On 11 April 1865, he made his last public speech, from the White House balcony, warning that reconstruction:

'...is fraught with great difficulty. Unlike the case of a war between independent nations, there is no authorized organ for us to treat with. No one man has authority to give up the rebellion for any other man. We simply must begin with, and mould from, disorganized and discordant elements. Nor is it a small additional embarrassment that we, the loyal people, differ among ourselves as to the mode, manner, and means of reconstruction.'

Those 'loyal people' was a reference to the radical congressmen who wanted to restrict and punish the former Confederate states – unlike Lincoln, who planned to 'let them down easy'. And even his most vengeful general in war, Sherman, saw no need to continue battering his defeated countrymen:

'I would not subjugate the

Left: The proud city of Richmond was reduced to rubble at the end of the war.
Right: The Catholic cathedral in Charleston (right) was also a war victim.

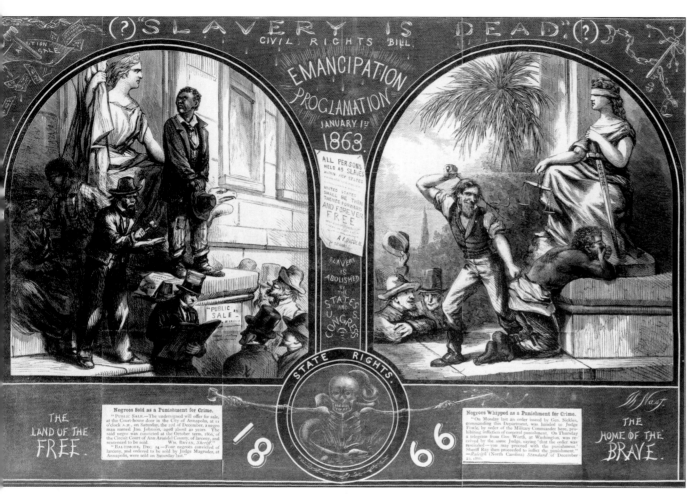

South. I pledge my honor when the South ceases its strife, sends its members to Congress and appeals to the courts for its remedy and not to "horrid war", I will be the open advocate of mercy and a restoration to home, and peace, and happiness of all who have lost them by my acts.'

Radical Disagreement

Since the very beginning of the conflict, the North had debated what to do with the South when it was defeated and forced back into the Union. Disagreement abounded about who should set the terms – the President or the Congress.

Lincoln held to his belief that the Southern states had never actually seceded since they had no Constitutional rights to do so. This meant that the US Government could not deal with the Confederate government as a political body but must instead concentrate on rebellious individuals. And so, on 7 December 1863, he announced his Proclamation of Amnesty and

Abolitionists publicized the cruelty of slavery to convince others to join their noble cause.

Life after war

PRESIDENT JEFFERSON DAVIS

President Jefferson Davis travelled with his wife to Canada when the charge of treason was dropped. He was released from prison in Richmond on a bail bond signed by, among others, Horace Greeley. In poor health, he went to England, where he was honoured and welcomed into society. He made several trips to Europe before feeling confident enough to return to the South. There be became the president of an insurance company in Memphis for a few years, then lived his final 12

years in Biloxi, Mississippi. He was impoverished when Mrs. Sarah Dorsey provided a cottage on her property for him and his wife, and there he wrote his history, *The Rise and Fall of the Confederate Government* (1881). When Mrs Dorsey died in 1879, he inherited her beautiful home, Beauvoir, overlooking the Gulf of Mexico. (Beauvoir was severely damaged during Hurricane Katrina in 2005, and the cottage destroyed.) He regained possession of his former Mississippi

plantation, Brierfield, which had been sold to his former slave, but he never moved there. He travelled throughout the South, receiving many honours, and died on 6 December 1889 in New Orleans, an unrepentant Confederate. He was never able to regain his US citizenship, but at the urging of President Jimmy Carter, it was posthumously restored by Congress in 1978.

After the war, US Senator Charles Sumner urged the government to give land owned by former Confederates to former slaves.

Reconstruction. This act would give a full pardon and restoration of citizen rights to anyone who took an oath of loyalty to the United States and promised to abide by the abolition of slavery. When 10 per cent of any state's voters made such an oath, that minority could establish a new state government and send representatives to Congress. The federal government would help in the transition to a free-labour economy, but it also reserved the right to prosecute Confederate military leaders.

By the end of the war, Louisiana and Arkansas had met Lincoln's criteria to return to their 'proper relation' with the Union, but the radical Republicans blocked their admittance to the Union.

Radical members of Congress disliked the President's approach, criticizing it as soft. It provided no real punishment and made it fairly easy for those who had supported the 'rebellion' to become full citizens again. It even offered the possibility of former Confederate senators moving into the US Congress. And Lincoln's act offered no guarantees of equality to former slaves, and made no offers of aid.

Two radical Republicans now moved to

counter Lincoln's proposal. Benjamin F. Wade of Ohio and Henry W. Davis of Maryland introduced the Wade-Davis Bill in Congress. On 2 July 1864, the bill passed, by a vote of 73–59 in the House and 18–14 in the Senate. This bill required half of a state's male white population to take an oath of loyalty before civil government was restored. Provisional governors would be appointed, and no Confederate officials or volunteer soldiers could hold state office. In fact, each state constitution had to specify that former Confederates would be banned from holding any position of leadership.

Confronted with such bitter sentiments, Lincoln simply pocket-vetoed the bill by refusing to sign or return it to Congress before it adjourned. His excuse was that he did not wish 'to be inflexibly committed to any single plan of restoration'. This infuriated the radical Republican Thaddeus Stevens, who complained, 'The President is determined to have the electoral votes of the seceded states. How little of the rights of war and the law of nations our President knows.'

The only recourse left to the radicals was to publish the Wade–Davis Manifesto. It appeared in

GENERAL ULYSSES S. GRANT

General Ulysses S. Grant, the Union's greatest war hero, was made General of the Armies in 1866. When President Johnson considered bringing General Lee to trial, Grant successfully fought against this, reminding him of the peace terms made at Appomattox Court House. He was appointed as US Secretary of War by President Johnson after the removal of Edwin Stanton, but the appointment was never confirmed. Nominated by the Republican Party, he was elected as the 18th US President in 1868 and re-elected in 1872. These were rough years, in which the country suffered through a depression and the problems of reconstruction. His second administration was marred by the scandals of

others in his government, especially in the Treasury Department and Indian Service. In 1884, after retiring, Grant was almost bankrupted by the collapse of an investment firm, Grant & Ward, in which he was a partner. To pay his debts, he sold his war mementoes and spent his last years, while suffering with cancer, dictating his memoirs to secure financial stability for his family. *Personal Memoirs of U. S. Grant* were completed shortly before his death, and have been acclaimed as one of the best war accounts ever written. He died at Mount McGregor in the Adirondacks near Saratoga Springs, New York, on 23 July 1885, and is buried in a mausoleum in New York City.

President Ulysses Grant was inaugurated 4 March 1869.

the *New York Tribune* on 5 August, denouncing Lincoln and his Reconstruction policy:

'The President must realize that our support is of a cause and not of a man and that the authority of Congress is paramount and must be respected; and if he wishes our support, he must confine himself to his executive duties – to obey and execute, not make the laws – to suppress by armed rebellion, and leave political reorganization to Congress.'

After the death of Lincoln, President Andrew Johnson was determined to maintain his idealistic programme of reconstruction. On 29 May, he issued two proclamations that reconstructed the previous Confederate states but offered nothing more than emancipation for former slaves, leaving individual states to handle the situation. The radicals wanted blacks to be immediately franchised and ex-Confederates disenfranchised – proposals bound to increase the Republican vote. And the Confederate states were to be treated as conquered territories controlled by the military.

President Andrew Johnson could not stop the radical Republicans' harsh reconstruction policy.

Life after war

GENERAL ROBERT E. LEE

General Robert E. Lee emerged from the war without funds or home, Arlington having been confiscated by the US Government. He declined many business offers, choosing instead to become president of small Washington College in Lexington, Virginia (renamed Washington and Lee University after his death). He revived the foundering school, beginning an honour system and establishing the nation's first journalism school as well as business and law schools. During the postwar years, Lee was foremost in urging his fellow Southerners to forget old hatreds, to help rebuild the country, and to take pride in being US citizens again. He signed the oath of allegiance in 1865 to restore his citizenship, but this was never approved because the document was misplaced (given by Secretary of State Seward to a friend as a souvenir). In 1870, he made a farewell tour of the South, and was hailed as its hero. The war had left Lee with a serious heart condition, and he died on 12 October 1870, four months after his Southern trip, his last words supposedly being, 'Strike the tent'. He was buried in a chapel he had built on campus. His citizenship was restored by Congress in 1975 during President Gerald Ford's administration.

General Robert E. Lee

On 9 April 1866, Congress passed the Civil Rights Act by one vote over the veto of Johnson. It stated that every person born in the United States was a citizen – without regard to race, colour or previous condition. This gave each citizen the right to

....

President Andrew Johnson.

make and enforce contracts; to sue and be sued; to inherit, sell and hold personal property; and to give evidence in court. Anyone who denied those rights to former slaves was guilty of a misdemeanour and, upon conviction, faced a fine of up to $1000 or imprisonment of up to one year – or both.

Johnson was not a leader prepared to compromise. Nor did he have the close political support enjoyed by Lincoln. After congressional elections in 1866, during which he

....

President Johnson is told of his impeachment.

CS GENERAL PIERRE G. T. BEAUREGARD

CS General Pierre G.T. Beauregard declined military commissions in the Egyptian and Romanian armies and returned to his native Louisiana to work in New Orleans. He became wealthy as a railroad director and served as adjutant general of the state, but was also involved in running a corrupt lottery. He died on 20 February 1893.

CS General Braxton Bragg

CS GENERAL BRAXTON BRAGG

CS General Braxton Bragg became a civil engineer in Alabama and Texas, dying on 27 September 1876.

showed his temperamental streak, radical Republicans opposed to his policies took a landslide victory and a two-thirds majority.

Congress was now determined to take control of affairs, and on 2 March, it passed the Reconstruction Act of 1867. This split 10 ex-Confederate states into five military districts, each commanded by a US Army major general. Some 20,000 troops would be sent south, including black militia. New constitutions were to be written, guaranteeing ratification of the 14th Amendment, which gave citizenship to the freed slaves and power to the federal government to protect them. Both races would be registered to vote. A loyalty oath would be required, and former Confederate leaders barred from office. On 23 March, Congress passed another Reconstruction Act, designed to reinforce the first one, and to protect the black vote at all cost.

Johnson used his veto and own interpretation of the act to delay the radical programme. This inspired the radicals to pass a Tenure of Office act over his veto, forbidding the President from removing certain government officials without the approval of Congress. When Johnson removed Secretary of War Edwin Stanton, suspecting him of working with the radicals,

he faced impeachment. Procedures began on 5 March 1868, and the votes, held on 16 May and 26 May, fell just one short of the two-thirds needed for conviction (by 35 to 19).

Blacks Under Attack

The 14th Amendment was first sent to the states on 13 June 1866. It was rejected by all former Confederate states, with the exception of Tennessee, which became the first of all states to approve it, on 19 July. Readmitted to the Union later that year, it was also the only one not given a military government. It would not be until 28 July 1868 that the Amendment would be finally ratified

On 30 July 1866, after black male suffrage was introduced into the Louisiana Constitution, race riots broke out across the South, and in New Orleans 48 blacks were killed and 160 injured. Racial violence continued in August, and this overall trend lost President Johnson support among moderate Northerners.

....

Rioters in Memphis, Tennessee burned a Freedmen's schoolhouse to protest against reconstruction.

Life after war

US GENERAL AMBROSE BURNSIDE

US General Ambrose Burnside became a successful politician, elected as the governor of Rhode Island for three terms, from 1866 to 1869, and as a US senator from 1875 to 1881. He was the first president of the National Rifle Association. He died on 13 September 1881.

US GENERAL BENJAMIN F. BUTLER

US General Benjamin F. Butler became a radical Republican. He served in Congress from 1867 to 1875 and from 1877 to 1879, managing the impeachment trial of President Johnson. He changed parties to be elected the Democratic governor of Massachusetts in 1882. He died in Washington on 11 January 1893.

Some Southerners recognized that such activity was likely to backfire. Edward A. Pollard, editor of the *Richmond Examiner,* believed that the superiority of white Southerners was now in dire danger. In his book *The Lost Cause* (1866), he wrote 'It would be immeasurably the worst consequence of defeat in this war that the South should lose its moral and intellectual distinctiveness as a people, and cease to assert its well-known superiority in civilization, in political scholarship, and in all the standards of individual character over the people of the North.'

On 8 January 1867, blacks were granted suffrage in Washington, DC, but Johnson vetoed the bill, arguing that each state must enfranchise its own citizens. Congress, however, overrode his veto.

The controlled programme of reconstruction brought six of the 10 states back into the Union in June 1868, the other four following in July 1870. Their governments were mainly controlled by Republicans in coalition with

Riots accompanied a Freedmen's procession through the streets of New Orleans.

US General George Armstrong Custer

US GENERAL GEORGE ARMSTRONG CUSTER

US General George Armstrong Custer remained in the army, named in 1866 as a lieutenant colonel in the Seventh Cavalry. He fought successfully against Cheyenne Indians in Kansas before being killed along with his men on 25 June 1876 by Sioux Indians led by Crazy Horse at the Battle of Big Horn.

CS GENERAL JUBAL A. EARLY

CS General Jubal A. Early was heading for Texas when the war ended, so he proceeded to Mexico. From there, he moved to Cuba and then Canada, where he penned his memoirs. In 1867, he returned to Virginia to practise law and later helped manage the Louisiana state lottery, which was run by former General Beauregard. Early was the first president of the Southern Historical Society. He died at Lynchburg, Virginia on 2 March 1894.

newly freed slaves, 'carpetbaggers' (Northerners who had moved South), and 'scalawags' (Southern collaborators).

The move to enfranchise blacks did not sit well with some in the North. 'The South deserves all she has got for her injustice to the negro,' Sherman wrote Halleck, 'but that is no reason why we should go to the other extreme.' And US Secretary of the Navy Gideon Wells noted in his diary: 'No one can claim that the blacks, in the slave states especially, can exercise the elective franchise intelligently. In most of the free states they are not permitted to vote.'

Not surprisingly, Southerners were bitter. They resented these artificial, and corrupt, governments; they objected to the power given to blacks; and they were suspicious of Northern organizations such as the Freedmen's Bureau, which aided former slaves, and the Union League, which indoctrinated them with Republican principles. To counter this, the former Confederates developed 'Black Codes', which were condoned by President Johnson and

Civil rights for former slaves came slowly but were assured by Constitutional amendments.

Life after war

US ADMIRAL DAVID FARRAGUT

US Admiral David Farragut was promoted to become the nation's first full admiral after the war. He commanded the US Navy's European Squadron, sailing on a goodwill tour of foreign seaports in 1867. He died at Portsmouth, New Hampshire on 14 August 1870.

CS GENERAL NATHAN BEDFORD FORREST

CS General Nathan Bedford Forrest was ruined financially by the war and settled in Memphis as president of the Selma, Marion and Memphis Railroad. He became active in the Ku Klux Klan and was suspected of being a Grand Wizard, although he later resigned in protest at the organization's violent activities. He died in Memphis on 29 October 1877.

US General John Frémont

US GENERAL JOHN FRÉMONT

US General John Frémont tried a railroad career, but lost his money and was convicted of corruption in 1873. He recovered his reputation and served as the territorial governor of Arizona from 1878 to 1883. He died penniless in New York City on 13 July 1890.

US troops are heckled by locals as they are withdrawn from the State House in New Orleans as reconstruction came to an end.

restricted the rights of former slaves. They also established various secret organizations, the most popular being the Ku Klux Klan, designed to frighten blacks into remaining in their place. A prominent member, and possible leader, was the former general Nathan Bedford Forrest, who had been involved in the Fort Pillow 'massacre' of blacks. The Klan was just one of the organizations that made the Civil Rights Act of 1866 a failure.

During these tensions in the South, eyes were turned to Richmond, where the trial of former president Jefferson Davis began on 3 December 1868. However, on 25 December, President Johnson proclaimed a general amnesty for all who took part in 'the Rebellion'. As a result, charges against Davis were dropped on 15 February 1869.

Horace Greeley

HORACE GREELEY

Horace Greeley risked unpopularity when he put his signature to the bail bond of Jefferson Davis, believing that his constitutional rights had been infringed. He urged the impeachment of President Johnson. In 1870, he established a temperance town in Colorado, which was later named after him. Burdened by debts, he ran for President in 1872, backed by a coalition of Democrats and liberal Republicans, but was defeated by the incumbent Grant. He died in New York City three weeks after the election, on 29 November 1872.

CS GENERAL WADE HAMPTON

CS General Wade Hampton worked hard for the return of Southern rule. He was elected governor of South Carolina, from 1877 to 1879, then served as a US senator from 1879 to 1891. He then became the US commissioner of Pacific railroads from 1893 to 1897.

The Consequences of Reconstruction

The reconstruction programme spanned 11 years. It officially ended on 24 April 1877, when Louisiana became the last state to have federal troops withdrawn (from New Orleans). By this point, Democrats had taken over all the ex-Confederate state governments – and would maintain 'the solid South' one-party system through most of the twentieth century. The Republicans, firmly established in the North, abandoned voters in the South, including their black supporters. This allowed the South to dismantle the reconstruction programme all too speedily. Whites were once again supreme, and the strict segregation of the races would remain in place until the latter half of the twentieth century.

The experience of reconstruction drove a hard wedge between the North and South, creating sectional and racial tensions. Confederate General Wade Hampton had predicted to President Davis after Lee's surrender: '*No suffering which can be inflicted by the passage over our country of the Yankee armies can equal what would fall on us if we return to the Union.*' In many ways, he was proved right. The war had

THE

SLAVERY CODE

OF THE

DISTRICT OF COLUMBIA,

TOGETHER

WITH NOTES AND JUDICIAL DECISIONS EXPLANA-
TORY OF THE SAME.

BY A MEMBER OF THE WASHINGTON BAR.

WASHINGTON:
L. TOWERS & CO., PRINTERS.
1862.

This Code came out 17 March 1862 for Washington's slaves, but on 16 April slavery was abolished there.

ruined many whites financially. Former slaves were now exploited as tenant farmers, living in shacks hardly better than their slave quarters. And the economy continued to rely on cotton, producing in the 1880s double the amount of cotton grown in 1860.

Reconstruction did have its positive side. Blacks won some freedoms. Judicial procedures were reformed, and courts improved. The taxation system changed for the better. Hospitals and other public buildings were built, along with the South's first free (albeit segregated) public schools. And the Southern states began the slow evolution from an agricultural economy to one based on commerce and industry. No indictments for treason were served, while the few Confederate leaders imprisoned were soon released (other than Jefferson Davis), and their property was not taken.

Let it not be forgotten that what had ended once and for all was the reality of slavery and the theory of secession. The federal government now had powers it had never taken before. The principle was established that a state could not resign its membership in the Union – a counter to President Davis's early plea, 'All we ask is to be

Life after war

CS GENERAL WILLIAM HARDEE

CS General William Hardee retired to a plantation near Selma, Alabama. He died on 6 November 1873 while travelling to Wytheville, Virginia and was buried in Selma.

CS GENERAL JOHN BELL HOOD

CS General John Bell Hood became a businessman in New Orleans, where he wrote his memoirs. He died there on 30 August 1879, a victim of a yellow fever epidemic that also killed his wife and one of his 11 children.

US GENERAL JOSEPH HOOKER

US General Joseph Hooker remained in the US Army until a stroke debilitated him in 1868, forcing him to retire. By then, he had attained the rank of major general. He died at Garden City, New York on 31 October 1879.

let alone.' And made real was his observation from 1865: 'If the Confederacy fails, there should be written on its tombstone, *Died of a Theory*.'

Nor has the theory ever been tested again. For General Sherman was right to predict, 'The mass of the people south will never trouble us again. They have suffered terrifically, and I now feel disposed to befriend them.' The feelings of the North were perhaps summed up best by the Rev Henry Ward Beecher. Speaking at the ceremonial raising of the US flag over Fort Sumter on 14 April 1865, he said, 'We have shown by all that we have suffered in war how great is our estimate of the importance of the Southern States to this Union, and we will honor that estimate now in peace by still greater exertions for their rebuilding.'

Shame and Pride

Was it a 'civil war' or just a 'war between the states'? Several of today's scholars choose the latter Southern term, on the grounds that a civil war is fought to establish the right to govern a

Southerners continued to plot resistence after the war's end, as depicted in this 1866 sketch.

CS GENERAL JOSEPH JOHNSTON

CS General Joseph Johnston worked in the insurance business while writing his memoirs. He was elected to the US Congress, serving from 1879 to 1881, and then was appointed as a US railroad commissioner by President Grover Cleveland. He, too, wrote his memoirs. Serving as a pallbearer at General Sherman's funeral on 20 February 1891, a chilly winter's day in St Louis, he refused to wear his hat as a mark of respect. He died a month later of pneumonia, on 21 March, in Washington, DC.

US GENERAL GEORGE MCCLELLAN

US General George McClellan went on a three-year trip through Europe after losing the 1864 election to Lincoln. He returned to resume his original career, becoming chief engineer of the New York City Department of Docks from 1870 to 1872. He was one of three men who reorganized the Atlantic and Great Western Railway, becoming its president in 1872. McClellan was then elected governor of New Jersey, serving from 1878 to 1881. He died suddenly on 29 October 1885 in Orange, New Jersey, and his memoirs, *McClellan's Own Story*, were published posthumously in 1887.

nation. This principle was never at stake, the Southern states fighting for independence from the Union. Other scholars insist that this is too pedantic a definition, pointing out that a civil war is fought between citizens of the same country. Moreover, the United States never recognized that the South was its own nation, implying that this was a 'war of rebellion'.

Simply put, the war was a moment when Americans fought Americans to free Americans. Sir Denis Brogan, the Scottish historian, described the conflict as 'the great purging experience of the American people, their shame and their pride'.

It cost nearly 550,000 lives, more Americans than died in any other war in the nation's history. Union military casualties numbered 646,393 overall. The dead totalled 364,512, with 140,415 of these killed on the battlefield; another 281,881 were wounded. The Confederacy had 233,821 casualties, with 133,821 killed (some 74,524 of these in battles) and about 100,000 wounded. An estimated

The Ku Klux Klan terrorized the freed slaves to keep them from politics and true civil rights.

Life after war

CS GENERAL JOHN MOSBY

CS General John Mosby went back to his law practice in Virginia, where he lost friends by becoming a Republican and supporting General Grant for President in 1872. Once in office, Grant appointed him as consul to Hong Kong in 1878, where he helped reform the Foreign Service office. In 1885, he returned to the United States, working with the Southern Pacific Railroad in San Francisco and becoming friends with a boy, George Patton, who later won fame as a general in World War II. From 1904 to 1910, Mosby was an assistant attorney for the US Department of Justice in Washington, and died in Washington on 30 May (Memorial Day) 1916.

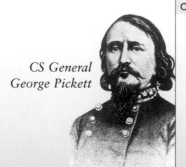

CS General George Pickett

CS GENERAL GEORGE PICKETT

CS General George Pickett avoided future military service, turning down an offer from President Grant to be US Marshal, and a generalship from Egypt. He went into the insurance business in Norfolk, Virginia, where he died on 30 July 1875.

The trial of former Confederate President Jefferson Davis began on 3 December 1868, but he received amnesty from President Johnson.

50,000 Southern civilians also died. To pursue the war, the Union spent some $5 billion and the Confederacy about $3 billion.

Once the war was over, the country turned its focus to repairing the damaged East and to taming and settling the West. But the fighting would not be forgotten, the scars running deep. For 81 years, Vicksburg refused to celebrate on 4 July, this also being the day that it surrendered. African-Americans were segregated in the US military until after World War II, and in the South until the 1960s. Many white Southerners refused to vote Republican for more than a century, until Richard Nixon's election in 1968.

'The New South' and 'The South shall rise again!' became mottos, but Dixie rose in unexpected ways. Today's region, with its chain stores and shopping malls, looks more American than Southern, and the influx of Yankees from the North and Hispanics from the South is changing the nature of the land that bred Robert E. Lee and Frederick Douglass.

The horror of the Civil War was perhaps best summarized by Sam Watkins, a private in the 1st Tennessee Regiment. His 1882 memoir, *Co. Aytch* describes his shock:

'Is it true that I have seen all these things? That they are real incidents in my life's history? Did I see those brave and noble countrymen of mine laid low in death and weltering in their blood? Did I see our country laid waste and in ruins? Did I see soldiers marching, the earth trembling and jarring beneath their measured tread? Did I see the ruins of smouldering cities and deserted homes? Did I see my comrades buried and see the violet and wild flowers bloom over their graves? Did I see the flag of my country, that I had followed so long, furled to be no more unfurled forever? Surely they are but the vagaries of mine own imagination.'

Watkins and his fellow soldiers would be alarmed at the modern backlash against the Confederacy and its symbols. Political correctness, led by African-American sensibilities, has banished Confederate battle flags from flying over the Alabama and South Carolina capitols and removed a small one from the Georgia state flag. The name 'Confederate' was deleted from a Memphis Street and is in jeopardy on a Vanderbilt University building. The names of Confederate heroes are also disappearing: Robert E. Lee High School in Birmingham, Alabama changed its name in 2001 to Martin Luther King High School. Alabama has reduced its slogan, 'The Heart of Dixie', to small type on its licence

US General Fitz-John Porter

US GENERAL FITZ-JOHN PORTER

US General Fitz-John Porter, who had been dismissed from the army for disobeying orders, was reappointed as a colonel on 5 August 1886. This he owed mainly to the efforts of Congressman Joseph Wheeler, the former Confederate general. Two days later, with his reputation restored, Porter retired. During his time out of the military, he had tried a variety of jobs, including serving as a mine superintendent in Colorado and as the New York City commissioner of police, fire, and public works. He also turned down an offer to join the Egyptian army in 1869. Porter died in Morristown, New Jersey on 21 May 1901.

US Secretary of State William Seward

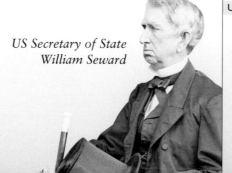

US SECRETARY OF STATE WILLIAM SEWARD

US Secretary of State William Seward survived the assassination attack by John Wilkes Booth's conspirator, and continued in his role under President Johnson, supporting his reconstruction plans. In 1867, he paid Russia $7.2 million for Alaska, which became known as 'Seward's folly' because of its icy wilderness. He retired from politics after the end of Johnson's term and took a two-year world tour, returning to Auburn, New York, where he died on 10 October 1872.

Slaves soon found that freedom was barely a step from slavery, with many working their old jobs on white farms for a meagre amount of money.

Life after war

US GENERAL PHILIP SHERIDAN

US General Philip Sheridan was sent to the Texas–Mexico border after the war, where his troops' presence was a factor in the defeat of Maximilian, the French emperor. Sheridan was then put in command of Reconstruction in Louisiana and Texas in 1867, but acted so harshly he was recalled after six months. In the winter of 1868–69, he conducted a successful campaign against Indians in the West and later helped to create Yellowstone Park for the government. He was promoted to lieutenant general when Grant became President in 1869, and spent 1870 and 1871 in Europe, observing the Franco-Prussian War for two months from the German side. Sheridan spent his last months writing his *Personal Memoirs* and was promoted to full general on 1 June 1888. He died two months later, on 5 August, in Nosquitt, Massachusetts.

US GENERAL WILLIAM TECUMSEH SHERMAN

US General William Tecumseh Sherman went to St Louis to help the army build the transcontinental railway and control the Indians. Sought after as a presidential candidate, he gave his now famous response: 'I will not accept if nominated and will not serve if elected.' In 1866, he was promoted to lieutenant general after Grant became a full general, and was subsequently promoted by President Grant to commanding general of the army, serving in that capacity from 1869 to 1883. During this time, he established Fort Levenworth, Kansas as a training centre. His memoirs, published in 1875, were very successful. He retired from active duty on 8 February 1884, living first in St Louis and then in New York City, where he died on 14 February 1891.

plates. Final victory is uncertain in this new battle pitting Southern heritage against 'slavery symbols', but the fight underlines the intense feelings that still exist, more than 140 years after the guns fell silent.

What Happened Next

On the day that President Lincoln was assassinated, he told Senator John Creswell of Maryland, 'The war is over. It has been a tough time, but we have lived it out. Or some of us have.'

Those people who did survive went on to a variety of professions. Some became notable successes in civilian life, others, however, struggled to adjust to life after the war. Some found happiness and satisfaction in their later years, others confronted sorrow and tragedy. The stories of some of the key figures are featured throughout this chapter, showing what they did in the aftermath of America's deadly battle with itself.

The US Navy decorated its ships with flags in Charleston Harbor to celebrate the war's victory.

CS Vice President Alexander Stephens

CS VICE PRESIDENT ALEXANDER STEPHENS

CS Vice President Alexander Stephens was arrested after the war and imprisoned for five months in Fort Warren in Boston. He was released on 12 October 1865 and returned to Georgia politics, being elected to the US Senate in 1866, but resigning because federal law barred former Confederates from holding office. He published *A Constitutional View of the Late War Between the States* (1868–70), thus giving the war the title that is used throughout the South even today. Stephens practised law until new legislation allowed him to be elected, in 1872, to the US House of Representatives, where he served from 1873 to 1882. He was elected as governor of Georgia in 1882, and died on 4 March 1883, a few months after his inauguration.

CS General Joseph Wheeler

CS GENERAL JOSEPH WHEELER

CS General Joseph Wheeler was released from prison at Fort Delaware on 8 June 1865, having been captured in Georgia in May. He moved to a plantation in Alabama and served in the US House of Representatives from 1881 to 1882, in 1883, and from 1885 to 1900. He was appointed a general of volunteers in the US Army in 1898 when the Spanish-American War began, landing in Cuba and fighting at San Juan Hill and Santiago. (Forgetful, he sometimes urged his troops to 'attack the Yankees'.) He later sailed for the Philippines, fighting there too. Wheeler retired to live in Brooklyn, New York, where he died on 25 January 1906. His later military action means that he is one of the few Confederates to be buried in Arlington National Cemetery.

Index